Africa's Fourth Industrial Revolution

With the rise of new technologies and disruptive innovations reshaping the global economy, the Fourth Industrial Revolution has been characterized as a fusion between the physical, digital, and biological worlds. From the increasing adoption of mobile devices to the entrepreneurial use of 3D printing, artificial intelligence, and robotics, trends across Africa speak to the continent's potential for growth and sustainable development in the Fourth Industrial Revolution. In this innovative and timely study, Landry Signé examines the meaning, drivers, and implications of the Fourth Industrial Revolution for Africa. Drawing upon comparative, continent-wide analysis, Signé powerfully challenges our understandings of Africa's transformation and sheds light on the potential of the Fourth Industrial Revolution to change and shape the Global South. By defining and investigating the Fourth Industrial Revolution, Signé develops a valuable framework for further study and suggests strategies that Africans and their global partners can use to capitalize upon this rapidly evolving technological landscape.

LANDRY SIGNÉ is Executive Director and Professor at the Thunderbird School of Global Management, Senior Fellow at the Brookings Institution, and Distinguished Fellow at Stanford University. He is a world-renowned professor and leading practitioner, who has won over seventy awards and distinctions globally for his academic, policy, business, and leadership accomplishments, including being recognized as a World Economic Forum Young Global Leader, Andrew Carnegie Fellow, Desmond Tutu Fellow, Rubenstein Fellow, and Wilson Center Public Policy Fellow. He has authored numerous key publications, including *Innovating Development Strategies in Africa* (2017), *African Development, African Transformation* (2018), and *Unlocking Africa's Business Potential* (2020).

T0384501

Africa's Fourth Industrial Revolution

LANDRY SIGNÉ
Thunderbird School of Global Management
The Brookings Institution
Stanford University

CAMBRIDGE
UNIVERSITY PRESS

CAMBRIDGE
UNIVERSITY PRESS

Shaftesbury Road, Cambridge CB2 8EA, United Kingdom

One Liberty Plaza, 20th Floor, New York, NY 10006, USA

477 Williamstown Road, Port Melbourne, VIC 3207, Australia

314–321, 3rd Floor, Plot 3, Splendor Forum, Jasola District Centre, New Delhi – 110025, India

103 Penang Road, #05–06/07, Visioncrest Commercial, Singapore 238467

Cambridge University Press is part of Cambridge University Press & Assessment, a department of the University of Cambridge.

We share the University's mission to contribute to society through the pursuit of education, learning and research at the highest international levels of excellence.

www.cambridge.org
Information on this title: www.cambridge.org/9781009200042

DOI: 10.1017/9781009200004

First published 2023

A catalogue record for this publication is available from the British Library.

Library of Congress Cataloging-in-Publication Data
Names: Signé, Landry, author.
Title: Africa's fourth industrial revolution / Landry Signé, Stanford University, California.
Description: Cambridge, United Kingdom ; New York, NY : Cambridge University Press, [2023] | Includes bibliographical references and index.
Identifiers: LCCN 2022030529 (print) | LCCN 2022030530 (ebook) | ISBN 9781009200042 (hardback) | ISBN 9781009200011 (paperback) | ISBN 9781009200004 (epub)
Subjects: LCSH: Economic development–Africa. | Africa–Economic conditions–21st century. | Africa–Economic policy.
Classification: LCC HC800 .S5376 2023 (print) | LCC HC800 (ebook) | DDC 338.96–dc23/eng/20220713
LC record available at https://lccn.loc.gov/2022030529
LC ebook record available at https://lccn.loc.gov/2022030530

ISBN 978-1-009-20004-2 Hardback
ISBN 978-1-009-20001-1 Paperback

Contents

Figures

Tables

Foreword

The world is at a crossroads, with a new technological era that is fundamentally changing the way we live, work, and relate to one another. This "Fourth Industrial Revolution," a term I first coined in 2015, is characterized by new technologies that are fusing the physical, digital, and biological worlds and that offer both great potential and great peril to societies as they drive structural transformation to systems of global production, labor, governance, and beyond.

In today's interconnected world, no country or industry can avoid feeling the direct or indirect repercussions of technological development. The question for states, firms, and individuals is not whether to participate in the Fourth Industrial Revolution but how to manage its enormous opportunities for growth and the troubling risks posed by immense market disruption and structural transformation. The pace and unpredictability of innovation during the Fourth Industrial Revolution will be unprecedented; these changes will force public and private sector stakeholders to adapt rapidly or risk falling behind.

Although extensively studied since the publication of my book entitled *The Fourth Industrial Revolution*, little work has been done to better understand Africa's role in the Fourth Industrial Revolution. This is why I have welcomed the opportunity to write the foreword for the pioneering book, *Africa's Fourth Industrial Revolution*, by one of the World Economic Forum's Young Global Leaders, Professor Landry Signé.

In this book, Professor Landry Signé examines what defines the Fourth Industrial Revolution and its key technological components, drivers, and global implications. He forecasts Africa's participation in the Fourth Industrial Revolution by analyzing consumer and industry trends shaping the continent and countries that are leading the way, evaluating specific opportunities, risks, and strategies for Africa presented by the Fourth Industrial Revolution. He provides guidance for government, business, academic, and civil society leaders to help capitalize on the Fourth Industrial Revolution and maximize returns from deploying new technologies. His book presents the duality of the Fourth Industrial Revolution to leaders across the African continent, as both an opportunity for leapfrogging and a risk of falling even further behind. Overall, Professor Signé demonstrates that the Fourth Industrial Revolution offers an unparalleled opportunity to address many of Africa's key challenges and can help catalyze the continent to unite if government, business, academic, and civil society leaders can work together to harness this potential.

This book will change the way you see Africa's transformation and potential in the Fourth Industrial Revolution. Everyone, especially leaders interested in understanding how the Fourth Industrial Revolution is changing the developing world and how policy and business leaders can shape it to capture its dividends and mitigate its risks, must read this book.

Professor Klaus Schwab Founder and Executive Chairman
of the World Economic Forum, Author of *The Fourth
Industrial Revolution* (2015) and *Shaping the Future
of the Fourth Industrial Revolution* (2018)

Preface

Professor Landry Signé's new book *Africa's Fourth Industrial Revolution* is an incisive, thought-provoking, timely, and ambitious look at how African countries can become global leaders in innovation and technology during the Fourth Industrial Revolution. Professor Signé offers a comprehensive and specific look at the main drivers, opportunities, and risks of the Fourth Industrial Revolution in Africa. He expertly uses extensive evidence to demonstrate how the Fourth Industrial Revolution will affect governments, businesses, entrepreneurs, research institutions, and other major stakeholders and discusses how these stakeholders can capitalize on the potential of new technologies, rather than being left behind.

As the sixth President of the Republic of Mauritius and distinguished scientist and academic leader, I am intimately familiar with the vital role that technology and innovation play in economic development. Mauritius embraced technology as a driver of development and now has one of the highest information and communication technology (ICT) penetration rates in Africa. Mauritius has become a hub for local and multinational ICT companies, and the ICT sector now employs thousands of Mauritians and is a major contributor to growth. Professor Landry Signé's book insightfully discusses the case of Mauritius, among other African current and emerging innovation leaders, drawing thoughtful recommendations and forward-looking strategies from my country's experience. His analysis provides an excellent guide for all African leaders as the Fourth Industrial Revolution unfolds and the importance of ICT continues to increase.

Professor Landry Signé is the ideal scholar to undertake this research. His internationally acclaimed work has focused on the transformation of the global political economy, with special attention to unlocking Africa and emerging economies' potential, and on understanding why nations and businesses succeed or fail and how to fix them so that no one and no country is left behind. His work provides world-class evidence-based insight, new strategic thinking, and innovative solutions to the most pressing issues facing Africa and emerging markets.

This insightful book has also been enriched with his unique global experience. In addition to being a forward-thinking and world-renowned university professor, global political economist, and Africanist affiliated with the Brookings Institution, Stanford University, and other leading institutions, Professor Landry Signé is also an influential leader, bridging the world of ideas and actions. He often travels the world to help companies, governments, and international organizations adapt and improve their efficiency and performance in a fast-changing world, sitting on boards and councils as well as advising top global leaders and C-level executives. He engages with the foremost political, business, academic, and society leaders to accelerate the transformation of Africa and the emerging world and has gained global distinction for his contribution to solving some of the world's most pressing challenges.

All African and global leaders, whether in government, business, academia, or other fields, must read *Africa's Fourth Industrial Revolution*. This book provides exceptional insight into the steps that African countries, firms, and entrepreneurs, and the friends of Africa on the global stage, must take to capitalize on the opportunities presented by the Fourth Industrial Revolution and become global leaders in innovation. The recommendations provided in the book include several policy measures similar to those that Mauritius implemented while undergoing technology-led economic development, among many other insightful, innovative strategies. Overall, the book provides the best guide for African and global leaders looking to better understand and capitalize on the Fourth Industrial Revolution. We need more incredibly wise thinkers like Professor Landry Signé.

H. E. Professor Ameenah Gurib-Fakim
Sixth President of the Republic of Mauritius

Acknowledgments

Writing a book requires the collaboration and unique contribution of many individuals. The author would like to sincerely thank David M. Rubenstein, Brookings lifetime trustee and chair emeritus; Brahima S. Coulibaly, Vice President and Director of the Global Economy and Development program; and Sanjeev Khagram, Dean and Director General of the Thunderbird School of Global Management, for their support of this research. Special thanks to Professor Klaus Schwab, the Executive Chairman of the World Economic Forum, and H.E. Professor Ameenah Gurib-Fakim, the sixth President of the Republic of Mauritius, who graciously wrote a foreword and preface for the book. The author would also like to express his sincere appreciation to the people who have made this work possible or provided constructive feedback, including anonymous reviewers. The author is grateful to William Hurt, Genevieve Jesse, Payce Madden, and Gael Signé for their important contributions. The author is also thankful to Aloysius Ordu, Karim El Aynaoui, Louise Fox, Nicholas Davis, Chido Munyati, Eyerusalem Siba, Merrell Tuck-Primdahl, Christina Golubski, Jeannine Ajello, Joshua T. Miller, David Batcheck, Dhruv Gandhi, Nisrine Ouazzani, Franck Ouattara, Elise Léa Julie El Nouchi, Hannah Pontzer, Moussa Balla Sissoko, Alana Ramirez, and Hanna Dooley who have supported this work. The author is enormously grateful to the peer reviewers for their insightful feedback as well as to Chris Maserole, Jessica Brandt, and Sarah Reed from the Brookings Artificial Intelligence and Emerging Technology Initiative. I would like to thank my fantastic parents and siblings, whose unconditional support has been a constant source of motivation: Joséphine, Michel, Nadège, Carine, Gaël, Marcelle, and Ange.

Last but not least, I am grateful to my dearest love, Nadine, who provided invaluable moral support, and to my son and daughter, Landry Jr. and Lana, for spreading joy and happiness in our life every single day. I dedicate this book to my daughter, Lana, and to the "4IR Generation."

1 Introduction
Understanding Africa's Role in the Fourth Industrial Revolution

We stand at the beginning of a new technological golden era, referred to as the Fourth Industrial Revolution, also known as "the 4IR."[1] Over the past few years, a dramatic wave of technological innovation has captured the attention of academics, firms, and policy-makers alike.[2] Current discussions surrounding the 4IR tend to focus on advanced economies in the West. However, the 4IR is not just taking place inside the labs of Silicon Valley. Pockets of innovation are expanding across the globe and beginning to shake the foundation of states and markets, including on the African continent. A new era of technology will inevitably empower new players in the international political economy. Firms, governments, and investors who can adapt to fast-paced disruptions will also take the reins of global leadership and prosperity.

The 4IR has implications for a broad range of domains, and much of the current research focuses mainly on production and manufacturing systems. However, scholars have argued that the 4IR will have dramatic impacts on consumption, labor, finance,[3] health and global living standards,[4] governance, security, and more.[5] Analysts who consider the 4IR's broader impacts tend to generate more diverse and dramatic predictions than those who focus solely on its implications for production and manufacturing. Schwab (2016), for example, analyzes the risks and benefits of twenty-three "deep shifts"[6] driven by a series of different

---

[1] Some scholars refer to the Fourth Industrial Revolution as "Industry 4.0," but the 4IR is much more complex, going beyond industry.
[2] See, for example: Schwab (2016a); Liao et al. (2017); Colombo et al. (2017); Manyika et al. (2017); Peters (2017); Alur (2015); Monostori (2014); Drath and Horch (2014)
[3] World Economic Forum (2017a; Manyika et al. (2013); Gentner (2016); Deloitte (2018a)
[4] Ekekwe (2018); Matchaba (2018); Zheng et al. (2018); Schwab (2016a)
[5] Schwab and Davis (2018); Sicari et al. (2015)
[6] Implantable technologies, our digital presence, vision as the new interface, wearable internet, ubiquitous computing, a supercomputer in your pocket,

technologies. He finds that there is excellent potential here for the 4IR to connect billions of people to digital networks and improve organizations' efficiency. However, there is significant risk that organizations will be unable to adapt to changes; shifting power will generate new security concerns, causing inequality to grow.[7] Even narrower approaches have estimated enormous consequences for the 4IR. But, in contrast, McKinsey & Company estimates that the Internet of Things alone could add $4 trillion to $11 trillion a year in value to the global economy by 2025.[8]

Not all predictions are optimistic. Skeptics worry about inequality and labor displacement generated by labor-saving technology, such as automation, in addition to heightened threats from hacking, data discrimination, and new surveillance tools.[9] Li, Yun, and Wu (2017) emphasize that efficiency improvements will come at the consequence of heightened social inequality and broadened structural unemployment.[10] Even optimistic views of the 4IR, such as those of the World Economic Forum (WEF), tend to acknowledge that Industry 4.0 will generate *both* opportunities and risks, winners and losers. As a result, proactive strategies to maximize benefits and minimize harm have become a growing global priority, which African countries must focus on developing.[11]

1.1 Unlocking Africa's Growth and Inclusive Prosperity: Innovation and Transformation

African economies have better performed at the beginning of the twenty-first century, compared to the two last decades of the previous century fueling excitement about Africa's growth potential.[12] Now, particular features of the 4IR present even further opportunities to

---

storage for all, the internet of and for things, the connected home, smart cities, big data for decisions, driverless cars, artificial intelligence and decision-making, AI and white-collar jobs, robotics and services, bitcoin and the blockchain, the sharing economy, government and the blockchain, 3D printing and manufacturing, 3D printing and human health, 3D printing and consumer products, designer beings, and neurotechnologies.

[7] Schwab (2016a, pp. 120–172)   [8] Manyika et al. (2015)
[9] Neudert (2018); World Economic Forum (2018a); Schwab and Davis (2018)
[10] Li, Yun, and Wu (2017, pp. 631–632)
[11] Schwab and Davis (2018); Meads (2017)
[12] Mahajan (2011); Drummond, Thakoor, and Yu (2014); Signé (2018a)

unlock Africa's growth transformation. At a macro-industrial level, 4IR technologies present Africa with the opportunity to circumvent traditional infrastructure deficits that have held back productivity.[13] Governments, firms, and entrepreneurs across the continent are beginning to exploit these opportunities through investments, start-ups, and public–private partnerships.[14] On an international scale, the McKinsey Global Institute has estimated that twelve disruptive 4IR technologies,[15] including mobile internet and automation, will have an estimated economic impact of $14 trillion to $33 trillion per year by 2025.[16] While many of these gains will accrue to advanced economies, many developing countries are uniquely situated to rapidly adopt the latest technology and use them to overcome traditional barriers to growth. For example, McKinsey suggests that 50 percent of the economic impact from mobile internet and 70 percent of the gains from expanding internet "cloud" technology can be captured by developing economies.[17] The pandemic has profoundly impacted the acceleration of the use, adoption, and innovation of 4IR technologies, which should be key components of the plans required for recovery and economic prosperity across different African regions.

Africa's growing leadership in the domain of mobile technology has demonstrated its ability to participate in a new global economy driven by digital assets, data, and knowledge goods.[18] It has also shown the potential that technological innovation holds for Africa to leapfrog traditional infrastructure deficits and accelerate growth. The rapid expansion in access to mobile phones across the continent has, for example, provided widespread connectivity without the need for significant infrastructure investments from the public sector. It has also enabled the development of platforms such as mobile money (see Section 6.1.1, Chapter 6), expanding access to credit for the unbanked, and driving growth across a variety of sectors. African companies' competitive advantage has benefited immensely from the increased volume of digital maturity.[19] Further

---

[13] Coulibaly (2017); Newfarmer, Page, and Tarp (2018, p. 34); Deloitte (2018, p. 5)
[14] Ndemo (2016); Siba and Sow (2017); Bayen (2018a, 2018b)
[15] Mobile internet, automation of knowledge work, the Internet of Things, cloud, advanced robotics, autonomous and near-autonomous vehicles, next-generation genomics, energy storage, 3D printing, advanced materials, advanced oil and gas exploration and recovery, and renewable energy.
[16] Manyika et al. (2013, p. 11)   [17] Manyika et al. (2013, p. 17)
[18] Chan (2018)   [19] Dannouni et al. (2020)

investments in these capabilities will accelerate the growth and innovation that is, in part, driven by Africa's rising young labor force, urbanization rates, and consumer spending. Africa cannot afford to sit on the sidelines during the 4IR. Global patterns of market disruption and structural transformation will inevitably penetrate Africa's borders, whether African stakeholders are prepared for these changes or not.

Skeptics of the 4IR's growth in Africa have stated that much of the continent has yet to widely adopt the innovations from the *Second* and *Third* Industrial Revolutions. Africa continues to trail the rest of the world. The continent does not have the necessary prerequisites to advance its position and participate in the 4IR, such as internet access and electrification.[20] Chirisa and Mavhima (2019) stress that African leaders need to assume a clear role on how "leapfrogging" into the 4IR should be informed by clear and unambiguous policy goals and strategies to create an avenue for sustainable development.[21] Otherwise, African countries could put themselves at risk (risks that could lead to the recolonization of the continent) and lose out on potential opportunities to build back better.[22] Despite Africa's deficits in infrastructure, however, the globalized, interconnected nature of the 4IR means that Africa cannot avoid facing the direct and indirect consequences of innovation and market disruption. Even African states that do not directly employ technologies such as automation will likely compete with economies exploiting 4IR technologies.[23] Moreover, international trade and investment may be vehicles for delivering 4IR products and equipment to the African continent. For example, a McKinsey survey conducted in June 2017 found that of the 1,000 Chinese companies operating in Africa, half of the firms had introduced a new product or service to the local market. Meanwhile, one-third had introduced a new technology, thereby allowing African countries to benefit from technology transfer.[24]

1.2 Methodology and Outline of the Book

Africa's position in the 4IR will depend on the answers to several critical questions. Mainly, what are the key implications of the 4IR for Africa?

---

[20] AfDB (2018, p. 66)   [21] Chirisa and Mavhima (2019, pp. 124–144)
[22] Onwughalu and Ojakorotu (2020, pp. 75–93)   [23] Coulibaly (2017)
[24] Sun, Jarayam, and Kassiri (2017, p. 11)

What barriers and drivers will shape Africa's ability to participate in the 4IR? What advantages and technological niches can African governments and businesses exploit to compete globally? Which leaders and key players on the African continent can drive innovation and leapfrog development? How can policy-makers, business leaders, civil society, academics, and other actors collaborate to ensure that Africa thrives under the 4IR and that no one is left behind? More broadly, how can Africa grow, develop, and become a global powerhouse under the 4IR?

This book will systematically analyze the origins, implications, catalysts, and challenges of the 4IR in Africa to address the questions stated above. This book will use a process-tracing method to identify opportunities and key players in the public and private sectors, from leading governments to firms, entrepreneurs, and individuals. I will also employ a comparative method to understand the variation among African players in the 4IR. By analyzing high-performing states, corporations, and innovators, I will identify strategies for all businesses and countries on the African continent to seize the reigns of the 4IR.

Measuring the development of the 4IR is complicated because it encompasses a wide range of technologies that rely on many different forms of infrastructure and underlying political and economic conditions to succeed. One approach has been to use digital maturity levels as a starting point for assessing preparedness for the 4IR since much of 4IR technology – such as artificial intelligence (AI), IoT, and blockchain – relies on digital interfaces. Digital maturity indexes initially included measures of ICT development and broadband access.[25] Over time, however, researchers have expanded the scope of these metrics to encompass digital usage and implementation, as well as the skills and conditions necessary for continued digital growth and innovation.[26]

An example of this is the Siemens digital maturity assessment (DMA), which assigns countries a score out of 100 based on variables in four different categories: economic maturity, business environment, infrastructure, and digital literacy and skills.[27] Some indexes – such as McKinsey and Company's industry digitization index – analyze the digital maturity of specific business sectors. For example, Prashant

[25] Jensen (2007); Muto (2008); Klonner and Nolen (2010); Batzilis et al. (2010); Gruber and Koutroumpis (2011); Crandall et al. (2007); Thompson and Garbacz (2008); Koutroumpis (2009); Qiang and Rossotto (2009); Katz et al. (2010)
[26] El-Darwiche et al. (2013) [27] Siemens (2017)

Gandhi, Somesh Khanna, and Sree Ramaswamy use twenty-seven indicators that fall into three categories: digital usage, digital assets, and digital workers.[28] The Siemens analysis also ranks industries by their culture of innovation, digital operations, and digital customer offerings.[29] Yet another branch of literature has begun to classify the digital maturity of specific cities and urban environments, such as the European Digital City Index and Cohen's Smart City Index.[30]

Another approach focuses more broadly on determining levels of innovation and competitiveness. The most well-known indexes here which attempt to measure these metrics include the Global Innovation Index (GII), the International Innovation Index, the Bloomberg Innovation Index, and the WEF's Global Competitiveness Index (GCI).[31] The GII is noteworthy for its complex blend of quantitative data and qualitative surveys and assessments. At the same time, recent iterations of the GCI have been explicitly influenced by the WEF's vision of the 4IR.[32] These indexes can identify environments where the 4IR may be more likely to grow and actualize, including on the African continent. This is critical since emerging technologies related to the 4IR have a vital role to play as the world and Africa recover from the COVID-19 pandemic to rebuild their economies.[33]

This book primarily utilizes the GII and GCI to analyze the preparation and progress of various African states in the 4IR. I chose these indexes due to their prominence in innovation literature and analysis, and their comprehensive combination of quantitative metrics such as education expenditure with some degree of qualitative and survey data.[34] One risk of using an index such as the GII is that it may oversimplify innovation by boiling down distinct political and economic phenomena into a single metric. As Kolodziejczyk argues, innovation indexes may, for example, misrepresent meaningful innovation by their over-reliance on patents. However, I address these

---

[28] Gandhi, Khanna, and Ramaswamy (2016)   [29] Siemens (2017)
[30] EDCI (2016); See also: Cohen (2014)
[31] Cornell University, INSEAD, and WIPO (2018); Andrew, DeRocco, and Taylor (2009); Schwab (2018); Vasconcellos, Fonseca e Fonseca, and Morel (2018); Jamrisko and Lu (2017)
[32] Kolodziejczyk (2018)   [33] World Economic Forum (2020)
[34] The GII model includes eighty individual indicators, which fall into three categories: "quantitative/objective/hard data" (57), "composite indicators/index data" (18), and "survey/qualitative/subjective soft data" (5). For more explanation, see Cornell University, INSEAD, and WIPO (2018, p. 370)

concerns by critically analyzing how African countries perform in the GII's distinct subcategories and by providing further policy and entrepreneurial contexts to illustrate leaders' strategies in the 4IR. Moreover, I will show how GII results may have ambiguous interpretations or run contrary to qualitative assessments or expectations about leading tech locations in Africa. While the same could be said about the GCI in terms of oversimplification and misrepresentation, I, too, address these concerns as competitiveness is essential for measuring a state's success and maturity. This sets the stage for policy-makers to understand and capitalize on long-term growth, given a country's ranking and contributing factors.[35] In doing so, I hope to demonstrate how policy-makers and academics can draw more nuanced insights and conclusions from innovation performance indices, such as the GII and the GCI.

This book proceeds as follows: In Chapter 2, I examine the definition of the 4IR based on a review of the literature and elaborate on key technologies that characterize Industry 4.0 in Africa. In Chapter 3, I discuss the implications of the 4IR for Africa in five key domains. Chapter 4 analyzes the supply- and demand-side drivers of and challenges to the 4IR in Africa, followed by illustrations of the continent's leaders in technology and innovation. In Chapters 5 and 6, I identify implications of the 4IR for key African industries in the primary, secondary, and tertiary sectors. Chapter 7 discusses cybersecurity and prioritizing technological development in business and policy for African stakeholders to maximize the continent's technical potential. Chapter 8 provides illustrations of the continent's leaders in technology and innovation, while Chapter 9 details Africa's emerging innovation leaders. Chapter 10 addresses health care and the critical role technological innovations play in generating returns for business and health outcomes that contribute to economic prosperity and sustainable development through the investment of health-related 4IR technologies. Chapter 11 summarizes the strategies to maximize Africa's potential for high returns and impact for the future of Africa and the global economy, including broader insights about how Africa can leverage its advantages to thrive in the coming decades.

---

[35] World Economic Forum (2020)

2 | *What Is the Fourth Industrial Revolution?*

The Fourth Industrial Revolution (4IR) is a way of acknowledging, describing, and understanding a range of ongoing changes in how the world functions. These changes are driven by a shift in the pace and scope of co-evolution in technological developments, production systems, and social behaviors, a moment of "punctuated equilibrium" as socio-technological beings.

Being a relatively new concept that brings together concepts across a number of scholarly fields in the social sciences – including science and technology studies, philosophy, history, management studies, and economics – there is no single, commonly-accepted definition of the 4IR. One study that invited eleven scholars to define and identify characteristics of the 4IR concluded with eleven different definitions.[1] Generally, however, most descriptions include broadly defined next-generation digital technology as an underlying basis and bridge for technological transformation. One standardized notion about the 4IR is that its technologies have innovative synergies and combinations with each other – "cyber-physical" systems incorporating a blend of big data, automation, sensor technology, and connectivity.[2]

As described by Schwab and Davis (2018), the 4IR is a normative concept designed to help policy makers and leaders of organizations to engage productively with these technologies and shape their impact on the world. For this reason, the metaphor at the heart of the 4IR consciously recalls both the era-shaping benefits and tragic human and environmental costs associated with prior industrial revolutions, prompting decision makers to consider the systemic and human consequences of funding, designing, developing, diffusing, adopting, using, and abandoning key technologies. In doing so, it aspires to be what Sheila Jasanoff has termed a "socio-technological imaginary": a collective, stable, and public vision of a desirable future, animated by a shared

[1] Lee et al. (2018, pp. 2–7) [2] Alur (2015)

understanding of how social life and order can be supported by advances in science and technology.[3] Contrary to discussions that focus on "Industry 4.0," the idea of the 4IR is not confined to discussion of manufacturing and production; like all industrial revolutions, the 4IR is as much a matter of altered human experience as it is a shift in the productivity frontier.

To better understand the 4IR, it is helpful to examine the context of the three previous industrial revolutions on which it builds (Table 2.1). The First Industrial Revolution of the eighteenth century began with steam power, which enhanced production and transport, reorganized the world of labor, supercharged urbanizations, and dramatically changed landscapes. The Second Industrial Revolution of the late nineteenth century marked the advent of electric power in homes and factories worldwide, creating the foundation of the modern world. The Third Industrial Revolution of the twentieth century included the acceleration of electronics, information technology, and digitization. Each of these revolutions relied on the seamless web of prior technologies, arranged in complex networks to support production, consumption, and social interaction, as the critical infrastructure on which to create new systems that re-ordered human relationships. The 4IR is the advent and impact of technologies that, building on prior industrial revolutions, fuse the digital, biological, and physical world.[4]

Rather than focusing on specific technologies, the literature bases its definition of the 4IR on general qualities and characteristics. Schwab identifies three distinct features of the 4IR: velocity, scope, and systems impact.[5] Velocity refers to the speed at which technologies are spreading and evolving. For example, the number of devices connected to the Internet across the globe is exploding. Advances in genetic engineering, through the Human Genome Project and new genetic editing techniques, have soared. Scope refers to the wide range of sectors, industries, and occupations affected by these technologies. For example, 3D printing, also known as additive manufacturing, could become a method of production for a wide range of light and heavy products, from circuit boards to wind turbines and anything in between. Finally, systems impact refers to the breadth and depth of changes that will occur to entire production, management, and governance systems.[6]

---

[3] Jasanoff (2015)   [4] As defined by Schwab (2016a)   [5] Schwab (2016a)
[6] Schwab (2016a)

Table 2.1 *Industrial Revolution timelines*

Wave	Period	Transition period	Energy resource	Main technical achievement	Main developed industries	Transport means
I	1760–1870*	1870–1900*	Coal	Steam engine	Textile, steel	Train
II	1870–1960*	1940–1960	Oil, electricity	Internal combustion engine	Metallurgy, auto, machine building	Train, car
III	1960–2000	1980–2000	Nuclear energy, natural gas	Computers, robots	Auto, chemistry	Car, plane
IV	2000–present	2000–2010	Green energies	Internet of Things, 3D printer, genetic engineering	High-tech industries	Electric car, ultra-fast train

*Adjusted by the author.
Source: Prisecaru (2016)

The World Economic Forum developed a Strategic Intelligence Map for the 4IR, which attempts to break down the 4IR into a web of broad themes and specific implications.[7] The map categorizes 4IR research based on several major categories: frontier technologies, disruption to jobs and demand for new skills, access and inclusion, agency and trust, technology innovation, ethics and identity, and agile technology governance. Robotic process automation (RPA) allows for a fast-emerging technology that can help automate large quantities of routines.[8] Within the public sector, RPA can be used to help efficiency and effectiveness, which is critical in maximizing resources and time for citizens, especially because of the COVID-19 pandemic.[9] During the pandemic, studies acknowledge that RPA helped to maintain 60 percent of business processes through robotization and software development.[10] Another name for RPA is "bots," which, in turn, are simple mechanisms used to structure data and eliminate human error.[11] With RPA as an essential tool for the Fourth Industrial Revolution, success will be dependent on the insight and practicality of RPA adoption across sectors.[12]

These broad themes connect to smaller branches that feature specific technologies and impacts, including blockchain, artificial intelligence and robotics, cybersecurity, sustainable development, digital economy and society, and the future of production, among others. The overlaps within the map illustrate that 4IR technologies and their implications are highly interconnected, often bridging previously separated themes within the domains of politics, economics, society, and technology.[13]

2.1 Key Technologies of the Fourth Industrial Revolution

The 4IR's key technologies will connect physical, biological, and digital systems; make decisions autonomously; transform production methods; and change the way humans interact with the world. Examining the technologies' characteristics provides a critical means to distinguish between the Third and Fourth Industrial Revolutions and better understand the implications of the 4IR.

Schwab and Davis (2018) divide current emerging technologies into four categories that illustrate the ways in which they are reshaping

---

[7] World Economic Forum (2019)   [8] Agostinelli, Marrella, and Mecella (2020)
[9] Rehr and Munteanu (2021)   [10] Siderska (2021)
[11] ACT-IAC Emerging Technology COI and Management Concepts (2021)
[12] Bornet, Barkin, and Wirtz (2021)   [13] Schwab (2016b)

human systems. The first *are technologies that radically extend the existing digital world*, creating entirely new forms of governance, computational capabilities, and sensing and featuring technologies such as quantum information technologies, the Internet of Things and distributed ledger technologies. The second *are technologies that "rematerialize" key aspects of the digital world to reform the physical world* and include robotics, advanced materials, and multidimensional printing. The third *are technologies that allow us to alter human beings and other organisms*, including creating entirely new beings and directly altering our perception of the world. These include biotechnologies, neurotechnologies, mixed reality, and synthetic biology. Finally, Schwab and Davis point to a number of *technologies that create impact at a systems level in altering our environment and radically shifting infrastructures*. These include emerging energy technologies, geoengineering, and space technologies. Table 2.2 provides us with an illustration of some of the key technologies associated with each category, and the next sections briefly define thirteen technologies.

2.1.1 Additive Manufacturing

Additive manufacturing, or 3D printing, is a means of producing objects that are much more customizable than traditional manufacturing and may become widely used in the future for creating an extensive range of small and large objects at relatively low cost. 3D printing offers small-scale manufacturers the ability to produce goods with lower economies of scale. It may thus transform systems of manufacturing and industrialization, particularly in Africa, where few large-scale manufacturers exist. In the long run, 3D printing may be used for many applications, such as being paired with biotechnology to print human organs for medical transplants.[14] In fact, the uptake of additive manufacturing is growing within Africa. In South Africa, for example, additive manufacturing is used as a prototyping and production tool in a wide range of industries and impacts the production systems of medium, small, and micro enterprises.[15] In addition, 3D printing can aid in the development of 36,000 classrooms in Malawi within ten years, which could take up to seventy years if built with standard procedures.[16]

---

[14] Schwab (2016a, p. 21)   [15] de Beer et al. (2016, p. 50)   [16] Pensulo (2021)

Table 2.2 *Key technology associated with the Fourth Industrial Revolution*

Category and key characteristics	Illustrations	Illustrations
Technologies that radically extend the existing digital world	• *Artificial intelligence* • *Machine learning* • *Distributed ledger technologies* • *Cloud computing* • *Edge computing* • *Ubiquitous, satellite-provided, high-speed Internet* • *Robotic process automation*	• *Big data* • *Quantum information technologies* • *Machine co-creativity and augmented design* • *Digital twins* • *Digital platforms* • *Smart sensors*
Technologies that "rematerialize" key aspects of the digital world to reform the physical world	• *Automation* • *Multi-dimensional manufacturing* • *The Internet of Things* • *Advanced materials* • *Cobots and human-robot collaboration* • *Multi-terrain, adaptable robots*	• *Natural language processing* • *Conversational voice interface* • *Mass personalization and micro-moments* • *Intelligent spaces and smart places* • *Computer vision and facial recognition*
Technologies that allow us to alter human beings and other organisms	• *Biotechnology* • *Genomics & gene editing* • *Nanotechnology* • *Virtual and augmented reality* • *Microchip implants*	• *Mixed reality* • *Augmented humans* • *AI-powered prosthetics* • *Neurotechnologies and brain-computer interfaces*

Table 2.2 (*cont.*)

Category and key characteristics	Illustrations	Illustrations
Technologies that create impact at a systems level in altering our environment and radically shifting infrastructures	• *Energy technologies* • *Geoengineering* • *Space technologies* • *"Smart" and predictive policing* • *AI-driven surveillance-based "smart" and "safe" cities*	• *Autonomous vehicles* • *Swarming drones* • *Cybersecurity and cyber-resilience* • *System integration* • *Reusable spacecraft* • *High-bandwidth, interconnected satellite constellations*

Note: These categories are not always mutually exclusive, given the fusing nature of technologies associated with the Fourth Industrial Revolution.

2.1.2 Advanced Materials Science

Advanced materials science, which seeks to optimize the use of raw materials and develop new sustainable materials, is changing how a wide range of consumer and industrial products is produced, from batteries and consumer electronics to water filtration. Recent advancements in materials science have multiple functionalities that will help in mechanical and civil engineering, manufacturing, metrology, nanotechnology, life sciences, and food sciences.[17] These advancements are due to the rapid development of 4IR technologies[18] fueling cyber-physical spaces. For example, new sensors and magnets drawing on the latest materials science may transform heat waste into electricity.[19] Advanced materials also have applications for improving resiliency and lowering the environmental impact of infrastructure. The logistics industry can use advanced materials to improve packaging, increase the efficiency of vehicles, and reduce the environmental impact of fuel, while adaptive cities can optimize energy systems and improve resource management.[20]

[17] Prakash et al. (2020)   [18] Zoltán (2019, pp. 1–6)
[19] Schwab and Davis (2018, p. 134); Gilga et al. (2017)   [20] de Beer et al. (2016)

2.1.3 *Artificial Intelligence*

Artificial intelligence refers to the ability of machines, computers, or computer-controlled robots to perform operations analogous to human intelligence, from learning, reasoning, recognizing complex patterns, and processing large amounts of information to draw conclusions, self-correct, and make recommendations. Artificial intelligence is *a key general-purpose technology for the 4IR that unlocks automation and robotics and is central to many other emerging technologies.* Artificial intelligence is hence one of the most discussed innovations of the 4IR.

Artificial intelligence has a wide range of applications, from personal assistants, such as Apple's Siri, to autonomous vehicles, to robots with the ability to interact with and adjust to their environment. Worldwide, financial firms are using AI to automate rote tasks and free up financial advisors to handle client services. At the same time, current applications of AI in health care allow for improved medical record-keeping and patient services.[21] In Africa, Nigeria leads the world in using AI for fast, remote medical diagnoses, which solves some health care issues without significant investment in infrastructure.[22] Partnerships will be essential in taking advantage of AI benefits such as lower bandwidth costs if data is processed locally.[23] Nations such as Canada, Israel, and Singapore joined together the public sector, private sector, and academia to create global competitive advantages in AI. Now it is time for Africa to do the same.[24]

Within the broad field of AI techniques and approaches, one of the most powerful sub-fields is "machine learning" (ML), which deploys data and algorithms to imitate the way that humans learn, gradually improving its accuracy. In turn, "deep learning" is a sub-field of machine learning. Machine learning represents a significant advancement in the practical applicability of AI algorithms and data sourcing.[25] It is a technology that can allow computer systems to mimic capacities similar to human intelligence, such as vision and speech, which can impact many sectors outside of tech.[26] Machine learning-based solutions provide future solutions to African agriculture by acquiring data and using it for historical and technical predictions.[27] Machine learning

---

[21] Agarwal et al. (2018)   [22] For example, see: Kontzer (2018)
[23] Deloitte (2020, p. 2)   [24] Candelon, El Bedraoui, and Maher (2021)
[25] Ly (2021)   [26] Ly (2021)   [27] Ly (2021)

would, for example, help employ precision agriculture, otherwise known as smart farming, by making predictions based on soil parameters, carbon and moisture content, yield production, and weed detection.[28] Precision agriculture will be critical for the future of food security in Africa; hence, the need for machine learning applications is stronger than ever.

2.1.4 Automation

Automation is a rapidly growing trend in global manufacturing. Growth in the stock of industrial robots rose 85 percent from 2014 to 2019, a trend that continues to increase, according to the International Federation for Robotics.[29] In fact, globally, despite the effects of the pandemic, overall growth trends are predicted to remain the same with as many as 500,000 units to be installed per year by 2024.[30] Automation has raised concerns about job displacement in manufacturing and other industries; however, it also has the potential to *create* jobs by enhancing productivity and creating complementary job niches to support automation. At a global level, the World Economic Forum estimates that automation will create 97 million jobs by 2025.[31] Automation has yet to penetrate deep into the African continent. Still, some innovative firms are already finding ways to enhance their production processes with industrial machines. Botswana's mining industry, the country's largest sector, uses mine robots to extract minerals at depths previously beyond human capacity.[32]

2.1.5 Autonomous Vehicles and Drones

Autonomous vehicles, including cars and trucks, and drones, can move through their environment with little or no human input using sensors and advanced control systems. Autonomous trucks are likely to massively disrupt the logistics and shipping sector as they eliminate the need for drivers. Meanwhile, autonomous cars have the potential to fundamentally change the ways that people travel, live, and work. For Africa, autonomous drones have the most immediate potential for

---

[28] Sharma et al. (2020)   [29] International Federation of Robotics (2020)
[30] International Federation of Robotics (2021)   [31] Kande and Sonmez (2020)
[32] Anyango (2018)

impact. They can deliver lightweight goods such as medical supplies to remote or rural regions with poor infrastructure and have additional applications in agriculture, surveying, and emergency response. In fact, Rwanda was the first African country to partner with a US startup, Zipline, to use drones for health care delivery. This project has since scaled up into other countries including Ghana, where Zipline has utilized drone delivery to provide medical supplies, COVID-19 testing, and vaccines to remote areas.[33] Drone delivery has also made the shipment of medical supplies, such as the COVID-19 vaccine, highly efficient, accounting for close to 13 percent of Ghana's initial vaccine shipment, and doing so in only three days.[34]

2.1.6 Big Data and Augmented Analytics

Big data – enormous data sets that can computationally analyze to reveal patterns and trends – is an underlying requirement for many other 4IR technologies, such as artificial intelligence, biotechnology, and blockchain. Big data comes in many formats, from structured, numeric data that is easily analyzed to unstructured, nonnumeric data from sources such as Twitter and mobile phone records that require significant manipulation before analysis. When appropriately structured and analyzed, big data can reduce organizational costs and speed up processes, develop new products and services, and improve decision-making.[35] While most big data currently comes from countries with widespread internet access, there is also significant potential for collecting data from sources other than the Internet. In Africa, data from mobile money transactions is underpinning the development of new algorithms to provide credit scoring services to the unbanked and underbanked. These algorithms depend on big data and machine learning technologies to accurately predict a consumer's risk of defaulting on their credit.

As data volumes grow exponentially in the 4IR, big data can be leveraged in the form of "augmented analytics". Augmented analytics is rooted in machine learning and natural processing languages to help boost business intelligence, data sharing, and analytics.[36] Essentially, augmented analytics automates data preparation and data sharing.[37]

---

[33] We Robotics (2020)   [34] Abusalem et al. (2021)   [35] SAS (2019)
[36] Sanjudharan and Ahmad (2020)   [37] Andriole (2019)

With big data expanding across different sectors, the cultivation of augmented analytics is critical in managing the disruption of data.[38] Business
intelligence tools such as augmented analytics will ensure a quick cleaning
of colossal volumes of data, which can allow firms to make real-time
informed decisions.[39]

2.1.7 Biotechnology

Biotechnology is evolving at an incredibly rapid pace in a variety of ways.
Thanks to the Human Genome Project, a genome can be sequenced in a
few hours and for less than a thousand dollars.[40] One of the latest gene-
editing tools, CRISPR, is currently being tested by scientists to combat
cancer and alter human DNA.[41] The 4IR has introduced a field called
metabolomics, which analyzes the cross section of biology, chemistry,
chemometrics, statistics, and computer science.[42] The emergence of this
new field is a huge achievement, thanks to the help of 4IR technologies.
Biotechnology also has implications outside gene editing, including the
development of improved crops, more resilient livestock, and the creation
of new medicines. South Africa is already capitalizing on the biotech
movement with startups in medicine, food preservation, water treatment,
and beyond.[43]

2.1.8 Distributed Ledger Technologies (e.g. Blockchain)

Distributed ledger technologies (DLTs), of which the blockchain is one
example, is characterized by the ability to create and exchange digital
records without a centralized, trusted agent.[44]

Cryptocurrencies such as bitcoin are some of the most famous
examples of blockchain in action, but the technology has a much more
comprehensive range of applications.[45] For example, DLTs could
become a tool for public registration of land and property in sub-
Saharan Africa, allowing millions of people to solidify formal property
ownership and access to capital.[46] DLTs could also be used for supply

---

[38] Dialani (2021)   [39] Henn (2021)
[40] Hayden (2014); Schwab (2016a, p. 24)   [41] Schwab and Davis (2018, p. 157)
[42] Tugizimana et al. (2020)   [43] See, for example: Mpala (2018)
[44] Swan (2015); Yli-Huumo (2016); Zheng et al. (2018)
[45] Zheng et al. (2018, pp. 363–367)
[46] Zheng et al. (2018, p. 365); Schwab (2016a, p. 50)

chain management and for verifying the origin of goods, potentially contributing to the ethical sourcing of traded products and helping to improve consumer safety. African countries such as Kenya, Nigeria, and Ghana are currently seeing the benefits of DLTs in fighting corruption and voter fraud and combatting inflation.[47]

2.1.9 Cloud Computing

Cloud computing refers to the on-demand, remote availability of computer system resources such as software, infrastructure, platforms, data storage, and computing power to users over the Internet. Cloud computing allows companies and individuals to minimize up-front ICT infrastructure costs and optimize their use of resources. It can provide a valuable service to back up data, particularly in countries where unreliable electricity has the potential to damage electronic devices. The adoption of cloud technologies will continue to rise in businesses throughout the 2020s.[48] Cloud platforms in the 4IR will provide digital infrastructure for smart cities due to their ability to store and analyze data. They will also provide data analytics, AI, and other capabilities to companies, individuals, and organizations; and will help institutions manage large volumes of data.[49] In some African countries, cloud computing has already become a solution to ICT infrastructure problems. The banking and education sectors have been the first to adopt the technology on the continent. Countries including Tanzania and Rwanda have begun data center projects to support cloud technology.[50]

2.1.10 High-Speed, High-Bandwidth Internet

High-speed, high-bandwidth internet, including 5G technology, will allow the digital economy and society to become even more complex and elaborate. New services and industries are developing entirely through internet forums and devices, from online retail and financial services to digitized public services managed by government agencies. These trends are especially prevalent on the African continent. Africa's growing mobile sector has entailed a robust digital marketplace, and

[47] Mwanza and Wilkings (2018)   [48] Deloitte Insights (2020)
[49] Tan (2018)   [50] Maaref (2012)

Kenya has become a model for digital growth. Many 4IR technologies, such as automated vehicles and the Internet of Things, will also rely on improved internet technology to function effectively.

2.1.11 The Internet of Things

The Internet of Things (IoT) is a physical network of devices that simultaneously exist and interact with the physical world while being connected to the Internet, thereby able to sense the world around them while receiving and sending data to other devices and applications.[51] Internet of Things has wide-ranging implications both on a small scale, with devices that connect home appliances, reduce home energy usage, and track personal activity, and on a large scale, with applications for transportation, national energy and water systems, manufacturing, health, and waste management. The largest current driver of IoT is the spread of connected mobile phones and devices, but there has also been rapid investment in, for example, the United States, China, India, and the United Kingdom in IoT infrastructure, such as "smart city" technology, which uses data to efficiently manage urban resources.[52] The amount of global IoT spending was predicted to increase by 24 percent in 2021 and by an additional 27 percent through 2025.[53] This growth will only continue to accelerate: The number of IoT devices is forecasted to reach nearly 125 billion by 2030.[54] In Africa, one study identified ten existing smart city zones, showing the application of IoT infrastructure on the African continent.[55] Rwanda is currently leading the way in African smart cities, with Ghana, Kenya, and South Africa also designing cities with solar-powered streetlights and automated lift car parks.

2.1.12 Nanotechnology

Nanotechnology, the development of microscopic materials and service robots, will have a transformative, potentially volatile impact in a wide scope of domains: Nanobots can deliver drugs not only to repair cellular damage but also to enhance chemical weapons and explosives.[56]

---

[51] Höller et al. (2014); Atzori, Iera, and Morabito (2010); Kortuem et al. (2010)
[52] Deloitte (2014)   [53] Wegner (2021)   [54] Howell (2017)
[55] Huet (2016)   [56] Schwab and Davis (2018, p. 134)

The potency of this technology has led a combination of US agencies to spend over $1.7 billion annually on nanotech research.[57] While most nanotechnology research and policy-making is currently concentrated in developed economies, government support programs for nanotechnology research are being developed in Nigeria and South Africa; the South African Nanotechnology Initiative, for example, has brought together a network of academic researchers in various nanotechnology-related fields in order to strengthen their nanotechnology capacity and drive growth.[58]

2.1.13 Virtual and Augmented Reality

Virtual and augmented reality (VR/AR) refers to "technology that overlays information and virtual objects on real-world scenes in real-time."[59] Augmented reality has a growing set of consumer and business applications across a range of industries, from developing interactive video games and enhancing educational experiences to designing complex manufacturing products and processes.[60] Virtual and augmented reality also serve as efficient technologies in facilitating reconstruction planning and damage control caused by natural disasters.[61] Ventures in AR are beginning to develop across the African continent, supported by cross-border efforts from entrepreneurs and firms. For example, over thirty-five teams from seven African countries competed in an AR Africa Hackathon event in April 2018, applying AR technologies to critical sectors such as health care, education, and tourism.[62] Winners from Nigeria developed an application using AR to authenticate medication as a measure against counterfeit drugs.[63]

2.2 Key Themes of the Fourth Industrial Revolution

Several key themes emerge from an analysis of the major technologies and general characteristics of the 4IR. The first of these are productivity and sustainability. The 4IR will allow countries, businesses, and individuals to harness new technologies to increase the speed, efficiency, and sustainability of production using technologies such as

---

[57] National Nanotechnology Initiative (2021)   [58] Alo (n.d.)
[59] Marr (2018)   [60] Ong and Nee (2013, pp. 2–5)
[61] Zhu and Li (2021, p. 10)   [62] Okonkwo (2018)   [63] Okonkwo (2018)

automation, artificial intelligence, and 3D printing. These technologies have the potential to augment growth as industrial productivity increases, online connectivity opens new international markets, and the production of small-scale, customized manufactured goods becomes viable. Growth based on 4IR technologies is also likely to be more environmentally sustainable than that of previous industrial revolutions, as developments in areas such as materials science and nanotechnology decrease the environmental impact of manufacturing and construction.

A second theme is that of disruption and structural transformation. The 4IR will drive rapid and massive changes to industries, jobs, and skills and will pose new challenges for governance and security. By 2025, 85 million job roles may be displaced by technology, while 97 million new job roles may emerge.[64] These new jobs will require a workforce with new skills in science, technology, engineering, ICT, and management, among other fields. Worldwide, governments will need to collaborate with the private sector and other key stakeholders to change education systems to reduce the impacts of joblessness due to automation and to improve cybersecurity. But as employment in low-skill industries decreases due to technology, new opportunities will arise in higher-skill industries that develop innovative uses for big data, cloud technologies, and artificial intelligence. This process is likely to change the structure of both developed and developing economies; in Africa, this structural transformation may mean that economic growth and development will have to occur through means other than indus-trialization, as technology will reduce the need for labor in industrial sectors.

Third, the 4IR will both require new levels of and present new opportunities for cooperation and inclusivity on a global scale. Some of the 4IR's technologies, such as cloud computing and 3D printing, offer new, promising means for inclusivity of developing countries with poor ICT infrastructure and of small, medium, and micro enterprises and entrepreneurs. These technologies can help reduce the up-front costs of infrastructure, make small-scale production more cost effect-ive, and improve access to software and other computer services for underserved populations. However, there remain significant risks that will remain concentrated in the economies of the developed world,

[64] World Economic Forum (2020)

leaving Africa and other developing economies to fall further behind. New technologies also have the potential to exacerbate within-country inequality, as the premiums to high-skill occupations increase and the need for low-skilled labor decreases. Without global cooperation to continue improving access to technology, particularly high-speed, high-bandwidth internet, and to mitigate the displacing effects of automation and other 4IR technologies, the 4IR may result in higher levels of intrastate and interstate inequality.

Finally, the 4IR poses new risks for security, privacy, and data integrity. Innovation and technology will need to be complemented with a robust and adaptive regulatory framework and strong, agile governance to ensure consumer protection and a stable transition into the 4IR. Cybersecurity will take on unprecedented importance as cyber warfare expands and the increasing interconnection of systems and importance of data provides new targets for attack. Again, global cooperation that incorporates both the public sector and technology companies will likely be necessary to ensure the privacy of citizens and the integrity of data.

Overall, the 4IR's cyber-physical systems and technologies are likely to have a transformative effect on the global economy and international relations. In Chapter 3, I turn to an examination of the likely impacts of the 4IR in Africa.

3 | *What Does the Fourth Industrial Revolution Mean for Africa?*

A growing literature base is beginning to examine Africa's prospects in the Fourth Industrial Research (4IR). Extensive research has already documented and analyzed the impacts of mobile internet and broadband penetration throughout the continent.[1] Research and initiatives on African "smart cities" have also gained traction as a method for urban development and sustainability.[2] Most recently, scholars have focused on the implications of the 4IR for African industrialization, development, and manufacturing.[3] Some scholars have primarily highlighted the risks African industry faces from the competition with automation in advanced economies and a growing digital divide. For example, Banga and te Velde (2018) remark on the comparatively low rates of digitalization and broadband in Africa; they argue that African countries face a limited window of opportunity to develop labor-intensive manufacturing before automation and 3D printing from advanced economies become cheap enough to outcompete African labor.[4]

Conversely, other scholars and researchers have suggested myriad opportunities for African development and "leapfrog" potential in the 4IR.[5] Naudé (2017) examines the role of entrepreneurs in developing 4IR innovation for Africa's manufacturing sector. Analyzing successful initiatives by African entrepreneurs with technologies such as 3D

---

[1] Wyche and Olson (2018); Deen-Swarray (2016); Lancaster (2017); Asongu and Nwachukwu (2016); Yeboah-Boateng, Osei-Owusu, and Henten (2017); Mothobi and Grzybowski (2017); Ndung'u (2018b); Ndemo (2016); Ponelis and Holmner (2015); Pepper, Garrity, and LaSalle (2016); Stork, Calandro, and Gillwald (2013)

[2] Slavova and Okwechime (2016); Siba and Sow (2017); Huet (2016); Tshiani and Tanner (2018); Kizza (2016); Deloitte (2015)

[3] Banga and te Velde (2018); Cilliers (2018); de Beer et al. (2016); Naudé (2017); Newfarmer, Page, and Tarp (2018); Hallward-Driemeier and Nayyar (2017)

[4] Banga and te Velde (2018, pp. 52–53)

[5] Newfarmer, Page, and Tarp (2018); Agarwal et al. (2018); Schmidt (2018)

printing identifies an opportunity for small-scale manufacturing to become more competitive and efficient. Cilliers (2018) finds that the 4IR may encourage the production of goods for regional, rather than global, markets and suggests a cluster of policy interventions for African countries to take advantage of this trend, such as investments in ICT infrastructure and educational access.[6] Finally, Newfarmer, Page, and Tarp (2018) highlight the role of "industries without smoke-stacks," characterized by, for example, growing ICT and service sector exports, which may provide a new sustainable path for African development in the context of the 4IR.

I argue that while African states, industries, and individuals will feel the changes of the 4IR everywhere, there are five key domains that stand out: economic growth and structural transformation; labor, skills, and production; poverty and inequality; democracy, power, and governance; and peace and security.

3.1 Economic Growth and Structural Transformation

By 2050, Africa will have more than half of its population under the age of twenty-five,[7] housing the world's largest youth-oriented potential workforce.[8] But, in the post-COVID-19 era, the African continent faces the challenge of regaining the successful trajectory of economic growth and employment opportunity before the pandemic hit. Here, 4IR technology represents a massive opportunity for growth in supporting African countries' positive development. The Fourth Industrial Revolution technology has the potential to create new formal wage jobs at such a rate that informal employment will be reduced in terms of total employment and increased earnings will be seen in the informal sector.[9] Benefits can also include reduction of production cost, productivity and earnings improvement, and the development and introduction of new business lines, which could be particularly advantageous to Africa's youth (who will account for the largest share of workers in the African workforce). Certain sectors will benefit more from the deployment of 4IR technologies than others, including the agricultural sector, where 4IR technology can reduce poverty and increase farm earnings; the manufacturing sector, where 4IR technology can encourage small-scale

---

[6] Cilliers (2018, pp. 19–20)   [7] Agence Française de Developpement (2019)
[8] Nsengimana (2018)   [9] Signé and Fox (2021, p. 3)

production at the domestic and regional market level; and the service sector, where opportunities for wage employment expansion are the highest.[10] Incremental change in these areas is expected, and African countries can continue to capitalize on these advancements by developing comprehensive strategies to overcome significant challenges.

As the 4IR unfolds, African countries will be increasingly integrated into the global economy, and one of Africa's critical economic challenges will be structural transformation. The difference between positive and negative outcomes from the advancement of the 4IR will come from a country's ability to balance its internal conditions and policy choices. Widening inequality remains a critical risk to overall economic development and transformation in some African countries. Poorer youth risk being left behind as they have less access to ICT services, electricity, quality education, and training.[11] The overall digital gender divide also puts women in disadvantageous positions that increases inequality in the continent. However, with multi-external stakeholder cooperation, African countries can help to lead investors to realize needed investments and reduce challenges.

3.1.1 Opportunities for Structural Transformation

However, different pathways to industrialization exist, and other sectors can also significantly contribute to economic growth. The potential of nonmanufacturing sectors: in particular, "industries without smokestacks," including tourism, telecommunication, ICT-based services, agro-processing, and horticulture – will become more critical in the context of the 4IR as a driver of industrialization, growth, and employment. The upside of Africa's current economic structure is that many countries can now have the potential to jump into advanced manufacturing and services with little resistance from entrenched, outdated manufacturing structures.

The ICT revolution has already driven growth in the industrial and service sectors, and 4IR technologies such as high-speed Internet, blockchain, and VR have further potential to cause rapid expansion of, in particular, Africa's service sector. On the global level, trade in services is already growing faster than trade in goods, and Africa's trade in services nearly doubled from 2005 to 2015, reaching $240

---

[10] Signé and Fox (2021, p. 3)   [11] Signé and Fox (2021, p. 4)

billion. The services sector also offers many advantages for developing countries, compared to manufacturing. Trade, in-services, can bypass logistical and customs barriers – major obstacles for Africa, particularly its landlocked countries – facilitated by technological change. Services also generally result in more inclusive, environmentally friendly, and gender-friendly growth.[12]

Many 4IR technologies, especially blockchain, artificial intelligence, IoT, and 3D printing, are likely to impact the future of trade significantly. The 4IR can increase commodity-exporting and efficiency and sustainability of small countries, enhancing cross-border trade by improving standardization and traceability.[13] Blockchain, for example, may help improve cross-border payment processes by reducing fees and currency exchange rate costs and enhancing the tracking of goods and services along the supply chain.[14] In this context, the African Continental Free Trade Area (AfCFTA), which entered into force in May 2019, has the potential to be a pivotal mechanism to ensure that African countries benefit from the 4IR's impacts on trade and can mitigate the risks it presents. The AfCFTA will allow for the creation of cohesive continental trade laws and regulations, which will better accommodate the rapid changes of the 4IR. It may also help ensure that landlocked and small countries have greater access to regional and global markets, thus mitigating the tendency of some 4IR technologies to enhance inequality. Finally, the AfCFTA will improve regional economic integration, thus improving the ability of businesses to learn from each other and integrate themselves into regional supply chains, potentially driving increased innovation.

The 4IR also offers opportunities for new forms of manufacturing that could drive growth, including more competitive small-scale manufacturing through additive manufacturing and mass customization, cheaper automation, and cheaper input costs.[15] The 4IR is also likely to present new opportunities for agriculture-driven transformation. ICTs have the potential to upgrade all stages of agricultural value chains: Precision agriculture can increase the productivity of farms using big data and autonomous vehicles to optimize the delivery of inputs; ICT platforms, such as those that connect farmers to service providers or markets, can help develop new business models to increase

---

[12] AfDB, OECD, and UNDP (2017, p. 167) [13] Tsagkalidis et al. (2018, p. 3)
[14] Tsagkalidis et al. (2018, p. 9) [15] Naudé (2018, p. 4)

youth participation; and blockchain technologies can guarantee food safety standards and lead to increased involvement in international food markets. New technologies are likely to make African countries highly competitive global food suppliers while presenting few downsides in terms of job loss and helping to improve inclusion, particularly in rural areas.[16] While questions remain about the ability of these sectors to absorb low-skilled labor, the move away from low-productivity agriculture and capital-heavy commodities is promising for economic growth.

Africa is poised to develop new business models based on 4IR technologies. Among the opportunities are business models that bring goods and services to consumers, including products-as-services, the sharing economy, and digital services and exports. The success of M-Pesa, in financial services, as well as the potential of autonomous drones for delivery and digital applications for agriculture, points to a future where 4IR solutions are tailored to the African context. These solutions can drive rapid growth and improve economic inclusion while also suggesting that some new technologies may be easier to adopt and adapt in Africa than in other regions.[17]

Data may become the "new oil" of the digital era, meaning that businesses will need to gather and exploit data efficiently to maintain a competitive advantage.[18] New digital platforms and blockchain transaction tools have low barriers to entry, inviting small firms and entrepreneurs on the African continent and across the world to gain access to the global digital economy. Yet significant, established tech firms such as Google, Facebook, Amazon, and Microsoft may gain an increasingly central role in global commerce as data consolidated by these companies become more integral to international business. In this context, African firms, states, and investors will need to be creative to find new technological niches in the global market to maintain the continent's competitiveness.

Innovative industrialization strategies could better target high-potential entrepreneurial activities to accelerate growth. Entrepreneurs play an essential role in bringing innovation to an economy, including new technologies, production methods, and experimenting with new products in local markets. Public and private support for tech hubs will

---

[16] AfDB, ADB, EBRD, IDB (2018)   [17] World Economic Forum (2017a, p. 9)
[18] Engelke (2018)

also help drive innovation and growth: Currently, South Africa, Nigeria, Egypt, and Kenya host more than thirty tech hubs, and most countries in Africa have at least one. Growth in Ghana and Côte d'Ivoire demonstrates West Africa's potential to become a technological destination. Meanwhile in East Africa, Kigali is poised as the next tech leader, having hosted the Africa Tech Summit and the GSMA Mobile 360 Africa conference recently.[19] Greater investment in these growing tech hubs is just as essential as funding to established hubs because expanding the locations of innovation will enhance the profile of all African tech companies on the world stage.

3.1.2 Consumer Markets and Distribution

The 4IR is transforming the distribution and types of services demanded by African consumers. The spread of ICTs provides new and innovative avenues for consumer spending, such as e-commerce, and has facilitated access to Africa's large and growing consumer market in new and varied ways. Africa's consumer market is much less saturated and developed than that of other developing regions, thus offering massive growth and investment opportunities.[20] Signé and Fox state that "new technology emerging from the 4IR can provide better material welfare by lessening the cost of consumer goods."[21] As the 4IR begins to offer new options for connectivity, localization of product offerings, and digital platforms, businesses will better be able to tap this consumer market and drive growth on the continent.

Within the next thirty years, it is expected that seven out of ten people will live in cities globally,[22] and African cities are expected to double in population within this time as well. In fact, Africa's current largest city, Lagos, is expected to expand at a rate of seventy-seven people per hour between now and 2030.[23] In addition, Africa's economically active population will increase from 56 percent of the continent to 66 percent.[24] The African continent is estimated to become one of the youngest continents globally. Fifty percent of the population under the age of twenty-five may give way to a promising future for the 4IR.[25] The fast-growing population, coupled with proper educational training and

---

[19] Engelke (2018)   [20] Signé (2018b, p. 17)   [21] Signé and Fox (2021, p. 11)
[22] World Bank (2020)   [23] Muggah and Hill (2018)
[24] Muggah and Hill (2018)   [25] Smith (2019)

job-creating policies, could be the continent's most effective tool in aiding socio-economic transformations.[26] Improved social and economic standards will enable the continent to boost consumption and build more robust markets. Current leading country markets include a combination of fast-growing, digitally mature, and business-friendly states, such as Ethiopia, Ghana, Kenya, Nigeria, Morocco, and South Africa.[27] Increased governmental spending on ICT can benefit the digitalization in sub-Saharan Africa and generate new economic growth,[28] such as successes found in leading countries' markets.

African consumers today have greater access to markets due to the increased adoption of mobile phones and the Internet throughout the continent. One analysis, conducted in 2018, found over 300 unique digital platforms (combined across eight focus countries) matching suppliers and consumers of goods and services operating in Ghana, Kenya, Nigeria, Rwanda, South Africa, Tanzania, Uganda, and Zambia.[29] The majority of these platforms provided access to services such as transportation and mail, and 27 percent were platforms for online shopping. More than 80 percent of these digital platforms were founded in Africa, and thirty-seven platforms serviced multiple countries.[30] Companies are also more easily connected to consumers, enhancing mobile marketing and promotional access that incentivize spending and brand loyalty. E-commerce will continue to grow because of the influx of online shopping due to COVID-19. For example, Nigeria's Paystack, a financial payment company, saw five times the increase in transactions compared to pre-pandemic figures.[31] The rapid increase of internet usage during the pandemic among African consumers will be vital in accelerating 4IR expansions across the continent.

Consumers will significantly influence the manufacturing and supply chain systems in the 4IR because data on consumer preferences can inform manufacturers and create new revenue streams from customizable products. For example, 4IR manufacturers will use 3D printing to design machines capable of producing customized goods in reduced time span to market.[32] In Uganda, a Canadian company has partnered

[26] Brown (2020)   [27] Brown (2020)
[28] Myoyella, Karacuka, and Haucap (2020)
[29] Makuvaza, Johnson, and Smit (2018)
[30] Makuvaza, Johnson, and Smit (2018)   [31] Oxford Business Group (2021)
[32] Jamwal (2016)

with local innovators to use 3D printing for prosthetic limbs custom-ized to individuals' needs in less time than it takes to cast and mold a prosthetic.[33] In Togo, 3D printing is used to print local entrepreneurs' prototypes for easy, quick distribution of anti-theft products for motorcyclists.[34]

The primary challenges to consumer market development rest in comparisons of Africa's purchasing power parity growth – or lack thereof – with an increase in income and labor productivity throughout the rest of the world. Sub-Saharan Africa's per capita income levels equal less than one-third the levels of any other world region and have risen worryingly slow since 2000, compared to the steady increase in the global mean level of income from 2000 to 2016.[35]

Africa's consumer markets are also constrained by their largely infor-mal configuration. South Africa and Angola host the most significant modern trade sectors, but formal retail only accounted for 39 percent and 34 percent of shopping visits, respectively, in 2015.[36] In Nigeria, 80 percent of consumers participate in roadside or "table-top" vending, and 95 percent of consumer spending occurs at these informal markets in Ghana, Cameroon, Ethiopia, and Egypt.[37] Investment is necessary to transform these informal markets into large-scale centers for consumer spending.

Overall, digital market opportunities underscore both trends of rising ICT access and demand and the need to bolster internet infrastructure to maintain growth. First movers may gain a significant advantage in these digital markets, as African consumers are known for developing brand loyalty, particularly to local vendors.[38] Just as Uber and Amazon have dominated in Western markets, firms such as Twende, a Tanzania-based e-hailing application, and Jumia, an online shopping platform, are becoming critical online players in Africa. Jumia has become the largest e-commerce platform in Africa, reporting a 50 percent rise in transactions during the first half of the year in 2020.[39] Yet even digital platforms represent only one avenue for the 4IR in Africa's consumer markets. New entry points continue to emerge as Africa's tech leaders and entrepreneurs find new ways to provide goods and services to previously underserved markets. Rwanda's successful humanitarian

---

[33] Gadzala (2018)   [34] Gadzala (2018)   [35] Signé (2018b, p. 3)
[36] Signé (2018b, p. 14)   [37] Signé (2018b, p. 14)   [38] Spivey et al. (2013)
[39] Oxford Business Group (2021)

application of drones to deliver medicine, for example, demonstrates a new way for African firms to sell products to consumers in remote regions.

The 4IR expands the territory for investment opportunities in Africa. Therefore, firms and investors look toward fast-growing markets on the continent and the untapped potential of regions and sectors that can now supply a range of goods and services using 4IR innovation. States that facilitate businesses and reduce the risks for private sector players to supply underserved markets can gain the most from what the 4IR has to offer consumers. National leaders also have an essential role in encouraging investment in consumer goods and risk management for domestic firms amid global competition.

Policy-makers and company leaders are responsible for coordinating their strategies for domestic entry into consumer markets and the protection of domestic buyers. Several methods include investing in market research to analyze domestic supply and demand potential, incentivizing localized product offerings, encouraging import substitution, and collaborating with technology innovators to incorporate 4IR technology with each step.

Governments across the African continent are facilitating the growth of digitalization and should focus on promoting the importance of ICTs internally while increasing the use of social media.[40] The development of Africa's consumer markets has enormous potential for future job creation within the industry. As incomes in emerging markets and among Africa's middle-class rise, production and trade within consumer markets can be transformed to provide for consumers' growing demand for technologically integrated products and services.

3.2 Labor, Skills, and Production

The 4IR will dramatically change global systems of labor and production, including in Africa. As manifestations of the 4IR increasingly penetrate the borders of African countries, skills and capabilities must adapt much more rapidly to the needs of African firms and competition with machines. On the one hand, Africa's working population is becoming better educated. The share of workers with at least a secondary

---

[40] Solomon and van Klyton (2020)

education will increase from 36 percent in 2010 to 52 percent in 2030.[41] Yet machines work faster than schools: Estimates of automatable work activities range from upwards of 40 percent across African countries.[42] Governments and industries may struggle to incorporate Africa's growing workforce with new production systems; Africa's labor force must make quick and drastic changes to adapt to the 4IR.

Automation using 4IR technologies, such as robotics and artificial intelligence, has had a significant impact on the manufacturing sector. Automation and artificial intelligence will allow business stakeholders either the opportunity to facilitate change or to fall behind.[43] In 2020, the International Federation of Robotics reported a 12 percent increase in industrial robots, summing up a total of 2.7 million operating in factories worldwide.[44] The accelerating adoption of automation technologies has been driven by the declining costs of robotics and improvements in robots and artificial intelligence abilities, resulting in greater manufacturing efficiencies and increased labor productivity.[45] A study by Boston Consulting estimates that automation will further raise labor productivity in manufacturing by between 10 and 30 percent over the next decade.[46]

Robots are particularly efficient at tasks that are "dull, dangerous, and dirty."[47] As a result, most industrial robots are used in manufacturing sectors, such as vehicles and transportation equipment, electronic and electrical equipment, and machinery. Africa imports significant numbers of these goods, suggesting a large domestic market that local manufacturers may be able to tap as they adopt robots and other technologies that improve efficiency and make local production more cost-effective.[48]

Currently, in Africa, most manufacturing robots are used in South Africa's automotive sector. But given the potential for robots to increase manufacturing productivity in high-demand sectors, there are a growing number of initiatives in several African countries pushing for their greater use. For example, the Ghana-based African Robotics Network had more than 380 members in 51 countries in 2016; in Uganda, the Fundi Bots initiative provides robotics education to children; and Egypt launched the EG Robotics initiative in 2015 to

[41] World Economic Forum (2017b, p. 7)
[42] World Economic Forum (2017b, p. 9)   [43] Atiku and Boateng (2020)
[44] IFR (2020)   [45] Naudé (2017)   [46] Sirkin, Zinser, and Rose (2015)
[47] Frey, Osborne, and Holmes (2016)   [48] Naudé (2017, p. 6)

promote robotic development in Egypt and the MENA region. The private sector drives most of these initiatives and receives little public sector support.[49]

3.2.1 Challenges Surrounding Labor and Skills

Given the potential impact of the 4IR on production, the composition of demand for labor and the skills required to participate in the workforce is likely to undergo significant change. Unlike in earlier industrial revolutions, the 4IR's technologies tend to replace low-skilled workers while complementing high-skilled workers. A binding constraint on whether an economy can participate in manufacturing in the 4IR is thus whether its workforce is sufficiently and appropriately skilled.[50]

Africa's current labor force is far from its potential. The World Economic Forum's Human Capital Index finds that sub-Saharan Africa captures only 55 percent of its total human capital potential on average, compared to a global average of 65 percent. Correspondingly, 41 percent of all firms in Tanzania and 30 percent in Kenya identify inadequately skilled workforces as a major constraint to their businesses.[51] On the whole, the continent is underprepared for the impending disruption to jobs and skills. In South Africa, for example, 64 percent of companies are looking to reduce the number of workers who lack the skills to use new technology and replace them with temporary workers with relevant skills.[52] Governments and industries may struggle to incorporate Africa's growing workforce with new systems of production. With 11 million African workers continuing to enter the job market every year with varying levels of skills and capabilities, Africa needs to cultivate digital skills as part of transitioning its population from low-skill, low-paying jobs to high-skill, high-paying jobs.[53]

As African firms modernize and develop, employment will require managerial skills, interaction with digital interfaces, and data analysis skills. The fastest-growing jobs on LinkedIn for Africa include occupations that require hard quantitative skills in addition to creativity and decision-making skills, such as entrepreneurs, business managers, and

---

[49] Naudé (2017, p. 7)   [50] Naudé (2017, p. 4)
[51] World Economic Forum (2017b, pp. iii–1)
[52] World Economic Forum (2020, p. 106)   [53] Newman, Page, and Tarp (2017)

data center managers. Notably, most of these professions can be complementary rather than substituting to labor-saving innovations, such as automation and AI. Just as labor-saving technology is reshaping employment around the world, 4IR innovations will require African laborers to develop a broader and more diverse skill set that can add value to new production systems.

Several factors hinder the opportunities of the 4IR, such as low GDP growth, high debt, and underinvestment.[54] However, investing in building human capital in science, technology, engineering, and mathematics (STEM) will help drive local innovation and growth.[55] This is especially true in data analysis, computer science, and engineering, as these are fields in which the 4IR could create a wide range of new jobs. Recent research from the World Economic Forum on human capital in the 4IR recommends that governments strengthen education systems, ensuring the future readiness of curricula. They also suggest investing in digital fluency and ICT literacy, providing robust technical and vocational education and training, and remaining open to education innovation, among other recommendations.[56] New technologies offer opportunities for the innovative delivery of education and training: Online courses, for example, are available globally from top universities through Massive Online Open Courses (MOOCs). Ultimately, those without access to the proper education or technical training will suffer,[57] which is why partnerships will be the key to developing 4IR skills. The diaspora presents another opportunity to present adequate incentives to those trained in robotics, AI, biotechnology, and other 4IR skills to return to their country of origin and educate the domestic workforce.[58] Businesses will also need to determine how the 4IR will affect employees and processes and act accordingly, upskilling and reskilling workers where necessary. The education system alone should not be relied upon to provide workers with 4IR-relevant skills: Businesses should provide essential skills training as part of an internal strengthening process.

In addition to building human capital, challenges also remain regarding the creation of quality formal sector jobs. On average, the high-skilled employment share of sub-Saharan Africa is just 6 percent,

---

[54] Itcovitz (2020)   [55] Itcovitz (2020)
[56] World Economic Forum (2017c, p. 10)   [57] Kazimierczuk (2020, pp. 1 and 2)
[58] Chen, Geiger, and Fu (2015)

compared to the global average of 24 percent.[59] The absence of skilled employment opportunities has led to high levels of unemployment among educated youth, most notably in North Africa. Addressing the disruptive effects of the 4IR will thus require a multifaceted approach that builds human capital, ensures that the skills taught by education providers align with the rapidly changing needs of industry, and expands the availability of high-skill formal jobs.

3.3 Poverty and Inequality

The 4IR can be harnessed as a tool for social innovation and poverty alleviation across the African continent. While many 4IR technologies are seen as threats to low-skilled laborers, new technologies also offer Africa's poorest with new job market opportunities. The spread of digital technologies can also empower the poor with access to information and services that can improve their standard of living. Further innovations such as AI, IoT, and blockchain can enhance opportunities for data gathering and analysis for poverty-reduction strategies.

The low levels of economic inclusion that have accompanied Africa's recent growth concern stability and the sustainability of development on the continent. Rapid growth in Africa has failed, for example, to create enough quality jobs for the estimated 36.3 million unemployed population. Poverty reduction has also been short of expectations. Leaving large sections of the population behind is likely to affect the sustainability of future economic growth by stifling the potential of aggregate demand and economic dynamism.[60] Inequality is also directly correlated with sociopolitical instability, which lowers investment and thus further lowers growth.[61]

The previous three industrial revolutions failed to reach most of Africa; a significant portion of the continent uses preindustrial machinery. There is a lack of basic infrastructure, which exacerbates current global and within-country divides. Without stable and widespread infrastructure, the 4IR could further drive inequality among and within countries. For example, a large proportion of the nearly 500,000 employed in the South African mining sector may lose their jobs to robots and other 4IR technologies.[62] In Egypt, it is estimated that

---

[59] World Economic Forum (2017b, p. 4)   [60] Ncube (2015, p. 1)
[61] Alesina and Perotti (1996, p. 1203)   [62] Harvey (2017)

49 percent of all work activities are susceptible to automation.[63] As seen in many advanced economies, where automation has contributed to growing inequality, new technologies threaten to further concentrate benefits and wealth among the already wealthy. Globally, countries with low levels of human capital and ICT usage risk falling even further behind.[64] However, the growth of mobile subscription rates and investments such as the World Bank's $1.2 billion for African broadband demonstrate a growing commitment to digital infrastructure that can become a powerful driver for poverty reduction.[65]

Innovative initiatives are beginning to form across the continent to encourage inclusive growth under the 4IR. For example, the NGO Educate! works with national education systems and secondary schools in Uganda, Rwanda, and Kenya to address youth unemployment by reforming school curricula and teaching methods to impart, to students, the skills needed for the 4IR. In South Africa, the Skills Development Levy directly supports the training and education of South African employees with industry-aligned training and skill development. The Skills Initiative for Africa, a joint initiative with Germany and the African Union Commission, promotes innovative technical and vocational education and training (TVET) approaches through institutional strengthening, capacity development, and an Africa-wide dialogue platform.[66]

The technologies of the 4IR also have the potential to improve economic inclusion. Mobile money platforms such as M-Pesa have received considerable attention for their ability to bring banking, insurance, and other financial services to many who had previously been excluded. But other, less well-known applications also have significant potential. Consider, for example, Poverty Stoplight, an application now operating in over forty-three countries[67] allows families to assess their level of poverty across fifty specific indicators, gauging their well-being and access to sanitation and transportation.[68] The application enables families to develop strategies for managing their social circumstances based on household priorities. It also allows governments and corporations to understand better the needs of citizens, consumers, and employees. In addition, a new program called the

---

[63] World Economic Forum (2017d, p. iii)   [64] Harvey (2017)
[65] Navas-Sabater (2015)   [66] Deloitte (2018b, p. 45)
[67] Poverty Stoplight (2021)   [68] Burt (2016)

Nutrition Early Warning System (NEWS) uses AI-based technologies and satellite imaging to predict and overcome natural disasters that pose nutritional challenges, such as malnutrition. As a result, the program will help to battle these issues using productive agro-food activities.[69]

Addressing women's inequalities in Africa is a critical aspect of economic inclusion. Chiweche (2019) explains that new technologies may reduce jobs in female-dominated industries.[70] However, 4IR technologies such as mobile money services are increasing women's economic empowerment, allowing women to move away from subsistence agriculture and into new nonfarm businesses.[71] Although disruptions resulting from the 4IR are to be anticipated, all groups need to be considered when building inclusive frameworks to alleviate negative impacts. Young women are a vital part of Africa's growing population[72] as well as to the success of the 4IR. Female-centric frameworks and training programs must be adopted, to ensure strategic solutions. Innovations in 4IR technologies will need to be supported by promotions of STEM education skills training for young girls and increased opportunities for female entrepreneurship.[73] These training initiatives will be critical in assimilating African women into a more inclusive 4IR.

Transformation, and long-term strategies for sustainable change, will have to include women. According to Byanyima and Kende-Robb (2021), women will be the driving force behind another wave of transformation across the continent.[74] They will continue to be leaders in emergency response scenarios. They have often played the role of frontline responders, and this was no different when the pandemic hit the continent. They were in charge of response systems; they saved numerous lives and contributed significantly to containing the spread of the virus. Now, however, they are stepping up their role as activists to demand their inclusion in decision-making and leadership positions since it is apparent what they are capable of doing. For this transformation to be effective, the tech sphere must include women. Internet penetration increased substantially due to the COVID-19 pandemic and only continues to grow each day. However, the pandemic also exposed how digitization is still implicitly unequal for women. It

[69] CIAT (2017)   [70] Chiweche (2019, p. 1)   [71] Signé and Fox (2021)
[72] Khan (2020)   [73] Khan (2020, p. 1)
[74] Byanyima and Kende-Robb (2021)

highlighted the inequities that prevent women from enhancing their access to education, health, and financial services. Sub-Saharan Africa houses the world's second-widest digital gender gap at 37 percent.[75] When women are afforded these tools, then fundamental transformation will begin to occur (change in the field of education, equitable health systems, and even trade).

As a result, a strong social net will also be necessary for supporting the workforce during the transition to new work patterns. Most of Africa currently has inadequate social protections and scores poorly on services such as health care coverage.[76] Still, progress in countries such as Rwanda, where over 90 percent of the population now has health care coverage, shows that the expansion of social services is an attainable goal.[77] New technologies could also have a transformative impact on the delivery of public services and effective governance. For example, by supplementing the growing mobile user base with a national biometric ID, there is potential for data collection to contribute to the pinpointed provision of basic services such as health care.[78] From the delivery of public goods, such as education, health, and social security, to market regulation and supervision, 4IR technologies promise to improve access to services and make economic growth more inclusive.

Finally, the potential of 4IR technologies underscores the importance of extending infrastructure to Africa's poorest: The 4IR cannot reach those who lack internet access or electricity. The 4IR's potential for sustainable and renewable energy generation may reduce electricity deficits, particularly in remote areas where installing a central electricity grid would be costly. Meanwhile, technological innovations related to environmental protection may help mitigate the effects of climate change, especially in poor and rural areas. Public and private sector investment in these technologies will help reduce Africa's infrastructure deficit and ensure that no one is left behind during the 4IR.

3.4 Governance and Power

The 4IR offers new opportunities for and threats to African governance. Effective governance is vital for service delivery, the security of

---

[75] Byanyima and Kende-Robb (2021)   [76] Chen, Geiger, and Fu (2015)
[77] Makaka, Breen, and Binagwaho (2012)   [78] Chen, Geiger, and Fu (2015)

populations and the state, and the improvement of institutional efficiency. Technology can improve governance if it is accompanied by integrated processes, comprehensive data management, and expanded communication that brings citizens into governance and innovation. Technology and governance thus have the potential to be mutually reinforcing. To capitalize on this potential, governments need to adapt to changing technological and regulatory environments in the 4IR, incorporating the public, private, and civil society sectors in discussions regarding the necessary infrastructure and institutional settings to encourage innovation in the 4IR.

The spread of connected devices will allow citizens to express their preferences and engage with governments, generating new data points for better-informed policy-making. Online public service provision can improve efficiency in tax collection and regulation enforcement. New technologies can be used as a tool for transparency and public accountability. Just as new data collection methods can gather information on citizens, they can also monitor and track government performance. "E-government" platforms, which perform these functions, have gained traction across the African continent, particularly in Ghana, Mauritius, Tunisia, Rwanda, Kenya, Egypt, South Africa, Mozambique, Morocco, and Botswana.[79]

On the flip side, 4IR tools may be exploited by autocratic states as mechanisms for surveillance, control, and repression.[80] Furthermore, even positive e-government tools will be susceptible to hacks, threatening citizen data and public trust. In short, the future of governance in Africa holds a great deal of promise but only if African states and citizens take proactive measures against new challenges that may arise from the 4IR tools.

Governments must effectively adapt to rapidly changing economic, technological, and business environments, support entrepreneurs and businesses, and address traditional and emerging aspects of the infrastructure and institutional environment to successfully capitalize on the 4IR. Already, the adoption of ICTs for public administration has occurred more rapidly and sustainably in countries where the digital transformation process is led by or supported at the highest level of government. The public sector plays a critical role in building human capital, creating an attractive environment for local and multinational

[79] Hafkin (2009, pp. 5–6); Wille (2017)   [80] Howard (2015)

businesses, and developing ICT infrastructure. Improving technology infrastructure is an essential contribution of government leadership. Countries that can effectively use ICTs for governance often have public data centers capable of hosting, storing, and managing information from different government institutions and private organizations. These governments also often digitize their public records and invest in the development of interoperability frameworks and legal and technological measures, which can result in further innovation.[81]

3.5 Technology and Governance in Africa

African countries currently leading the 4IR predominantly have robust and responsive governments that enable participation and innovation from the private sector, entrepreneurs, and research institutions. Many of these countries have established government agencies responsible for technology and innovation (see Chapters 7 and 8 for more information). In South Africa, for example, the State Information and Technology Agency was formed to streamline existing technologies and implement new systems in all government departments. The goal is to improve internal organizational processes, provide better information, improve service delivery, increase government transparency, reduce corruption, reinforce political credibility and accountability, and promote democratic practices through public participation.[82] In Morocco, the Ministry of Industry, Investment, Trade, and the Digital Economy supports research in advanced technologies and the development of innovative cities in Fez, Rabat, and Marrakesh.[83] Meanwhile, the Digital Development Agency, another critical government body, coordinates the efforts of the public and private sectors, serves as a primary reference for foreign investors, works to accelerate the implementation of facilitating policies, and aims to energize the Moroccan digital ecosystem.[84]

The UN's 2018 e-Government Development Index (EGDI) rated four African countries – Ghana, Mauritius, South Africa, and Tunisia – as having high e-government development due to their large number of online public services. More than thirty other African countries, including Nigeria, Rwanda, Cameroon, and Togo, were rated as having made

---

[81] OECD (2018)   [82] Mphidi (2008)   [83] UNESCO (2016)
[84] Mellah (2018)

significant progress in e-government.[85] About half of all African countries have electronic ID systems, and biometric polling cards have been
used in fourteen African countries. South Africa, for example, has
widespread biometric identification with a centralized repository for
biometric data and a large commercial data analysis sector. Other
countries, such as Côte d'Ivoire, have issued smartcard-equipped ID
cards that also carry biometric data.[86] Zimbabwe has introduced a
mobile app that helps citizens stay informed and allows scrutiny of
parliament's work by offering users access to parliamentary acts and
bills, publications, events, news, and live recordings. Odekro, a similar
initiative in Ghana, also provides online access to bills, motions, and
parliamentary debates.[87] The governments of Guinea-Bissau and São
Tomé, and Príncipe are using digital solutions to assist in the execution
of core tasks around revenue collection and management, human
resource audits, and basic health and education service delivery. The
governments of Angola, Cape Verde, and Mozambique are focused on
using technology to enhance administrative efficiency by addressing
problems of systems inoperability.[88] Nonprofits and the private sector
have also driven some e-government innovation. Kenya's Ushahidi, for
example, is an open-source software system that uses Google Maps and
allows users to report geo-tagged voting irregularities and political
violence. During Kenya's 2008–2009 political crisis, Ushahidi was able
to identify outbreaks of violence more quickly and more frequently than
traditional media.[89]

While these innovations show promise in improving and supplementing traditional methods of governance, the adoption of e-government
platforms has not yet served the needs of the majority of citizens in
African countries. According to the EGDI, Africa has pushed the most
significant number of countries into a higher EDGI group. Still,
infrastructure and human capital development may hinder these countries from moving any higher.[90] Services such as e-taxation, e-payment,
and e-billing are helpful for the middle and upper classes. E-government
initiatives that support and cater to the poor, however, such as those
designed to promote skills development or promote microenterprises,
are still lacking.[91]

---

[85] Daramola (2019)   [86] Sutherland (2017, pp. 83–112)
[87] *Africa News* (2017)   [88] OECD (2018)   [89] Turianskyi and Gruzd (2016)
[90] United Nations (2020)   [91] Daramola (2019)

Similarly, while e-government policy elements are being diffused from Europe and the United States to Africa, in many cases, these policies are not adapted to local contexts. They lack any assessment of risks or potential impacts of the proposed measures or consideration of local implementation ability.[92] Additionally, political leadership in many African countries lacks the drive needed to bring about change in the public sector and rarely sees e-government as a priority. Most African countries do not have the legal framework required to support and enable digital governance or the spread of new technologies.[93] There remains a need to prioritize, redesign, and recontextualize e-government initiatives in Africa to address the needs of the majority of citizens. If governments are too slow to adopt new technologies, they will fail to generate the efficiency gains needed for effective public services. Figure 3.1 gives a breakdown of e-government development by regional distribution.

Although governments will need to act carefully to address and mitigate these challenges, overall, digital technologies offer massive opportunities to reinvent government institutions to be better adapted to the 4IR and improve welfare and opportunities for all citizens. Governments can apply 4IR technologies to a variety of situations to improve effectiveness. Virtual reality can allow government officials in the military, law enforcement, emergency response, and other professions to simulate dangerous or infrequent situations and improve response time and efficacy; data visualization can allow for the comparison of infrastructure plans or transit scenarios; and machine learning can help determine the need for infrastructure maintenance and improve public health and safety.[94] E-democracy also offers opportunities to facilitate citizens' active participation in the democratic process, including voter registration, voting, and election monitoring. Technology can help citizens feel connected to politics and assert their demands for better governance and more transparent and accountable societies.[95] E-government platforms can also create empowering spaces for small businesses; one such method is the provision of open cloud platforms that can support small enterprises with computing infrastructure, software services, and access to a large consumer market.[96]

---

[92] Sutherland (2017, pp. 83–112)   [93] Mphidi (2008)   [94] Briggs (2018)
[95] Turianskyi and Gruzd (2016)   [96] Daramola (2019)

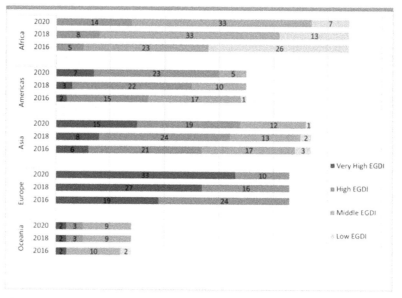

Figure 3.1 Regional distribution of countries by E-Government Development Index Level: 2016, 2018, 2020.
Source: United Nations, E-Governance 2020 Survey, p. 26

Implementing transformational e-government will depend heavily on changing the mindsets of those involved, starting with government leaders, due to the coordination needed to make e-government practices successful. African governments will have to confront the challenges of transparency, ineffective records management, and inefficient feedback mechanisms.[97] Regional initiatives should be further developed and expanded by creating, for example, regional digital government standards or joint programs for knowledge and skills development. Regional groupings could serve as a source of mutual support and inspiration. They could enable and sustain effective digital government transitions to create the necessary conditions for developing and providing regional services, including services for business creation and trade.[98] Furthermore, intergovernmental organizations could partner with 4IR entrepreneurs and private sector actors in Africa to train government officials in new technologies, such as AI and digital forensics, with the goal that officials will better recognize

[97] Minishi-Majanja and Ondari-Okemwa (2009, pp. 17–35)   [98] OECD (2018)

and support positive new technologies. This partnership could also help governments more quickly identify negative uses of new technologies, such as fabricated media so that they can remove inflammatory content and de-escalate national tensions.[99]

3.6 Global Power and Governance

At the interstate level, the 4IR may also result in a drastic upheaval to systems of global governance as we know them today: Innovation will play a greater role in deciding global power and interstate cooperation will become more critical as states grapple to regulate technological tools that defy borders, such as IoT and AI.[100]

Multilateral cooperation will become more complicated as 4IR innovations change the ways that states interact. While technologies that enable transparent, verifiable exchanges such as blockchain may increase trust in interstate transactions and communication, interconnected devices also open new avenues for global espionage and surveillance, which may heighten tensions between countries and hamper global governance.[101] In the context of a global system already plagued by rising trends of isolationism, nationalism, and the growing influence of authoritarian politics, the 4IR may precipitate new sources of digital and technological conflict.[102]

International politics and the spread of technology are becoming increasingly intertwined: Freedom House, for example, has signaled an alarm on China's efforts to use technology transfers as a method of geopolitical influence and norm setting.[103] In eighteen out of sixty-five countries surveyed by Freedom House, Chinese firms provided high-tech surveillance tools to governments for identifying threats to "public order." For example, Chinese tech giant CloudWalk is working in Zimbabwe to build a national facial recognition database and monitoring system, which will share data to the Chinese firm for improving its own AI facial recognition capabilities.[104] Privacy and security may become serious challenges as governments collect, store, and use

---

[99] Besaw and Filitz (2019)
[100] Banga and te Velde (2018); Schwab (2016a); Coulibaly (2017)
[101] For example, see Clapper (2016)
[102] Freedom House (2018); Galasso et al. (2017); Duara (2018); see also Bremmer (2017)
[103] Freedom House (2018, p. 8)   [104] Freedom House (2018, p. 8)

increasing amounts of citizens' personal data. Governments will need to ensure individual privacy and protect information systems from cyber threats.[105] Biometric technologies may fill some of the gaps in official information about individual citizens but may do so at the cost of citizens' control over their own identities.[106]

3.7 Peace and Security

New technologies offer both a promising means to maintain security and a new source of threat and vulnerability. Technologies such as drones may become integral to efforts to combat terrorism and crime: For example, the Moroccan startup ATLAN is developing drones powered by AI to scan for environment-related crimes such as illegal fishing and poaching.[107] However, while African governments can use technology such as drones, artificial intelligence, and IoT to monitor and deter violence, the 4IR may increase the ability of hackers to shut down critical infrastructure and offer Africa's extremist groups new AI tools such as "chatbots" to spread propaganda and hate speech.[108] Fragile and conflicted affected states are especially at risk due to the lack of stability; rumors and misinformation can continue to spread through various messaging apps and jeopardize current peace-building initiatives.[109]

New technologies also have the potential to make it easier to overturn weak governments without necessarily leading to improved governance and thus may increase leaders' determination to seek tools of political control.[110] There is further potential for the exacerbation of ethnic and religious divisions through the use of technologies such as social media and messaging platforms and through more advanced technologies such as artificial videos and voice recordings ("deep fakes"). These issues can be difficult to manage during contentious elections, particularly in transitioning democracies and among populations with a low level of technology awareness. Furthermore, if the disruptive effects of technology are too great or too rapid, rising unemployment and inequality could lead to social unrest.[111] African states will need to analyze and address these developments to successfully ensure internal stability during the 4IR.

[105] Mphidi (2008)   [106] Breckenridge (2005, pp. 267–282)   [107] Scott (2018)
[108] Neudert (2018)   [109] Dahshan (2020)   [110] Crocker (2019)
[111] Lye (2017)

3.8 Cybersecurity

Cybersecurity has become a major concern due to the 4IR's incursion into social, political, and economic systems. The disruption that will accompany the increased accumulation of technology within states and firms will inevitably change the security landscape. For example, in 2020, Uganda's telecoms and banking sectors experienced a major hack, in which $3.2 million was stolen as a result of a compromised mobile money network.[112] All stakeholders affected by the 4IR must be aware of cybersecurity issues that may impede the adoption of 4IR technology and successful creation of regulations that influence the promotion of technology and innovation.

African countries still rank relatively low in terms of cybersecurity resilience: According to the 2018 International Telecommunication Union's Global Cybersecurity Index, African countries are the least committed to cybersecurity globally.[113] There are six primary risks and consequences of poor cybersecurity for African businesses:[114]

1. Legal and regulatory noncompliance: African companies may fall behind standards required by trade partners, such as the European Union's General Data Protection Regulation.
2. Losses of productivity: Data loss or theft and delays caused by recovering from a cyberattack can hamper profitable activity and damage productivity. For example, the 2017 Wannacry attack, which hit 150 countries worldwide, affected Kenyan financial institutions and forced the Renault Tanger-Méditerrannée automobile plant in Morocco to close for a full day.[115]
3. Financial losses: Direct financial costs of cyberattacks have already grown significantly for African businesses. In 2017, Nigeria and Kenya lost an estimated $649 million and $210 million due to cybercrime, respectively.[116]
4. Prosecution, penalties, and associated fees: Data breaches compromise individual privacy, exposing companies to the risk of costly lawsuits that may involve millions of consumers. South Africa's largest data leak of 2017 resulted in stolen personal data of more than 60 million people.[117]

---

[112] Signé and Signé (2021)   [113] Signé and Signé (2021)
[114] Signé and Signé (2018)   [115] Signé and Signé (2018)
[116] Signé and Signé (2018)   [117] Signé and Signé (2018)

5. Theft of intellectual property and sensitive information: The potential loss of classified data such as commercial plans, patents, or government security information can compromise years of labor and research, particularly in Africa, where legal standards for curbing intellectual property theft are not aligned with international norms. Furthermore, a 2016 study by the Business Software Alliance found that 57 percent of software installed in Africa and the Middle East is unlicensed, opening the door for cyberattacks and data breaches.[118]

6. Reputation: Cyberattacks expose companies to public scrutiny, causing damage to a firm's image with customers, employees, investors, and partners.

In response to these risks, African governments and businesses must, more than ever before, strengthen their cyber-risk protection systems in order to sustain their activities in an increasingly connected world and avoid damaging effects on their finances and reputation. A harmonized approach across both public and private sectors will ensure coordinated efforts to combat cybercrime and the safety of individuals' and companies' data in the pursuit of economic growth, personal freedom, and an improved society in the 4IR.

---

[118] Business Software Alliance (2016, p. 7)

4 | Drivers of and Challenges to the Fourth Industrial Revolution in Africa

Scholars and industry analysts have identified many factors that may drive African innovation and growth in the Fourth Industrial Revolution. These drivers can be disaggregated into two broad categories: supply-side and demand-side. Supply-side drivers include the role of research and technological development, the availability of a technically trained workforce, and the existence of a conducive environment for innovation to thrive, such as financing and policy support. Demand describes public and private consumers' willingness to pay for innovation itself or innovative goods or services; the significant impacts of demand-side drivers on innovation are to serve as selecting mechanisms when innovation outputs are iterative, to provide feedback to improve innovation, and to stimulate firms and entrepreneurs to pursue innovation.

Drivers, of course, differ on a country-by-country basis. The strength and maturity of Africa's innovation ecosystems vary widely, as do the primary sources of innovative activity – government, academic institutions, firms, and entrepreneurs. These variations are discussed in more detail in Chapters 7 and 8. However, the following analysis provides context on drivers that are seen widely across the continent, particularly among Africa's 4IR leaders.

To determine the supply- and demand-side drivers of the 4IR in Africa, I analyze the literature and the GII's indicators of countries' innovation preparedness and ability. The GII can be broken down by its seven distinct pillars: institutions, human capital and research, infrastructure, market sophistication, business sophistication, knowledge and technology outputs, and creative outputs. Each pillar is divided into three sub-pillars, which are calculated as the weighted average of two to five individual indicators. These unique indicators, which are based on both quantitative and qualitative data, provide a detailed look at the innovation environment in a country. By examining individual country statistics and aggregating this data across

49

African countries to analyze trends, I can determine the predominant factors driving successful African innovation.

4.1 Supply-Side Drivers

On the supply-side, Africa enjoys several advantages that will give firms and entrepreneurs room to grow and court investment in the 4IR:

National governments across Africa recognize the imperative to modernize and step in to support Africa's entry to the 4IR. Many of Africa's 4IR leaders have strong leadership from governments and have adopted strategic plans for ICT development and innovation: In Mauritius, Tunisia, South Africa, and Morocco, for example, government support has been a significant driver of innovation. The 2013 East African Northern Corridor Agreement integrated ICT development as a strategic priority.[1] Both the governments of Rwanda and Nigeria have launched large public research initiatives into "smart city" technology, which incorporates internet and digital services into urban infrastructure to increase efficiency and improve the quality of life in cities.[2] On the GII, institutions' role in innovation is a relative strength for Africa, and African countries that perform well on the GII also tend to enable strong institutional environments (Figure 4.1).

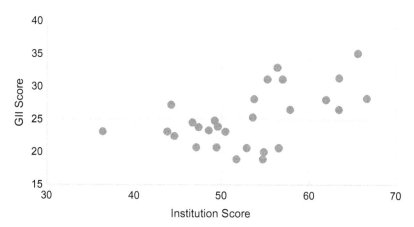

Figure 4.1 Institutions and innovation.
Source: Cornell University, INSEAD, and WIPO (2018)

[1] Meads (2018)   [2] Siba and Sow (2017)

Improving regulatory and business environments encourages investors and companies to establish themselves on the African continent, driving innovation and inclusion.

Much of Africa faces only limited legacy drawbacks from building new infrastructure. While infrastructure is not currently a relative strength of Africa on the GII, with most countries receiving middling to low scores, there are significant opportunities to turn this current weakness into an advantage. Most states and urban centers can immediately start with the latest technology without the high costs of replacing and maintaining legacy systems or integrating new technologies with older infrastructure.[3] For example, the expansion of affordable internet-enabled devices in Sub-Saharan Africa and South Asia cost only 34 percent of monthly income in 2019, compared to 44 percent in 2018.[4] The Fourth Industrial Revolution technologies also offer new means of developing more environmentally friendly, cost-effective infrastructure (for example, the use of advanced materials) and overcoming gaps in traditional infrastructure (for example, the use of drones).

Africa is already experiencing disruptive innovation and developing a vibrant class of entrepreneurs. Entrepreneurship was the second-fastest-growing profession on LinkedIn in Africa between 2011 and 2016, experiencing 20 percent growth.[5] African entrepreneurs are already finding niches for 4IR technology across the continent.[6] GII indicators reinforce the story around this driver, as African countries score relatively high on the indicator for the intensity of local competition. Such competition and entrepreneurship can push Africa to the forefront of innovation in the Fourth Industrial Revolution.

The affordability and availability of mobile devices such as tablets provide new platforms for African businesses to innovate and connect with consumers. In 2020, 495 million people subscribed to mobile services in Sub-Saharan Africa (46 percent of the region's population), marking an increase from 2019 that resulted in 20 million more subscribers.[7] In addition, mobile internet penetration is projected to reach 50 percent of the Sub-Saharan African population by 2025 (615 million mobile service subscribers).[8] Mobile devices currently provide

[3] Coulibaly (2017); Newfarmer, Page, and Tarp (2018, p. 34); Deloitte (2018a, p. 5)
[4] GSMA (2020, p.15)   [5] World Economic Forum (2017a, p. 14)
[6] Naudé (2017, p. 8)   [7] GSMA (2021b)   [8] GSMA (2021b)

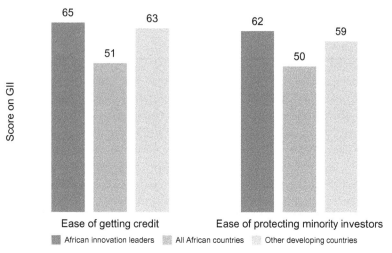

Figure 4.2 Credit and financing on the GII.
Source: Cornell University, INSEAD, and WIPO (2018)

robust platforms for banking and financial services across the African continent. Still, there are significant additional opportunities for their use, including developing online shopping platforms and health and education services – particularly as mobile internet speeds improve and more Africans begin to use smartphones.

Access to credit and financing for businesses and entrepreneurs is improving, and innovative new models for funding are being developed. On the GII, African countries, particularly Africa's innovation leaders,[9] score relatively well for the ease of getting credit and the ease of protecting minority investors (Figure 4.2). At the same time, investment levels remain low, compared to other regions. The growing success of major Africa-focused companies such as the Africa Internet Group, Africa's first $1 billion startup, is attracting new investors to the region, who are beginning to see the opportunities that Africa presents. New sources of financing models such as international lending and private–public partnerships are necessary for creating pro-investment environments. Additionally, new technologies such as AI and big data provide increasing opportunities for innovative credit scoring methods, which will continue to increase access to financing.

---

[9] Egypt, Kenya, Morocco, Nigeria, Rwanda, South Africa, Tunisia, and Mauritius; see Chapters 7 and 8 for more detail.

4.2 Demand-Side Drivers

Demographic and consumer trends across the continent also have exciting implications for technological growth and implementation in Africa.

Africa's rapidly growing population holds great potential to spur investment and growth for new technologies. Africa's working-age population will increase from 370 million adults in 2010 to over 600 million in 2030,[10] with over 11 million young people entering the job market in Africa every year.[11] Africa's youthful workforce and consumer base is a definite competitive advantage at a global level. By 2025, more than one-fifth of Europeans will be sixty-five or over, and the aging Western population may spur shifts in investment toward Africa's vibrant marketplace.[12]

Rising incomes and spending patterns will further drive Africa into the 4IR. By 2030, Africa's high- and middle-income groups are expected to grow by 100 million people. Household spending is projected to grow at an average rate of 5 percent, surpassing 3.8 percent across the developing world.[13] A large portion of this spending will go toward new technology and infrastructure that will accelerate the 4IR. In fact, spending on transportation and ICTs is expected to grow faster than spending on other sectors.[14] Stronger cooperation among regions, with the help of the AfCFTA, will facilitate economic growth through coordination and regional trade and foreign direct investments.[15]

Africa's growing urban population will increase concentrations of innovators and entrepreneurs, providing more opportunities for knowledge spillovers. Projections by the United Nations indicate that over half of Africa's population will live in cities within the next twenty-five years.[16] Urban consolidation[17] will complement the growth of industries

---

[10] World Economic Forum (2017a, p. 7)   [11] Coulibaly (2017)
[12] Deloitte (2014, p. 5)
[13] Aykut and Blaszkiewicz-Schwartzman (2018, pp. 13–14)
[14] Aykut and Blaszkiewicz-Schwartzman (2018, p. 14)   [15] UNCTAD (2020)
[16] Slavova and Okwechime (2016, p. 215)
[17] Africa's urban population growth rate increased by 5.2 percent throughout 1950–2015 and is projected to grow by 3.7 percent by 2050 – outperforming all other regions in previous and forecasted growth rates, compared to the developed world and East Asia. For example, over the same periods, the developed world's urban population grew by 1.3 percent from 1950 to 2015, and only 0.5 percent projected growth from 2015 to 2050. East Asia's urban

and the emergence of entrepreneurs, creating environments where businesses learn and benefit from each other. The increase in the middle class, urbanization, and technology helps to enhance Africa's value chains locally and abroad.[18] These opportunities will boost innovation within the private sector and help aid in AfCFTA initiatives.[19]

Urbanization has already resulted in tech hubs – defined as "physical spaces designed to foster and support tech start-ups" – which are popping up throughout Africa and will have an expansive effect on the creation and sustainability of start-ups.[20] Briter Bridges and AfriLabs have identified 643 active tech hubs throughout Africa; South Africa has 78 tech hubs, Nigeria has 90, Egypt has 56, Kenya has 50, and Morocco has 34.[21] These are just the top five countries, but other tech hubs exist in Ghana, Tunisia, Uganda, Zimbabwe, Côte d'Ivoire, and Senegal. Countries with less-developed innovation ecosystems such as Chad, Cape Verde, Mauritania, Swaziland, and Djibouti have at least one tech hub.

Africa's accelerating bandwidth and telecommunications demands will attract further investment in internet provision, providing the basis for growth in the 4IR. International bandwidth demand in Africa grew at a compound annual rate of 54 percent between 2016 and 2020, the fastest increase in demand of all regions during that period.[22] As incomes continue to grow across the continent and more people have access to smartphones, tablets, and computers, demand for high-speed, high-bandwidth internet and mobile internet will only increase.

Given these powerful supply and demand drivers of innovation on the continent, the 4IR is poised to impact the African continent dramatically. It is no surprise that investors and firms are increasingly recognizing Africa's potential: Venture capital raised by African start-ups rose by 53 percent from 2016 to 2017,[23] and this rapid growth may accelerate as firms and entrepreneurs agglomerate in Africa's expanding urban markets.

population also only grew by 4.3 percent from 1950 to 2015 and is projected to grow by 1.3 percent from 2015 to 2050. These numbers are comparatively lower than those in the African region (*Source*: Aykut and Blaszkiewicz-Schwartzman 2018 p. 17)

[18] UNECA (2020)   [19] UNECA (2020)   [20] Bayen (2018a)
[21] Shapshak (2019)   [22] Brodsky (2021)   [23] Adegoke (2018)

4.3 Challenges to and Risks for the 4IR in Africa

While these drivers should inspire a degree of optimism for Africa's participation in the 4IR, the continent faces several barriers to innovation and risks generated by new technology. The African continent can address these challenges through coordinated action between governments, academic institutions, the private sector, and regional and intergovernmental bodies where relevant. These coordinated efforts will be necessary for Africa to fully capitalize on the 4IR.

First, Africa's progress so far has been mainly consumer-driven, meeting the demand for goods and services such as mobile connections and digital applications. Producers have yet to benefit to the same extent; industrial use of the latest technologies is low relative to consumer use. Africa lags behind the annual installation and accumulated stock of industrial robots. For example, in 2015, only 0.1 percent of the global installation of robots took place in Africa, and only 0.3 percent of the global stock of operational robots was located in Africa.[24]

Second, although mobile internet penetration in Africa has grown dramatically, fixed broadband penetration has not kept pace, remaining below 1 percent of the continent's population.[25] Some have argued that mobile internet cannot offer a complete substitute for fixed broadband due to differences in speed and reliability.[26] Low fixed broadband penetration may hamper Africa's ability to adopt 4IR innovations that depend heavily on solid internet access. However, the lack of fixed broadband also represents a continuing opportunity for investors and firms to expand internet access and quality throughout the continent as Africa's consumer demand shifts to technology.

Third, while Africa's mobile sector has significantly benefitted consumers, it has not been a vital source of job creation, productivity, or infrastructure for long-term industrial growth.[27] The challenge of job creation may apply to many of the opportunities created by the 4IR, as the ICT sector tends not to be too labor-intensive. It requires highly skilled human capital, thus limiting its capacity to absorb Africa's large low-skilled worker population.

---

[24] UNCTAD (2017)   [25] UNECA (2017, p. 5)   [26] Lewin et al. (2009, p. 4)
[27] Schwab and Davis (2018, pp. 53–56)

Fourth, gaps in research, infrastructure, and education between African countries and advanced economies skew 4IR investments to the developed world.[28] African firms are innovative but need more support.[29] Foreign direct investment in Africa remains low, at around $46 billion in 2018, and little of this FDI is directed toward the ICT sector or the development of 4IR technology.[30] One reason for this lack of investment is Africa's low levels of human capital, which make productivity and, thus, returns to investment lower than in most other regions. However, by finding new ways to train workers to apply twenty-first-century skills, African states may overcome traditional gaps in education. The Youth for Technology initiative, for example, has opened 3D printing academies for young girls in Kenya and Nigeria, teaching them the entrepreneurial skills needed to develop products with this technology and then bring those products to the market.[31]

Fifth, AI and automation may displace workers and make traditional low-skilled, labor-intensive industrialization more difficult. Policy-makers will need to be mindful of how AI and automation will impact socio-economic inclusion.[32] In addition, African states may have greater difficulty in finding entry points in the global market and exploiting their comparative advantage to move up the value chain of goods. African manufacturing has already suffered from slow growth and gaps in technical maturity: In 2013, the manufacturing sector's average share of GDP in sub-Saharan Africa was about 10 percent, roughly the same share as in the 1970s.[33] Furthermore, Africa's share in industrial robots sold in 2015 was fifteen times lower than its share of global GDP, the lowest ratio of any region.[34] In particular, manufacturing, and export-led manufacturing, which has driven much of the recent economic growth in Asia, may not provide the same opportunities for Africa.

Sixth, African states that manage to acquire and adopt 4IR technologies may grapple with widening domestic inequalities driven by the cost of tech access and the rural–urban infrastructure divide. A Rwandan smart city project in Kigali, for example, has been criticized for inaccessible housing prices that the city's majority cannot

---

[28] Schwab and Davis (2018, pp. 53–56)   [29] Fu (2020)
[30] UNCTAD (2019)   [31] Naudé (2017, p. 8)   [32] Gwagwa et al. (2020)
[33] Newman, Page, and Tarp (2017)   [34] Banga and te Velde (2018, p. 9)

afford.[35] Beyond the outskirts of urban environments where 4IR tech is most likely to flourish, rural African regions that face shortages in Internet and electrification may fall behind in productivity growth and real wages, compared to their urban counterparts. If rural areas cannot meet the pace of their urban counterparts, risks of marginalization between developing nations and the developed world will increase.[36] The widening distinction between "haves" and "have-nots" that has dominated discourse in many developed countries may come to characterize African economies if the benefits of the 4IR are not strategically distributed or targeted for development purposes.

Finally, while 4IR technologies have high positive political and economic potential, they also have the potential to be misused by corrupt governments in Africa for purposes of surveillance and control. Internet of Things, sensor technology, and AI tools such as facial recognition create unprecedented avenues for personal data collection that may place privacy and individual security at risk.[37] The evolution of this technology may contribute to the global trend of "digital authoritarianism." Freedom House identifies this term as characterized by censorship, surveillance, and disinformation campaigns on the Internet.[38]

These disadvantages and risks mean that African tech start-ups and industries may struggle to compete globally. Therefore, African countries may face growing unrest from unemployed youth, especially from those who cannot harness the benefits of the 4IR due to low human capital, skills mismatches, or remote geography. In the worst-case scenario, failure to close critical deficits of education and infrastructure could severely widen the gap between African states and businesses and their competition in the developed world. However, if these challenges are appropriately addressed, current and new drivers of innovation could spur significant growth and development across the continent as the 4IR unfolds across Africa. Chapter 5 showcases some of the key opportunities that the 4IR presents for various sectors, building upon the drivers and challenges discussed above to show where the most substantial opportunities for growth lie.

---

[35] Siba and Sow (2017)   [36] Adhikari and Lehmann (2020)
[37] Howard (2015); Lightfoot and Wisniewski (2014); Roman, Najera, and Lopez (2011)
[38] Freedom House (2018)

5 | Capitalizing on the 4IR in Africa in the Primary and Secondary Sectors

Transformation, Implications, and Economic Opportunities

The 4IR has an important impact on the primary and secondary sectors. These traditional sectors include manufacturing and industrialization, infrastructure and construction, oil and gas, and agriculture and agro-processing, and are in many cases more established within African countries than the service sectors. Because of this, firms and entrepreneurs working within these industries have excellent potential to adopt new 4IR technologies that can significantly increase productivity, improve safety and sustainability, and increase profitability.

5.1 Manufacturing and Industrialization

The development of Africa's manufacturing sector is critical for industrial development and economic growth. However, many experts doubt Africa can achieve the same industrial growth through manufacturing experienced in East Asian countries such as South Korea and China. That skepticism arises from Africa's growth experience over the last thirty-five years. Instead of job-generating growth through capital-intensive resource-and energy-based industries, Africa has experienced periods of low agricultural productivity and development in the employment-intensive urban retail sector, stagnating productivity and manufacturing employment.[1] However, there have been positive trends in African manufacturing growth across the continent over the last forty years.

Africa's manufacturing sector grew faster than the world average, at 3.5 percent annually, from 2005 to 2014. Sub-Saharan Africa's manufacturing exports doubled from $50 billion in 2005 to over $100 billion in 2014.[2] Manufacturing has also driven higher productivity growth. Countries such as Ethiopia and Burkina Faso, which have had high manufacturing employment growth, also recorded high labor productivity growth

---

[1] Bhorat et al. (2017) [2] te Velde (2016)

between 2005 and 2014.[3] Additionally, manufacturing has received the highest levels of investment of any sector, accounting for 22 percent of foreign direct investment (FDI) in 2015.[4] High investment levels suggest manufacturing is following an upward trend, particularly in regional high-performers, such as South Africa, Nigeria, Egypt, Ethiopia, Rwanda, and Morocco. Deloitte's 2016 Global Manufacturing Competitiveness Index ranked South Africa, Egypt, and Nigeria within its top forty countries based on twelve drivers of manufacturing competitiveness: 1) talent, 2) cost competitiveness, 3) workforce productivity, 4) supplier network, 5) legal and regulatory system, 6) education and infrastructure, 7) physical infrastructure, 8) economic, trade, and financial tax system, 9) innovation policy and infrastructure, 10) energy policy, 11) local market attractiveness, and 12) health care system. Still, Africa lags significantly compared to OECD member countries – which had $6.7 trillion in manufacturing value-added in 2016.[5]

The future of African manufacturing is thus a critical element of Africa's journey into the 4IR. Ambitious public and private efforts to promote innovation and take advantage of the 4IR could revitalize African manufacturing as a source of growth.

5.1.1 The 4IR's Impact on Manufacturing and Industrialization

The sector's democratization and dematerialization will characterize the 4IR's impact on manufacturing. Technologies such as 3D printing will increase the involvement of small and micro enterprises in manufacturing. Artificial intelligence is used for maintenance processes to improve machinery as well as machines' design and adaptiveness. Nanomaterials and carbon fiber composites will lead to the dematerialization of manufacturing as less stock is needed to be kept. Products will use fewer physical inputs, and long production runs will be less necessary. In these cases, 4IR technology will be implemented in the production process in terms of inputs and production machinery and used to facilitate production organization, workers' training, and employment processes.[6]

At the sector level, digitization is likely to increase productivity, increase demand for new and existing products, decrease production

[3] Naudé (2018)   [4] *FDI Intelligence* (2016, p. 8)   [5] Signé (2020a)
[6] Naudé (2018b)

costs, enable new firms to enter markets, reduce the cost of trade, and increase global value chain participation. These impacts will expand to the labor market, where there is likely to be an increase in jobs in some sectors and new jobs, particularly in high-skill areas.[7] However, labor-saving technologies, such as robots and AI, contribute to the improvement of manufacturing production processes and reduce the comparative advantage of low-labor-cost countries, increasing labor force pressures and making it imperative to upgrade the quality of the workforce. New technologies will increase disruptions within manufacturing supply chains. Therefore, businesses must build production networks with these occurrences in mind.[8] Globally, the introduction of 4IR technology in the manufacturing sector is concentrated in the electronics, computers, and transportation industries. Notably, some labor-intensive goods, including textiles, apparel, and leather products, are the least affected by automation in manufacturing, even with high levels of global trade. These industries are likely to continue to grow regardless of the adoption of new technologies in African manufacturing.

Morocco's manufacturing industry provides a positive illustration of the opportunities for 4IR technology to promote sectors' transformation. Morocco's manufacturing sector is critical to the country's GDP and labor market, representing 18 percent of total output between 2010 and 2016 and employing 11 percent of the labor force.[9] The production of automotive vehicles is expected to grow at a compound annual rate of 5.6 percent between 2020 and 2026 (reaching $39.87 billion by 2026), encouraging firms such as Renault, Hyundai, and Ford to invest in Moroccan manufacturing.[10] Still, while the automotive industry has experienced recent growth, the World Economic Forum's Readiness for the Future of Production Report 2018 ranked Morocco 73rd out of 100 countries in terms of its ability to transform its manufacturing for the 4IR.[11] To address these challenges, the Moroccan government has encouraged further investment in manufacturing and technology, adopting its Industrial Acceleration Plan in 2014 to accelerate the transformation of electrical wiring, harness systems, maintenance, repair, operations, and engineering in the aeronautics subsector. This policy shows the opportunity for growth that

[7] Banga and te Velde (2018)   [8] McKinsey Global Institute (2020)
[9] Khurana and Shaban (2018)   [10] Mordor Intelligence (2021)
[11] Mordor Intelligence (2021, p. 14)

Table 5.1 *Negative impact of digitalization in African countries*

Sector-level impact	Labor market impact
Substitution of labor with automation	Decrease in jobs; more likely to affect unskilled workers
Replacement of skilled labor with cognitive robots	Decrease in skilled jobs and movement of skilled laborers to unskilled jobs
Re-shoring of manufacturing to developed economies	Decrease in jobs in developing countries
Global trend toward automation (in developed economies)	Decline in wages for laborers in developing economies to maintain competitiveness against cheap automation

Source: Banga and te Velde (2018, p. v)

can be made possible with targeted policies and straightforward frame-works for transforming the manufacturing sector in response to the 4IR.

5.1.2 Challenges and Constraints

The 4IR will present significant challenges for vulnerable labor markets that cannot accommodate automation and digitalization. Table 5.1 outlines the negative implications for African countries that do not adopt comprehensive strategies to adapt training and skills development for the 4IR.

Skills attainment is a significant constraint to implementing 4IR technology in manufacturing. During the period 2003 to 2012, tertiary enrollment rates on the continent were the lowest of any region glob-ally, averaging only 7.5 percent.[12] Inadequate digital skills impede employment rates for local populations and innovation potential for firms. Ethiopia, Senegal, South Africa, and Nigeria's manufacturing sectors all employ more than 10 percent of the population yet rank low on drivers of production that enable firms to implement 4IR technol-ogy.[13] Similarly, many African countries do not have adequate

---

[12] Naudé (2018b, p. 6)   [13] World Economic Forum and A.T. Kearney (2018)

structures for technology and innovation or access to global value chains and global trade and investment.

5.1.3 Opportunities and Strategies

The Brookings Institute's recent work indicates that Africa's "industries without smokestacks," including agro-processing, tourism, transport, and telecommunications and ICT-based services, have excellent growth potential.[14] In the shifting global landscape of the 4IR, more manufacturing opportunities may also become available in African markets, mainly through cutting-edge manufacturing practices using 3D printing and IoT "smart" production systems. Smart production systems could significantly improve the metal manufacturing subsector, which would greatly benefit Africa. The continent is home to the largest global reserves of aluminum, chromium, cobalt, diamonds, gold, manganese, phosphate, platinum-group metals, and vanadium.[15]

Investment in developing the next generation of entrepreneurs and high-skilled workers, such as targeted business training; promoting science, technology, engineering, and mathematics; and on-the-job training, will improve African countries' labor market resilience to the 4IR. A strong foundation for the future of investing will rely heavily on good governance, investment protection laws, and regulatory systems.[16] At the same time, African governments and entrepreneurs must be creative in finding niches within the 4IR that can serve as entry points for long-term industrialization and growth. One such opportunity might be found in 3D printing, as 3D printers are declining in price, are much more mobile than other manufacturing equipment, and have much lower energy requirements than other forms of production.[17] 3D printing catalyst growth and innovation when entrepreneurs operate in beneficial regulatory and financial environments.

5.2 Infrastructure and Construction

The 4IR offers a series of innovations to improve efficiency and costs in Africa's infrastructure and construction. African infrastructure is generally seen as lagging behind that of other developing regions. Estimates show

---

[14] Coulibaly (2018)   [15] Assegaf et al. (2017)   [16] Arnold (2019)
[17] Naudé (2017, pp. 7–8)

that closing Africa's infrastructure deficit will require an additional $150 billion investment by 2025.[18] Not only that, but most companies in the industry still use manual methods and traditional business practices, which has prevented the growth of the sector's productivity.

Despite these gaps, several ambitious public projects have improved the quality of infrastructures over the past decade, such as Ethiopia's Growth and Transformation Plan, which has generated an estimated $20 billion in construction projects each year.[19] Between 2018 and 2019, the total value of ongoing construction projects in Africa increased from $471 billion to $497 billion.[20]

5.2.1 The 4IR's Impact on Infrastructure and Construction

As the African construction and infrastructure space continues to grow, the opportunity for 4IR innovations to enhance infrastructure projects will become even more lucrative. Connected sensor technologies, mobile devices, and new software applications can "boost productivity, manage complexity, reduce project delays and cost overruns, and enhance safety and quality."[21] Augmented reality tools can assist workers and planners with modeling construction projects more efficiently.[22] 3D printing, blockchain, and artificial intelligence can support building design and streamline construction contracting.[23] The Fourth Industrial Revolution innovations can also make infrastructure projects more sustainable and energy-efficient, as IoT and digital infrastructure improve real-time energy monitoring and usage.[24] Given Africa's success in expanding digital platforms and developing a robust mobile sector, digitization applied to construction is a real opportunity to enhance the continent's efforts to close critical gaps in infrastructure.

5.2.2 Challenges and Constraints

The 4IR may disrupt the construction and infrastructure sector in Africa and globally, leading to unemployment as new technologies replace

---

[18] Lakemeeharan et al. (2020)
[19] V.e.n.t.u.r.e.s and Construct East Africa (2015, p. 3), citing a report by Access Capital
[20] Deloitte (2020, p. 3)   [21] Gerbert et al. (2016, p. 3)
[22] For example, see Barrow (2018)   [23] Nasman et al. (2017, p. 3)
[24] Nasman et al. (2017, p. 7)

manual processes. There remains significant uncertainty about how the future infrastructure will look and function. New technologies may lead to new, environmentally sustainable construction practices or, conversely, may lead to the rapid and unsustainable expansion of urban areas. Other trends such as climate change, shifting demographics, and urbanization create further uncertainty for the sector's future. Regardless, current business models will not be sufficient for infrastructure and construction companies to succeed in the 4IR. These companies will need to follow industry trends closely, remain adaptable, and employ adequately skilled personnel as the 4IR unfolds, or they will risk losing their competitive edge.

5.2.3 Opportunities and Strategies

The World Economic Forum estimates that, within a decade, full-scale digitization could generate an estimated $1 trillion to $1.7 trillion in cost savings for the construction industry. New technologies can also reduce the sector's negative externalities by improving environmental sustainability and reducing the energy use of infrastructure. Therefore, the infrastructure and construction sector must attract new, highly skilled workers with the abilities to use 4IR technologies; remain agile and adaptable in the face of a rapidly changing infrastructure ecosystem; and digitize processes and quickly adopt new technologies to maximize the use of big data, digital models, and other advanced technologies in the construction process.[25]

Additionally, African governments should support the sector as the 4IR unfolds to reduce its disruptive effects on employment and the industry as a whole. Governments can use their standing as regulators and the infrastructure sector's biggest customers to support companies' efforts to incorporate innovative technologies and remain adaptable. By sponsoring initiatives that encourage innovation, enabling schools and universities to build human capital in STEM fields, and revising building codes to promote innovative industry practices, the public sector can ensure that the infrastructure and construction sector reaps the benefits of the 4IR.[26]

5.3 Oil and Gas

The 4IR could be a boon to Africa's oil and gas exporters. In 2016, Africa held 7.6 percent of the world's proven oil reserves and 7.5

---

[25] World Economic Forum (2018c)   [26] World Economic Forum (2018c)

percent of proven gas reserves.[27] Over the past two decades, discoveries of oil and gas reserves on the African continent have driven the energy sector's growth. Resource reserves are controversial due to their association with political instability, corruption, and lack of diversification due to the "resource curse."[28] However, some states, such as Kenya and Ethiopia, have made recent substantial improvements in political accountability and may be capable of managing their resources effectively to overcome the resource course, following the example of Botswana's successfully managed diamond industry.[29] Other oil-exporting states will have to adapt to changes in energy needs and production capacity to overcome the decelerating growth rates.

Recent discoveries – including large oil deposits in Uganda and Kenya, gas reserves in Tanzania and Mozambique, and oil and gas in the region between Mauritania and Guinea – indicate the potential for more African involvement in the global energy market. Despite slowly recovering global prices, drilling in Africa is increasing.

5.3.1 The 4IR's Impact on Oil and Gas

The 4IR has significant implications for the oil and gas sector. Blockchain, advanced sensors, and AI can augment operational data from wells and basins, providing the basis for predictive maintenance and real-time yield monitoring.[30] Such efficiency improvements can yield sizable gains. Digital solutions proposed by the International Energy Agency could expand global revenues upwards of 5 percent.[31] By implementing digital tools such as AI, IoT, and blockchain, oil and gas companies are innovative in updating their value chains.[32] Digital tools are also gaining traction in the renewable energy sector. Connected devices assist renewables with integration into existing grids and improve response to energy demand with real-time data.[33] These tools may make renewables more competitive against natural

---

[27] PwC (2016, p. 4)
[28] For a recent review of this literature, see Vahabi (2007); foundational texts include Ross (1999), Collier and Hoeffler (1998), and Auty (1993), among others.
[29] Meijia and Castel (2012)
[30] Fraser, Anastaselos, and Raviumar (2018, pp. 1–2)   [31] Digitalist (2019)
[32] EY Global (2021)   [33] EY Global (2021, pp. 17–19)

resource energy sources. As digitalization expands on the African continent, stakeholders in oil and natural gas will have new opportunities to enhance production and threats from renewable competitors.

Already, digital disruption is one of the primary factors allowing African firms to keep costs low to mitigate the impact of oil and gas price decreases by automating inspection and safety procedures. While new technologies have only been partially adapted to African firms, there is an opportunity to expand the benefits of 4IR technology throughout the entire energy sector. This would have a significant impact on the industry in Africa because major global oil and gas companies, such as Exxon, BP, Shell, and ConocoPhillips, increasingly turn to the continent when expanding their operations. These large companies are more likely than African firms to implement 4IR technology in the short term and often partner with local firms and employees who benefit from technology transfer. In one example, Sound Energy, a British firm partnered with Morocco's National Hydrocarbons Office, used 3D mapping to appraise wells in eastern Morocco for hydrocarbons and 4D modeling to understand the potential risks in exploring this region.[34] This data was then available at the national level for state-operated exploration and production firms to utilize in their production pursuits.

The Fourth Industrial Revolution technology can also substantially reduce waste, increase production, and create a more optimal exploration and production system for African oil and gas companies. Investments in renewable energy, fuel efficiency, and energy storage are becoming highly profitable but often have environmental consequences or other externalities. Addressing negative externalities is one of the primary benefits of transforming the oil and gas sector for the 4IR. New technologies can make it possible to overcome the hypothesized "Environmental Kuznets Curve".[35]

Amid a global drive to invest in renewable energy over traditional sources, including coal, oil, and gas, the Environmental Kuznets Curve should be factored into the development of Africa's oil and gas sector in the 4IR. Economic growth from increased production does not have to become

---

[34] "Sound Energy" (2019)

[35] The hypothesized "Environmental Kuznets Curve" measures environmental degradation in terms of the stages of economic development (example, preindustrial economies, industrial economies, and postindustrial economies – service economy) (*Source*: Panayotou 1993).

environmentally detrimental when IoT better tracks materials, energy flows, extraction, production, and distribution. Introducing robots to the oil and gas extraction process can significantly reduce the social cost of dangerous exploration and material extraction. Additionally, investments in 4IR mapping and exploration technologies are more likely to provide high returns due to decreased risk and higher potential for discoveries.

5.3.2 Challenges and Constraints

Some states are merging national policies with private development of their energy sectors, while other states remain limited by state-owned enterprises in the energy sector. These state enterprises, sometimes monopolies within the country, are deeply ingrained in national systems and place many constraints on the sector's productivity, including through financing, local patronage networks, corruption, and a short-sighted focus on profits. Nepotistic systems of ownership impede innovation and risk strategizing for the inevitable impact of the 4IR on the oil and gas industry. Challenging operating environments, policy instability, and infrastructure deficits also hinder African energy-exporting countries' investment opportunities in oil and gas.[36] The industry also suffers from a lack of talent, regulatory uncertainty, political instability, and inadequate total infrastructure. The Niger Delta region, for example, is particularly challenged by oil theft, pipeline vandalism, and accusations of environmental negligence from the perspective of the local communities facing staggering pollution levels.[37]

Furthermore, the 4IR may negatively affect job opportunities in oil and gas industries throughout Africa, where AI, 3D printing, and robots are beginning to be used for inspections, exploration, and maintenance. The oil and gas sector may see an overall loss in employment positions as autonomous trucks, robots, and other fully integrated technologies. South Africa alone, where almost 500,000 are employed in the mining sector, could face significant unemployment issues when 4IR technology becomes central to the industry.[38]

5.3.3 Opportunities and Strategies

African countries, particularly in West Africa, have consistently produced oil and gas since emerging on the global market as export

[36] Botes, Marais, and Lane (2019)   [37] Slav (2019)   [38] Harvey (2017)

economies from the 1970s to the 1990s. New entrants in East and West Africa, such as Mozambique, Tanzania, Senegal, and Mauritania, have capitalized on discoveries and partnerships with energy majors to join the global energy trade. Senegal has moved from having a negligible presence in the energy sector to become one of the top ten producers in sub-Saharan Africa over the last five years.[39] Countries with more established production infrastructure but that have not yet adapted to digitization and 4IR technology – including Nigeria, Ghana, and South Africa – are still poised to adjust their oil and gas sector for the 4IR. An example of early technologies that could quickly adapt are drones to inspect facilities, robots to conduct monitoring and safety checks, and virtual reality to simulate well-drilling. Each 4IR technological adaption will require capital investment but will reduce overall costs of energy exploration, extraction, and production. Data skills will translate to safe operations and help in regulations of automation platforms.[40] Better integration of digital skills and technology will provide abundant opportunities to help create value in oil and gas companies.[41]

Despite fluctuating oil prices, a slight price increase in 2017 may indicate the beginning of an upward trend in costs that will stimulate investment in "megaprojects." Mozambique's Coral Sea South LNG project represents the most significant opportunity for hydrocarbon production on the continent within the next several years.[42] Eni East Africa currently leads the construction of a $4.67 billion floating processing facility set to be completed in 2022. BP has already purchased the rights to the 3.4 million tons of gas to be pumped out of the location each year for the next twenty years. The revenue from this project will fund exploration and technological inclusion throughout Mozambique and Eni East Africa's projects.

National policies intending to transform the oil and gas sector for the 4IR must first consider the compounding benefits of infrastructure development, financial reform, and regulatory stabilization instead of traditional risk analysis. Egypt is currently leading the way in coordinating its industrialization and modernization strategy with the latest gas discoveries in the country.[43] Two specific strategies that are both immediately implementable and sustainable in the long-term include the following.

---

[39] "Seven" (2017)   [40] Narayanan (2020)   [41] Holmås et al. (2019)
[42] Holmås et al. (2019)   [43] "Egypt Riding" (2018)

5.3.3.1 Planning 4IR Investments to Lay the Foundation for Energy Security

Without anticipating future demand, even in a volatile energy market affected by great power competition and political instability in other world regions, Africa cannot be a significant energy source for developed and emerging economies. National governments must transform their financial incentives and regulatory environments to encourage foreign and domestic investment in 4IR technology within the oil and gas sector. Partnering with multinational oil and gas companies to receive the benefits of technology transfer is one strategy that may allow countries to better capitalize on their oil and gas reserves.

5.3.3.2 Integrating Renewable Energy Strategies with 4IR Modernization Policies

The Fourth Industrial Revolution will inevitably advance the prospects for societies to become solely reliant on renewable energy sources. Still, since much of 4IR technology relies on sufficient electricity supplies, the oil and gas sector will continue to fuel economies for decades. The COVID-19 pandemic has led to a greater demand for greener and sustainable energy; coupled with the increased volatility in oil pricing, businesses need to consider advancing digital technologies.[44] Integrating renewables in high-pollution areas will help African governments achieve climate change targets to reduce CO_2 emissions and become more environmentally sustainable. Still, the oil and gas industry will likely fund much of this transition. These energy sources will be critical in expanding electricity access to lower-income individuals who are priced out of renewable energy sources in the short term.

5.4 Agriculture, Agro-Industries, and Agro-Processing

The future of African agriculture in the 4IR is critical to millions of stakeholders across the continent. For the foreseeable future, agriculture will continue to be a key sector for African employment. Farming alone accounts for 60 percent of total employment in sub-Saharan Africa, and the food system is projected to add more jobs than the rest of the economy between 2010 and 2025.[45] Furthermore, as incomes rise across the continent, growing consumer demand for food and

[44] Business Chief (2019)   [45] Ehui (2018)

beverages will coincide with business-to-business growth in agro-processing. By 2030, food and beverages will represent the most considerable portion of consumer spending at $740 billion, while agriculture and agro-processing will be the most significant sectors for business-to-business expenditures, at $915 billion.[46] Food imports are also increasing globally, and countries relying on these imports spend $35 billion annually, which could rise to $100 billion annually by 2030.[47]

Africa's agricultural productivity still lags behind the rest of the world and is under particular threat from climate change. Indeed, without adaptation efforts, climate change may have severe impacts on crop yields by as early as 2030.[48] However, the 4IR presents significant opportunities to modernize and improve the productivity of the agricultural sector, which has the potential to create employment opportunities and reduce food insecurity.

5.4.1 The 4IR's Impact on Agriculture, Agro-Industries, and Agro-Processing

The spread of ICTs and the inception of the 4IR have had a compounding effect on improving agriculture and agro-processing. New technologies will combine big data and AI concepts with helping in precision farming, such as monitoring, diagnosing insects, measuring soil moisture, and monitoring crop health.[49] The spread of mobile devices has also allowed for developing a knowledge-based agricultural community that promotes the spread of best practices through internet forums and services. As of 2015, an estimated 71 percent of African farmers used ICTs to improve their farming practices, and 90 percent of those farmers agreed on the benefits of ICTs to food security, increased yield, sustainable production, and income improvement.[50]

Ghana-based companies Farmerline and Agrocenta offer farmers mobile and web technology for agricultural advice, weather information, and financial tips. Hello Tractor is a startup in Nigeria and Kenya that allows farmers to hire affordable tractors via mobile phone. The company has served up to half a million farmers since launching

---

[46] Signé (2018b)   [47] Kariuki (2018)   [48] FAO (2016)
[49] Ane and Yasmin (2019)   [50] Theunissen (2015)

in 2014,[51] and reports yield increases of 200 percent for its clients.[52] Zenvus, a Nigerian startup, measures and analyzes soil data to help farmers apply the right fertilizer and optimally irrigate farms.[53]

As the cost of mechanization and automation declines, a wide range of 4IR products could play a pivotal role in Africa's battle to achieve food security against the threats posed by climate change and population growth. Innovations in food refrigeration and dehydration have led to reductions in food waste, a component of agricultural production that contributes to poverty, hunger, and disease and can be easily remedied with low-cost, quickly produced technologies. Empowering businesses will be imperative to leading agriculture to increased yields, lower costs, and reduced environmental impact.[54] Solar refrigerators in Kenya, for example, enable farmers to cool milk products and reduce spoilage. Similarly, the "Sparky Dryer," a dehydration machine invented by a Ugandan engineer, uses biofuel to dehydrate produce and reduce food waste.[55] African entrepreneurs and startups also use IoT to help farmers optimize productivity and minimize waste through data-driven "precision farming" techniques.

5.4.2 *Challenges and Constraints*

The greatest challenge to transforming the agricultural sector in the 4IR will be the lack of coordination between traditional industrialization and agrarian reform policies and 4IR innovation in the public and private sectors. State funding for digitalization in agriculture is not provided in developing infrastructure, which provides new processes and development strategies.[56] Continent-wide transformation requires a comprehensive approach to developing agro-industries and connecting local production to global value chains to create self-sustaining income and value-added production increases.

Climate change remains a significant threat to African food production as extreme weather events become more common. Deforestation is also a substantial contributor to agricultural challenges such as soil depletion throughout sub-Saharan Africa, particularly in West and Central Africa.[57] Globally, addressing environmental changes and

---

[51] Bhalla (2021)   [52] Bhalla (2021)   [53] Ehui (2018)
[54] Nijhuis and Herrmann (2019)   [55] Kariuki (2018)
[56] Marinchenko (2021)   [57] Hollingworth (2019)

climate patterns will require a concerted effort to monitor and solve challenges with new technologies. The lack of international coordination on climate issues means that African countries may need to take the lead, adopting national strategies that use traditional methods and 4IR technologies to improve agricultural productivity and reduce the effects of climate-induced food insecurity.

5.4.3 Opportunities and Strategies

Food insecurity is prevalent in many African countries, and the 4IR offers potential new technologies to help address this issue. Food waste accounted for 37 percent of the total food produced in 2011 (fruits and vegetables accounted for 50 percent of this loss).[58] The U.N. estimates that if the 37 percent of food wasted could instead be saved, it could feed approximately 300 million people across Africa.[59] The Fourth Industrial Revolution technologies offer innovative ways to reduce food waste by improving storage and cultivation practices, a massive opportunity to reduce food insecurity on the continent.

Improvements to the productivity of the agriculture sector also have significant implications for income growth in Africa. The importance of farm labor and income to developing countries' populations in sub-Saharan Africa, where on-farm activities represent almost 50 percent of all rural income in Ethiopia, Malawi, Nigeria, and Tanzania.[60] Information on competitive pricing monitored crop information, disease prevention tips, and disaster mitigation support can transform the agriculture sector to improve income, production, and demand throughout the continent.

Furthermore, increasing the efficiency of the agro-industry and agro-processing sector may be one of the 4IR's most significant contributions to Africa's economic growth, given the potential of these "industries without smokestacks." In Ethiopia and Senegal, food and beverage processing accounts for 70 percent of agro-industry value-added.[61] Food and beverage subsectors represent, overall, 30 to 50 percent of total manufacturing value and thus present a significant opportunity for growth should food waste and production processes be improved with 4IR technologies.[62]

[58] Kariuki (2018)   [59] Kariuki (2018)   [60] FAO (2017)   [61] FAO (2017)
[62] FAO (2017)

6 Capitalizing on the 4IR in Africa in the Tertiary Sector

Transformation, Implications, and Economic Opportunities

The African continent is ripe with opportunities for technological disruption to positively transform economic activities, enhance business and government, improve living standards, and accelerate development. The 4IR encompasses a broad scope of disruptive technologies with complex implications for various industries and public and private life. The synergies among 4IR innovations further complicate attempts to predict the precise impacts of such technologies in any context. Despite these challenges, however, an analysis of observable trends, comparative advantages, and growing tech initiatives can assist African firms, policymakers, entrepreneurs, and investors in identifying nascent opportunities for 4IR application. Failure to recognize and capitalize on 4IR opportunities, conversely, would impose considerable risks on African stakeholders. Without attempts to move beyond existing models of innovation, entrepreneurship, and digital growth on the continent, African businesses risk falling further behind, exacerbating the global "digital divide," and lowering their international competitiveness.[1]

This chapter breaks down the current developments and prospects for the Fourth Industrial Revolution within service sectors, including banking and financial services, tourism, information and communication technologies, and health care. The 4IR has transformative implications for many of these industries. This is partly due to its ability to connect people and firms to global markets and its synergies between cyber and physical systems. The sectors analyzed below thus reflect some of the most transparent and most promising terrains for the 4IR in Africa. These are coupled with illustrations of emerging opportunities for African governments, businesses, and entrepreneurs.

---

[1] Chan (2018); Banga and te Velde (2018)

6.1 Sectoral Comparison

6.1.1 Banking and Financial Services

The 4IR is dramatically shaping the future of banking, financial services, and capital investment and development in Africa. Sub-Saharan Africa is leading the world in terms of digital financial inclusion: leading the way in this industry for over a decade and, in 2020, accounting for 43 percent of all new accounts (the highest growth globally).[2] In addition, penetration is even higher in countries where mobile money platforms were first introduced, such as Kenya and Tanzania. Kenya's M-Pesa was a catalyst for the rapid expansion of financial access via mobile and digital devices, which continues to grow across the continent. In 2020, sub-Saharan Africa hosted 548 million registered mobile money accounts, the most of any region in the world.[3]

Mobile financial services have begun to expand to include a broad array of services, including credit, insurance, and cross-border remittances. There is significant scope for further improvement and new applications using 4IR technologies such as blockchain and machine learning. Africa's concurrent rise of financial inclusion in formal institutions and through mobile and digital technologies suggests that rather than having a disruptive effect, the 4IR in Africa may be able to fill traditional gaps and generate new opportunities.

6.1.1.1 The 4IR's Impact on Banking and Financial Services

In 2012, only about one-quarter of adult Africans had access to traditional or digital financial services. Constraints on access to credit, insurance, and other financial services hindered the ability to grow small-scale businesses, plan for future household expenses, make investments in health and education, and deal with emergencies, particularly for women, rural populations, and the very poor.[4] After just six years, in 2018 the rise of digital financial services provided by the financial technology (FinTech) sector and telecommunications companies drove a massive increase in financial inclusion. Forty-three percent of adult Africans now have access to financial services, and in countries such as Kenya, Tanzania, and the DRC, the financial

---

[2] GSMA (2021, p. 14)   [3] GSMA (2021, p. 14)   [4] IFC (2018)

inclusion rate more than doubled between 2012 and 2018.[5] While East Africa, and particularly Kenya, is a clear leader in financial innovation, technologies have spread over Africa, and access and use are rapidly growing. In Zimbabwe, for example, currency shortages have resulted in a dramatic uptake in mobile money and other electronic financial platforms.[6] Transactions on these platforms increased from 10 million transactions in June 2017 to 18 million in November 2017.[7] And in Côte d'Ivoire, the majority of the population prefers to use mobile money for payments and money transfers, rather than traditional banks.[8]

The 4IR is reaching beyond basic banking services. Indeed, applications such as M-Akiba in Kenya are creating micro-investment opportunities in government bonds and other assets. Weza Tele provides mobile services in commerce, supply chains, distribution, and payment integration; the company was bought for $1.7 million by AFB in 2015.[9] Nigeria's Paga platform incorporates mobile money services with digital bill payment and online purchasing and is preparing for international expansion after receiving $10 million in funding from the Global Innovation Fund.[10] Electronic banking is playing a transformative role in Africa, and it will continue to help better the efficiency and the quality of services throughout the financial sector.[11]

Credit risk models can also use 4IR technologies of advanced analytics and machine learning to increase accuracy.[12] In Kenya, IBM has analyzed purchase records from mobile devices and then applied machine learning algorithms to predict creditworthiness, giving lenders the confidence they needed to provide $3 million in loans to small businesses.[13] In Senegal, the MaTontine company incorporates a credit scoring system to access small loans and other financial services.[14] Growth in the mobile money market helps to fuel the entrepreneurial sector, job market, and state revenue.[15] With the incorporation of blockchain as a medium for verifiable property records and transactions in African markets, these technologies may dramatically expand the scope of formal credit access into previously informal sectors of the economy. In one example, Twiga Foods, a Nairobi-based start-up logistics platform for kiosks and food stalls, collaborated with IBM to incorporate blockchain technology to make

[5] IFC (2018)   [6] Mazambani, Rushwaya, and Mutambara (2018, p. 132)
[7] Flood (2018)   [8] World Bank (2016a)   [9] Jackson (2015)
[10] Bright (2018)   [11] Nnamani and Makwe (2019)   [12] Ganguly et al. (2017)
[13] Kinai (2018)   [14] Vidal (2017)   [15] Rouse and Verhoef (2016)

the lending process transparent and accessible for all involved parties, from the lending bank to the loan applicant. Their eight-week pilot processed more than 220 loans and provided an effective platform for users with limited IT literacy to access financing.[16]

Overall, all signs point to the future of investment and equity in Africa developing through the web, and the 4IR will only accelerate this trend. There is significant room for geographic growth: While East Africa and Ghana are mature mobile money markets, penetration remains low in Morocco, Egypt, and Nigeria, some of Africa's most populous countries.[17] And while Africa is a world leader in mobile banking, other 4IR-enabled financial innovations found in more developed markets have yet to take hold on the continent fully. Emerging FinTech companies, particularly in the United States and EU, offer loans and financial planning services, wealth management services with "robo-advice" and "robo-retirement," micro-investment opportunities, and global marketplaces for trading currencies, commodities, and more.[18] While these technologies could significantly disrupt the financial environment in developed markets, they are more likely to fill gaps where services are currently not widely offered in Africa. Innovations may also increase access to formal financial services. In Nigeria, for example, the adoption of biometric identification systems has allowed citizens to register for formal banking more easily.[19]

6.1.1.2 Challenges and Constraints

Countries lagging in adoption may face challenges catching up when the 4IR makes financial innovations the global norm. To date, there has been significant heterogeneity in the take-up of financial innovation in Africa. On the micro level, a high proportion of women, young people, and people living in rural areas remain financially excluded. On the macro level, despite growth, the adoption of these financial innovations in Central and Southern Africa remains relatively low. At the same time, many large countries, such as Nigeria, have not yet been able to capitalize on banking and finance innovations fully.

Why has Kenya, but not Nigeria then, seen rapid and widespread adoption of innovative financial services? A study by David-West and

---

[16] Kinai (2018)   [17] Chironga, De Grandis, and Zouaoui (2017)
[18] Axxsys (2018)   [19] GSMA (2018a)

Iheanachor (2016) suggests three primary supply-side constraints in the areas of business and regulatory environment, operations, and physical access. In Nigeria, lack of policy cohesion on financial innovation, high fees on financial services, low ownership of mobile devices among vulnerable populations, low awareness of digital financial services, and a lack of distribution agents in rural areas have contributed to low take-up.[20] Conversely, in Kenya, with the adoption of M-Pesa, the Kenyan Central Bank played a proactive role in spreading mobile money while reassuring the market of its oversight. At the same time, M-Pesa's operator, Safaricom, built a distributed network of agents across the country.[21] These early steps created an environment conducive to other financial innovations and encouraged entrepreneurs to enter the financial services sector.

For governments, central banks, and financial providers, there is a need to strike the right balance between leveraging opportunities and managing risks. To enable stakeholders to capitalize on market potential fully, governments and central banks must take steps to keep up with the pace of innovation. Currently, central banks are less familiar with regulating telecoms and FinTech companies than traditional financial institutions, so many financial services companies have escaped formal regulation in Africa.[22] At the same time, governments must also carefully consider and plan tax policies to avoid pushing taxpayers to alternatives to escape excessive taxation, reversing some of the gains made in financial inclusion through 4IR technology.[23]

6.1.1.3 Opportunities and Strategies

The continued global impact of the 4IR on banking and financial services presents massive opportunities for Africa. Given rising incomes across the African continent and the low costs and barriers to entry in the mobile service sector and blockchain, stakeholders in African financial markets can expect a robust market with intense competition but high growth potential. As African markets mature, demand will increase for financial products outside of person-to-person payments. There is clear scope for not only the continued increase in the use of mobile money services but also the introduction and spread of other financial services, such as loans, micro-investment, and financial planning.

---

[20] David-West et al. (2018)   [21] Riley and Kulathunga (2017)
[22] Aglionby (2018)   [23] Ndung'u (2019)

The capital potential of the informal sector remains largely untapped, and there is a space for firms and entrepreneurs to expand microfinance and credit services using blockchain, machine learning, and other verification tools to this sector. The gains from "formalizing" informal industry with proper records and credit access will be enormous. The informal sector constitutes 36 percent of sub-Saharan Africa's GDP[24] and accounts for $20 billion in Kenya alone.[25] Several initiatives have already cropped up in West Africa and Kenya to use blockchain as a medium for verifying property records and transactions in African markets, which may dramatically expand the scope of formal credit access into previously informal sectors of the economy.[26] Since blockchains are immutable, fraud – and thus the cost of risk – is reduced, and since blockchains execute in real-time, the time it takes to process and issue loans is shorter.

The 4IR also offers banks the tools needed to take advantage of the opportunities posed by the African market and utilize innovations to accelerate retail banking's revenue growth. Africa's retail banking penetration remains low, at just half the global average for emerging markets. In addition, retail banks struggle to find consumers, given widespread low-income levels, the popularity of cash, and little information around individuals' credit. 4IR-enabled digital solutions can be used to improve credit risk models and operational risk and compliance. Digital credit risk management uses automation, connectivity, and digital delivery and decision-making to allow for faster decisions and superior risk assessments than current manual processes.[27] There are also opportunities to increase the effectiveness of anti-money laundering (AML) operations through blockchain and distributed ledger technologies. These and similar solutions can help traditional banks take advantage of the rapid growth of the African middle class and further accelerate the growth of the African banking market, already the second-fastest growing in the world.[28] Overall, the 4IR's impact on banking and financial services in Africa may serve more to fill existing gaps and encourage financial inclusion than to disrupt the existing financial ecosystem.

[24] World Bank (2021)   [25] World Bank (2021)   [26] Gebre (2018)
[27] Ganguly et al. (2017)   [28] Chironga et al. (2018)

6.1.2 Tourism

Tourism has increased rapidly in recent years and has begun to contribute significantly to African economies. The African Development Bank estimates that visitors to the continent, in 2015, generated $39.2 billion in international tourism receipts and contributed to 9.1 million direct travel and tourism jobs.[29] Overall, between 2000 and 2017, the continent saw an increase of 36 million international tourist arrivals.[30] However, of the 1.4 billion people traveling internationally in 2018, only 67 million arrived in Africa.[31] While tourism is well-developed in countries such as Seychelles and Mauritius, the industry remains in the early stages of development elsewhere. The Fourth Industrial Revolution technologies can help draw more international travelers to experience the African continent's rich natural resources and culture.

6.1.2.1 The 4IR's Impact on Tourism

Big data analysis and cloud computing are changing the tourism industry. Digital tools allowing airplane passengers to book flights and check in online are already staples of the airline industry. The cloud, AI, and blockchain may further facilitate travelers' access to transportation or other services. In particular, blockchain has the potential to revolutionize tourism on the African continent by reducing the visa and entry process for international travelers and the business registration process for those within the tourism industry with access to international travelers' data. Africa's competitive digital platforms will help drive the growth of these services on the continent, as shown by the success of online travel agencies developed by AIG and transportation applications such as Twende.

The 4IR also has implications for the safety of international travelers and the reduction of crime. Information and communication technology tools and apps can help combat crime and create accessible tourism products useful for social issues regarding responsibility.[32] Interpol and VoguePay launched a blockchain-based digital platform in 2018 to enable citizen engagement and collaborate with more partner networks on crime monitoring to protect travelers and local citizens.[33] These

---

[29] AfDB (2016, p. 4)   [30] Signé and Johnson (2018)
[31] UNWTO (2019, p. 3)   [32] Eusébio, Teixeira, and Carneiro (2021)
[33] IFC (2018)

blockchain technologies encourage the participation of citizens and businesses in the promotion of safe cities and landmarks for locals and tourists to the country. In addition, sensor-based technology, smart tourism, and virtual and augmented reality will help the African tourism industry grow.[34]

6.1.2.2 Challenges and Constraints

Africa's tourism sector currently underperforms due to the continent's underdeveloped infrastructure and institutions. While 4IR technologies can reduce or eliminate some of the challenges posed by these issues, problems related to unsafe roads, unsanitary water, poor access to emergency services, and inconsistent electricity will need to be primarily addressed through traditional means. Related to these issues is the high cost of doing business in Africa, which has particularly acute implications for the tourism sector due to the importance clients give to the price-to-value ratio. The high costs of developing tourist attractions in Africa are passed to consumers, who may not receive a corresponding high-quality experience due to mismanagement or low quality of customer service.[35]

Additionally, in the absence of effective environmental conservation policies, the natural assets that bolster Africa's potential for tourism are deteriorating. Africa is currently facing widespread deforestation and the potential extinction of some wildlife species due to habitat loss and poaching. Despite some efforts by African governments to address these issues, most of the continent continues to perform poorly in environmental sustainability.[36] The Fourth Industrial Revolution solutions may be able to mitigate some of these challenges through the use of improved energy sources and sensor networks, among other technologies.

6.1.2.3 Opportunities and Strategies

By 2030, consumer spending on tourism, hospitality, and recreation in Africa will reach about $260 billion, almost twice the amount spent in 2015. As of 2018, only ten countries in Africa had $1 billion or more in tourism revenues, indicating the enormous potential for growth of the sector across the continent.[37] Given the nascent state of the tourism

---

[34] Waluyo and Tan (2022)   [35] Signé (2018c)   [36] Signé (2018c)
[37] Signé and Johnson (2018)

industry in Africa, massive opportunities exist for 4IR technologies to fill the sector's gaps, including infrastructure, logistics, communication, and security, rather than disrupt it.

According to some estimates, by 2025, digitization will add $1 trillion in value to the aviation, tourism, and travel industry globally.[38] New players in the online space will capture about $100 billion of these gains, primarily online travel agencies and platforms such as Airbnb.[39] Moreover, smart city infrastructure and connectivity can assist travelers in navigating foreign urban environments. Building on top of existing smart city infrastructure efforts, cities such as Kigali and Nairobi could develop "smart tourism" experiences by connecting tourists to city attractions and local businesses.[40] Further tourism opportunities exist with virtual and augmented reality: Virtual reality tools can assist with 3D planning of tourist locations and marketing via enhanced "virtual tours."[41] Using 4IR innovations, stakeholders in African tourism and travel can capture a larger share of the international tourism market.

6.1.3 Information and Communication Technology (ICT)

The ICT sector is at the forefront of the 4IR due to its ability to drive technological change and innovation. Globally, the industry has exploded in recent years. In Africa, growth in the ICT sector has mainly taken place in mobile telephones. Indeed, mobile subscriptions in sub-Saharan Africa increased from 44 per 100 people to 93 per 100 people between 2010 and 2020. Growth has also occurred in computer and internet access and usage. Internet access in the region increased from 24.8 percent to 28.6 percent between 2017 and 2020.[42]

ICT growth has been a powerful driver of development. One study found that increases in fixed and mobile telephone penetration rates had significant and positive effects on economic growth in Africa.[43] In contrast, another study found that increases in fixed and mobile telephone penetration rates lead to increases in labor productivity growth.[44] While many observers see African infrastructure deficits as a persistent barrier to ICT development, ICT itself can be an infrastructure solution. Digital

---

[38] World Economic Forum and Accenture (2017, p. 5)
[39] World Economic Forum and Accenture (2017, p. 5)
[40] Gretzel, Zhong, and Koo (2016)   [41] Guttentag (2010, pp. 640–642)
[42] World Bank and ITU (2020)   [43] Andrianaivo and Kpodar (2011)
[44] Wamboye, Adekola, and Sergi (2016)

platforms and services from education to banking can allow industries to develop without traditional physical infrastructure.[45]

Fast-growing consumer demand in the ICT industry is fueling internet growth and new digital products and services. ICT is second only to the transportation sector in consumption growth, representing the leading role ICT is likely to play in development during the 4IR.

6.1.3.1 The 4IR's Impact on ICTs

The growth and development of Africa's ICT sector are fundamentally intertwined with the 4IR. Since ICT services such as internet provision underlie other 4IR developments, continued expansion of ICTs can facilitate more entrepreneurship and job growth, such as accessible manufacturing practices and service provision through 3D printing and mobile applications.[46] New technologies should supplement labor and not replace it, so it is critical for governmental investment in education and reskilling programs.[47] Furthermore, ICT adoption has a positive and significant impact on innovation among African firms.[48] Conversely, many 4IR technologies fall within the purview of the ICT sector, such as cloud computing, AI, big data, and blockchain, among others. The ICT sector is thus likely to continue growing significantly as the 4IR unfolds across Africa and the world.

6.1.3.2 Challenges and Constraints

Access to high-speed, high-bandwidth internet will be vital for some 4IR technologies, such as IoT and cloud computing, to effectively function and support further growth in the ICT sector. However, the divide in access to the Internet between Africa and the rest of the world remains significant and continues to increase. Additionally, there is an intra-African digital divide between countries with access to international bandwidth and landlocked countries or countries without improved bandwidth access.[49] The intra-African digital divide is particularly apparent between North and sub-Saharan Africa. However, there are also significant disparities between sub-Saharan leaders, such as Nigeria and South Africa and other African countries.

Furthermore, the ICT sector is not very labor-intensive, so while the 4IR may create new employment opportunities in ICT industries, it is

---

[45] Ponelis and Holmner (2015, p. 166)   [46] Naudé (2017, p. 8)
[47] Madden (2020)   [48] Cirera, Lage, and Sabetti (2016)   [49] NEPAD (2012)

unlikely to become a significant driver of employment. The high skill requirement of jobs in the sector means that its job creation is somewhat limited to less abundant higher-skilled workers.

6.1.3.3 Opportunities and Strategies

Because fixed broadband access remains low, compared to mobile access, fixed broadband represents an area with high growth potential for investment. However, improving mobile broadband offers an increasingly viable alternative to fixed broadband access as mobile internet speed and reliability increase. For example, 5G networks are up to ten times faster than 4G networks.[50] 5G networks have proven to be less costly at a national level, benefitting countries with capacity strains and low broadband coverages.[51] Though most African subscribers rely on 2G networks, countries such as South Africa, Kenya, and Namibia have demonstrated potential to become early adopters of 5G on the African continent.[52]

A computer-literate populace with skills in data analysis, engineering, and software development, among other skills, will be necessary for countries to strengthen their ICT sectors and take the lead during the 4IR. African governments should also build human capital by strengthening educational institutions and investing in promising new technologies to supplement traditional education. Public sector investment should be targeted toward STEM education and focus on improving the quality of teaching and learning to develop critical thinking skills, while also expanding the availability of ICT tools, including computers, tablets, and the Internet, in schools.

6.1.4 Health Care

African countries face numerous health challenges, and climate change and disease resilience present short- and long-term challenges that require innovative solutions. According to the World Health Organization, Africa and the rest of the world face significant threats to health in 2019, including noncommunicable diseases, fragile and vulnerable settings, antimicrobial resistance, Ebola and other high-threat pathogens, and weak primary health care.[53] Africa, in particular,

---

[50] Frost & Sullivan and Principal (2018, p. 5)   [51] Oughton et al. (2021)
[52] Oughton et al. (2021, pp. 6–7)   [53] World Health Organization (2019a)

faces the additional challenges of limited physical infrastructure and a lack of qualified professionals. The Fourth Industrial Revolution technology can help mitigate these threats and build sustainable health care systems, even in fragile states or communities.

6.1.4.1 The 4IR's Impact on Health Care

The 4IR is already reshaping African health care systems, optimizing patient care, and improving medical outcomes. Mobile technology has become a platform for improving medical data and service delivery. For example, about 27,000 public health workers in Uganda use a mobile system called mTrac to report medicine stocks across the country. The SMS for Life program, a public–private partnership between Novartis and eight African countries, reduces medicine shortages in primary health care facilities by using mobile phones to track and manage stock levels of malaria treatments and other essential drugs.[54] Rwanda became the world's first country to incorporate drones into its health care system, using autonomous air vehicles to deliver blood transfusions to remote regions.[55] Initiatives applying artificial intelligence to health care demands have launched in several countries across the continent, such as a Nigerian start-up that has developed a machine learning system to detect childbirth asphyxia, the third-highest cause of under-five child deaths.[56] Technology has also improved disaster response. During the West African Ebola outbreak in 2014, for example, WhatsApp became an easy method of dispersing information, checking symptoms, and communicating under quarantine.[57]

Health care providers throughout the continent have managed to capitalize on 4IR technology to address major threats. Illness detection and pharmaceutical production have most immediately benefited from digitization. In Ghana, for example, mPharma predicts demand for prescription drugs to help pharmacists negotiate prices with manufacturers and save consumers money.[58] Artificial intelligence is being slowly implemented in Ethiopia to help medical professionals correctly diagnose cervical cancer and other abnormalities that become visible after women come into clinics for checkups.[59] IBM Research Africa uses AI to determine the optimal methods for eradicating malaria in

---

[54] Access to Medicine Foundation (2016)   [55] Matchaba (2018)
[56] Adepoju (2017)   [57] Atieno (2017)   [58] Adepoju (2017)
[59] Champlin, Bell, and Schocken (2017)

specific locations and using game theory and deep learning data analytics to diagnose pathological diseases and birth asphyxia.[60] AI offers low-cost solutions to improving health care access and quality.[61] The 4IR will take these advancements even further, with medical records ensured and safely shared among doctors using blockchain or expanded access to medical advice through the application of artificial intelligence algorithms mimicking human intelligence and analysis.[62]

While applying AI and other 4IR technology to Africa is still in its infancy, African countries are making coordinated efforts with international partners. For example, one European Commission-funded project known as CareAI combines AI and blockchain for medical data storage to diagnose infectious diseases.[63] The technology is designed to serve patients lacking medical records. CareAI not only targets refugee camps in Europe but also has immense potential for African countries that suffer from a scarcity of medical professionals and inadequate medical record-keeping.[64] The future of health care will depend on how well health care professionals embrace emerging technologies[65] in the 4IR.

6.1.4.2 Challenges and Constraints

Despite the achievements and growing potential of the 4IR in the health sector, several steps need to be taken to overcome the challenges to full technological development. Researchers and practitioners have linked political and economic factors to Africa's vulnerability to disease.[66] One of the significant barriers to the complete transformation of the sector is the lack of ICT infrastructure to connect 4IR technology to both urban and rural health systems. The infrastructure challenge can also affect communities' relationships with national governments and health systems. For example, when Ebola broke out in West Africa, local communities did not trust government officials with their health information. This distrust contributed to the spread of Ebola and likely undermined community engagement and future prevention.

Additional challenges may result from a lack of will to use ICT-enabled health care platforms from providers or patients. Health care providers may find ICT solutions overly expensive or complicated or

---

[60] Akinwande (2018)   [61] Owoyemi et al. (2020)   [62] IBM (2017)
[63] Ekekwe (2018); see also: Duricic (2018)   [64] Ekekwe (2018)
[65] The Medical Futurist (2020)   [66] Mistra (2019)

may have liability concerns regarding the use of new technologies. On the patient side, most ICT platforms, particularly those that improve the provision of information, still require patients to engage with the technology proactively. Particularly in areas where knowledge of health care is low, these ICT platforms may have low take-up.[67]

These health challenges may create a cycle of instability in preventative health care, regulatory environments, and disaster containment. As a result, the 4IR may limit ushering in more efficient, effective health care.

6.1.4.3 Opportunities and Strategies

The 4IR's innovations promise not only new avenues for health care industry development and transformative, life-saving social impacts. Innovations in biology and technology, such as biometric sensors, can entirely transform the health care and patient-caretaker systems. Additional investment, however, will be needed in both new technology and Africa's human capital and infrastructure for the continent to reap the full benefits. One opportunity that may benefit Africa in the coming years is the $400 million health care fund established by Quantum Global Group to invest in private medical centers, pharmaceuticals, biotechnology, medical equipment, and medical support services across the continent.[68]

African citizens must also be encouraged to take control of their health and their families by using the numerous applications and mobile platforms available to reach credible health information and preliminary treatment. These mobile options are cost-effective methods of spreading health care knowledge. New public and private partnerships can support the large-scale adoption of eHealth services that build on the digitization of the Third Industrial Revolution to underline the sector's total transformation in the 4IR.

---

[67] Shekar and Otto (2014)   [68] Bastos de Morais (2017)

7 | *Leaders in the Fourth Industrial Revolution on the African Continent*

To understand how African countries might catch up or lead in the 4IR, one can start by looking at the significant variation in digital maturity within the African continent itself. Understanding and nurturing adaptability will be the key to uplifting African states.[1] Digital economy assessments will help pave the way for sector reforms and infrastructure investments in Africa.[2] This chapter will evaluate the burgeoning tech opportunities, strategies, and innovative performance of five African countries leading the 4IR on the continent. The chosen countries have demonstrated high performance on the GII or GCI. Many have also become vital host sites for regional tech hubs. The GII and GCI scores of all five countries are summarized in Tables 7.1 and 7.2, respectively.

The GII aims to measure multidimensional components of innovation, which it recognizes as a central driver of economic growth and development. As such, it measures seven features of each country: institutions, human capital and research, infrastructure, market sophistication, business sophistication, knowledge and technology outputs, and creative outputs. The first five components comprise an innovation input sub-index, while the latter two comprise an innovation output sub-index.[3] The GCI aims to measure the drivers of long-term competitiveness in countries and, similar to the GII, emphasizes the role of human capital and innovation. The GCI measures twelve components of each country: the enabling environment, including institutions, infrastructure, ICT adoption, and macroeconomic stability; markets, including product market, labor market, financial system, and market size; human capital, including health and skills; and innovation ecosystem, including business dynamism and innovation capability.[4]

---

[1] Linsky and Darabya (2019)   [2] World Bank (2019)
[3] Cornell University, INSEAD, and WIPO (2018, pp. 55–57)   [4] Schwab (2018)

Table 7.1 *2018 GII scores and rankings for leading African countries*[5]

Country	2018 GII score/ranking	Strongest GII subcategory (rank)	Weakest GII subcategory (rank)
South Africa*	35.1/58	Market sophistication (23)	Infrastructure (84)
Tunisia*	32.9/66	Human capital & research (33)	Market sophistication (111)
Mauritius	31.3/75	Market sophistication (45)	Knowledge and technology outputs (115)
Morocco	31.1/76	Infrastructure (50)	Business sophistication (115)
Kenya*	31.1/78	Business sophistication (49)	Human capital & research (112)

*Indicates that a country performs better on the 2018 GII rankings than other countries at a similar level of economic development.[6]

Table 7.2 *2018 GCI scores and rankings for leading African countries*[7]

Country	2018 GCI score/ranking	Strongest GCI subcategory (rank)	Weakest GCI subcategory (rank)
South Africa	60.8/67	Financial system (18)	Health (125)
Tunisia	55.6/87	Health (58)	Labor market (129)
Mauritius	63.7/49	Product market (19)	Market size (117)
Morocco	58.5/75	Financial system (44)	Labor market (119)
Kenya	53.7/93	Labor market (60)	ICT adoption (113)

There is a significant overlap between the components measured on the GII and GCI, and as such, results on the two indexes tend to be

[5] Schwab (2018, p. xx); see pp. 321, 332, 289, 294, and 276, for each country's respective profile in the order presented in Table 7.1.
[6] Following the methodology described in Cornell University, INSEAD, and WIPO (2018, p. 36), a curve is fit for the relationship between GII scores and GDP per capita (PPP). Countries whose plotted GII score and GDP per capita fall above this curve have a greater-than-expected GII score for their level of GDP per capita and thus outperform other countries at a similar level of economic development.
[7] Schwab (2018)

Table 7.3 *South Africa GII and GCI rankings*

Category	Ranking
GII score (among African countries)	1
GII score (among all countries)	58
GCI score (among African countries)	2
GCI score (among all countries)	67

similar. However, while the GII is used as the primary analysis index due to its direct relation to innovation, the GCI provides valuable supplementary and contextual information. It is used to provide a richer picture of each country.

Top innovation performers on the African continent are examined for three reasons. First, the African countries leading the way into the 4IR may offer insights to those falling behind, particularly states such as South Africa and Kenya that outperform on the GII rankings relative to other countries at a similar level of economic development.[8] Second, strengths and weaknesses for innovative potential and 4IR capacity vary even among the top-performing states on the continent; thus, stakeholders from the most advanced African countries can still learn valuable lessons from their peers. For example, the two top-scoring African countries on the 2018 GII rankings are South Africa and Tunisia. As Table 7.1 illustrates, South Africa's strongest GII subcategory, market sophistication, is Tunisia's weakest subcategory. This indicates that Tunisia may draw from the South African model for improving its investment environment. Third, understanding the location, strategy, and innovative environment of top-performing countries is crucial to predicting the trajectory of the 4IR on the African continent.

7.1 South Africa

South Africa, one of the highest-performing economies on the African continent, is also a regional leader in 4IR innovation and significantly outperforms other countries at its income level. On the GII, South Africa performs best in its degree of market and business sophistication. For example, South Africa outperforms its peers among its income group in

[8] Cornell University, INSEAD, and WIPO (2018, p. xxxv)

Table 7.4 *Tunisia GII and GCI rankings*

Category	Ranking
GII score (among African countries)	2
GII score (among all countries)	66
GCI score (among African countries)	4
GCI score (among all countries)	87

terms of university-industry research collaboration, market capitalization as a percentage of GDP, and intellectual property payments as a percentage of total trade. University-industry partnership, in particular, has been responsible for catalyzing impactful innovation.

On the GCI, the country's financial system, innovation capability, labor market, business dynamism, and macroeconomic stability rank exceptionally high and are significant factors contributing to South Africa's current levels of innovation and preparedness for the disruption of the 4IR. Government support programs for innovation and R&D, thriving metropolitan tech hubs, and a relatively sophisticated and diversified economy further solidify South Africa's place as a regional leader in innovation (Table 7.3).

Strong support for innovation comes from the government, universities, the private sector, and entrepreneurs. In 1996, South Africa's adoption of national science, technology, and innovation policy committed the country to use innovation to support the development and overcome the legacy of apartheid. Since adopting this policy, South Africa has seen a threefold increase in research publications and a rise in doctoral graduation rates and enrollment at schools and universities.[9] South Africa's universities are some of the best on the African continent. Collaboration among university researchers, the government, and the private sector is a major driver of innovation.[10]

Innovative activities in the country are concentrated in large metropolitan areas such as Cape Town and Johannesburg, which encourages agglomeration economies to form and create opportunities for entrepreneurs and startups to learn from each other. Cape Town has between 700 and 1,200 active startups, making it home to the largest number of

[9] Kubayi-Ngubane (2018)   [10] Tshabalala (2017)

IT-based companies in Africa, while Johannesburg has between 200 and 500.[11]

On a national level, the composition of South Africa's economy shows a relatively high level of sophistication, with 2.8 percent of 2017s GDP originating from the agriculture sector, 29.7 percent from industry, and 67.5 percent from services.[12] Employment is diversified across various sectors, with most of the labor force employed in the community and social services, trade, finance and business services, manufacturing, and construction.[13] The country has a particularly robust medium-tech manufacturing sector: Medium- and high-tech exports comprised nearly 50 percent of all manufactured exports in 2015, up from 31 percent in 1996.[14] Given this economic sophistication and diversification, there is a considerable scope for 4IR technologies, adapted foreign technologies, and private R&D to drive economic growth and corporate profitability.

However, research and development intensity, often a proxy for innovation, in South African manufacturing firms is considerably lower than in OECD countries. It is relatively low compared to other African innovators such as Kenya (with the exception of the mining and fuel sub-sectors, which have patents and R&D levels comparable to the United States, Canada, and Australia). Furthermore, South Africa's R&D expenditure, relative to GDP, declined slightly from 2004 to 2012. However, the estimated return to an R&D activity in South African manufacturing firms is high compared to OECD countries.[15] South Africa should thus continue to pursue policies (outlined below) that encourage increased R&D expenditure.

7.1.1 Noteworthy Innovations

Supported by comparatively high levels of mobile and broadband penetration, tech entrepreneurship is flourishing, particularly in the burgeoning hubs of Cape Town and Johannesburg.[16] For example, South African entrepreneur Neil du Preez developed Mellowcab, a high-tech electric pedicab manufactured from recycled materials, to fill the gap for commuters who need micro-transport within a 3-kilometer radius.[17] Sectors such as agriculture and forestation are investing heavily in drones and

---

[11] World Bank (2017, p. 35)   [12] CIA (2019)
[13] Statistics South Africa (2018)   [14] World Bank (2015)
[15] Schaffer et al. (2018, p. 1)   [16] KPMG (2017)   [17] Nsehe (2014)

robotics. Startup Aerobotics, for example, uses aerial imagery from drones and satellites and machine learning to detect pests and diseases on farms and optimize crop performance for farmers.[18] At the University of Pretoria, the Virtual Reality Mine Design Centre uses innovative VR technologies to train students and mine staff in a simulated mining environment.[19]

In the banking and finance sector, South African financial institutions and a thriving fintech community are researching and applying the utility of blockchain and cryptocurrencies.[20] South Africa has also been an early adopter of additive manufacturing: Businesses and entrepreneurs in the areas of jewelry, tooling, and prototyping are known to use it, and several universities and government institutions are actively supporting R&D in the field.[21] In one example, entrepreneurs in South Africa – in collaboration with government and research institutions – developed additive manufacturing for titanium metal parts; under this new system, production times are up to eight times faster.[22] South Africa also plays a leading role in supporting continent-wide uptake of and preparedness for 4IR technologies by hosting a variety of African innovation-related summits and conferences, including the South African Innovation Summit, the Open Innovations Conference, Africa Tech Week, and Women in Tech Africa.

7.1.2 Strengths and Challenges

Government support programs are a significant strength of South Africa's innovation ecosystem, although there is scope to improve their effectiveness. South Africa uses the R&D Tax Incentive, introduced in November 2006, as a tax-based incentive and other measures to stimulate private sector R&D. The Department of Science and Technology oversees this incentive. They also manage various programs and agencies that promote innovation, including the Council for Scientific and Industrial Research, which oversees R&D in areas including health, energy, high-tech manufacturing, and mining. The Technology Innovation Agency, which funds strategic technological innovation with the aim of commercialization; the Technology for Human Resources in Industry Program, which encourages R&D collaboration between the private sector, universities, and science

---

[18] Steyn (2018)   [19] Smit (2013)   [20] KPMG (2017)   [21] Campbell (2015)
[22] Naudé (2017, p. 8)

councils; and the Support Program for Industrial Innovation and Industrial Innovation Partnership Program.[23] Legally, South Africa's strong intellectual property rights encourage and protect domestic innovation.[24]

South Africa has a robust research system, with excellent universities and world-class science facilities, which has contributed to the training of innovators and entrepreneurs and the development and application of new technologies. In fact, the Times Higher Education's World University Rankings for 2022 includes three of the country's universities ranked among the world's top 300.[25] International collaboration on research publications is high compared to other African and emerging economies, indicating integration into the global scientific community. Public research institutions also account for most of South Africa's patents.[26] However, despite relatively high education expenditure as a percentage of GDP and high-quality educational institutions, gross enrollment in tertiary education is low, at only 23.8 percent,[27] indicating an area for improvement.

South Africa's private sector is relatively dynamic and diversified, encouraging innovation and collaboration across various economic sectors. Several multinational companies have offices in the country, including Google and Microsoft, providing technology and knowledge transfer opportunities. Additionally, South Africa is the top FDI destination in sub-Saharan Africa.[28] These strengths have allowed South Africa to take its place as a leader in African innovation. As the 4IR further entrenches itself on the continent, South Africa can continue to lead by supporting regional integration in trade and business.

South Africa's challenges now involve accelerating the pace and extent of innovation, ensuring macroeconomic stability, and leaving no one behind. To take full advantage of the 4IR, South Africa will require a business climate that is more conducive to the entry and growth of new firms and risk-taking and experimentation. Legal reforms, the spread of best practices from leading metropolitan areas to local governments throughout the country, and 4IR solutions such as e-government can help improve the business environment and stimulate growth and innovation.[29]

[23] Naudé (2017, pp. 10–11)   [24] World Bank (2017, p. 35)
[25] *Times Higher Education* (2021)
[26] *Times Higher Education* (2021, pp. 34–35)   [27] World Bank (2018)
[28] World Bank (2018, p. 33)   [29] World Bank (2018, p. viii)

South Africa's Department of Trade and Industry predicts that the 4IR will present challenges where South Africa currently lags. These areas include enabling infrastructure, such as broadband and communications; unemployment, through the risk of job loss from automation; education and skills, by replacing less-skilled jobs with higher-skilled ones; and the integration of primary, secondary, and tertiary industrial sectors.[30] Given the reliance of many 4IR technologies on internet connectivity, enhancing internet penetration should be an urgent priority for South Africa to maintain its status as a regional innovative leader. Many companies – such as BCX, Cisco, Google, and Microsoft – are investing in ICT capacity building in South Africa.[31]

The 4IR presents many opportunities for South Africa. It is well-positioned to take advantage of its current status as a regional leader in technology and innovation. Despite the risks posed by automation, research from the World Bank suggests that greater innovation and R&D are likely to result in net job creation rather than job loss.[32] By building on existing innovation system strengths, continuing to improve the governance and design of existing innovation policies and agencies, encouraging increased private sector participation, and expanding the availability of funding for entrepreneurs and startups, South Africa can further improve its current innovation environment to solidify its status as a leader during the 4IR.[33]

7.2 Tunisia

Tunisia has developed momentum as an innovator in the North African region. In 2018, the country moved up eight places on the GII rankings and became an outperformer relative to other countries of its income group.[34] This momentum has coincided with a series of public reform efforts, civil projects, and investment initiatives. Tunisia's success on the 2018 GII rankings is fueled by high performance in three categories:

---

[30] DTI (2018)
[31] Sibanda (2019) – These companies are investing heavily to help make up for the lack of digital talent found in South Africa. For example, Cisco is using a networking academy to help and create an ICT talent pool and BCX is advancing skills in ICT infrastructure, software programming, cybersecurity, fintech, and AI through partnerships. Meeting demand is crucial and South Africa needs more initiatives such as these to help and close the talent gap.
[32] World Bank (2017, p. vii)   [33] Schaffer (2018, pp. 38–39)
[34] Cornell University, INSEAD, and WIPO (2018, p. 332)

human capital and research, knowledge and technology, and creative outputs. The 2018 GII report suggests that Tunisia may be gaining and developing technical capacity from international trade. The country ranks in the top 40 of all 126 countries for both high-tech imports as a percentage of total trade (10.6 percent) and high-tech exports as a percentage of total trade (4.6 percent).[35]

Tunisia performs somewhat worse on the GCI than the GII; its ranking is brought down primarily by low scores in the areas of macroeconomic stability, product market, and labor market. As in the GII, Tunisia outperforms in skills and human capital, mainly due to its excellent school life expectancy, the number of teachers, quality of research institutions, and R&D expenditure. It is also ranked relatively high in the GCI pillars of business dynamism, institutions, and financial system. Tunisia's government has been a primary contributor to the country's level of innovation and competitiveness through investment in research and education. Still, the strength of the country's entrepreneurial ecosystem offers another promising sign for taking advantage of the 4IR (Table 7.4).

The ICT sector is a priority in Tunisia, both as a source for innovation and a vehicle for developing other economic sectors. Currently, the ICT sector accounts for 7.5 percent of Tunisia's GDP and employs about 86,000 people within 2,120 private companies, 219 shared service centers, and eight development centers that serve multinational companies. The country also has three ICT-oriented "technoparks" and eighteen "cyberparks" dedicated to scientific and technological training, research, and production. Tunisia's ICT sector is also open to international involvement through exports, foreign investment, partnership, and outsourcing with developed and developing countries, particularly with other African countries.[36]

The digital economy of Tunisia is supported by growing efforts to develop ICT infrastructure and human capital. In May 2018, national telecom operator Tunisie Télécom successfully tested a 5G network in Tunis. Tunisia's Ministry of Communication Technologies and Digital Transformation announced that Tunisia will launch 5G licenses by the end of 2023.[37] Already, the Tunisian telecommunications network is

---

[35] Cornell University, INSEAD, and WIPO (2018, p. 332)
[36] Government of Canada (2020)
[37] Ecofin Agency (2018); International Trade Administration (2022)

among the most sophisticated in Africa, driving relatively high connectivity. More than 66 percent of Tunisia's population used the Internet in 2019,[38] a number that continues to grow rapidly. The country also had nearly 30,000 websites in 2015–2016.[39]

Tunisia also has a high-quality and dynamic entrepreneurship ecosystem and is particularly strong in product innovation, risk capital, and opportunity perception.[40] This strength contributes to the emergence of a tech startup scene in Tunisia supported by government and private sector initiatives. One such initiative, the TSIndex, launched in March 2017, is a crowd-sourced online platform that measures the impact of Tunisian startups on the local economy and gathers data on startups' business activities, such as turnover, number of employees, exports, and online transactions. The tool supports startups in assessing the business environment and brings more transparency and insight into the rising startup pillar of the Tunisian economy.[41]

7.2.1 Noteworthy Innovations

Tunisia was a pioneer in 4IR technology in Africa. Tunisia was an early adopter of digital currency. In 2009, Tunisia became the first country in the world to operate an electronic currency known as the e-Dinar. The e-Dinar wallet now accounts for 2.5 million transactions per year on 700,000 prepaid debit cards.[42] The Tunisian Association for Environmental Nanotechnology launched the first applied project in North Africa in 2010, which works to monitor and purify the waters of the Medjerda River.[43] When it comes to the Internet of Things, Tunisian utility company STEG has partnered with company Orange to offer smart electricity meters that cut meter-reading costs and reduce the risk of fraud.[44]

The World Economic Forum named five Tunisian startups on its list of the 100 Arab startups shaping the 4IR. Two of these startups deal with AI. Barac helps organizations detect fraud and cyberattacks as they happen by using a combination of real-time data and AI. Simple Expert uses AI to provide accurate budget estimates to app developers. Another two deal in agriculture, using high-tech solutions to improve

---

[38] World Bank (2019)   [39] Oxford Business Group (2020)   [40] Kallel (2018)
[41] World Economic Forum (2018d, pp. 1–29)   [42] Chakchouk (2017)
[43] Boumedjout (2010)   [44] Orange (2017, p. 16)

agricultural productivity, accelerate sustainable agriculture, and tackle resource scarcity. The last, startup GoMyCode, provides education technologies to schools to create high-end computer science education for all Tunisians.[45]

Digitalization will continue to play a massive role in helping Tunisians mitigate the economic impact of the COVID-19 pandemic. The Mashrou3i project uses digital technology to help small businesses in the country's interior regions rebuild sustainable models that can endure future disruptions and challenges.[46] Projects such as the Mashrou3i will continue to grow with the help of investments. In 2019, the World Bank announced two new projects totaling $175 million to support the government's "Startup Tunisia" program, which aims to grow startups, SMEs (small to medium-sized businesses), in addition to the digitalization of social security and educational systems for the country's youth population.[47]

7.2.2 Strengths and Challenges

The Tunisian government has played a significant role in furthering the country's preparedness for the 4IR. They have, among other initiatives, developed an electronic money platform (the e-Dinar) and an electronic procurement system, contributed to the diffusion of ICT through trade facilitation policies and programs, and supported the nationwide expansion of internet cafes ("PubliNets"). They have also implemented a series of measures to modernize the legal and regulatory framework for telecommunications, including creating the National Telecommunications Authority and National Frequency Agency. The Tunisian government's development plan supports many projects in the ICT sector, including spreading broadband internet access, digitizing government administration services, promoting ICT-enabled services for export, and encouraging foreign companies to hire Tunisians.[48]

Tunisia's government has identified the country's strong performance in entrepreneurship as an essential source of innovation but recognizes that obstacles remain that prevent Tunisian startups from succeeding nationally and internationally. To address barriers to startups' success, the government convened a task force of both public and

---

[45] World Economic Forum (2017d)   [46] Mashrou3i (2020)
[47] World Bank (2019)   [48] *Exportiamo* (2018)

private sector leaders to identify the needs of startups and entrepreneurs and propose a set of government actions to eliminate barriers. The Startup Act of April 2018 was a reaction to discovering bureaucratic obstacles faced by innovative entrepreneurs.[49] The Act supports startups with funding, grants them exemptions from corporate taxes, allows private and public sector employees up to a year off from their current jobs to run startups, provides a government-sponsored salary to founders, and assists firms in filing for international patents.[50]

Outside government involvement, the relative strength of Tunisia's research institutions and human capital is also driving innovative activities across the country. Tunisia's human capital is among the strongest in Africa and has massively improved in the past several decades. In 1988, Tunisia hosted only three higher education institutions. By academic year 2018/2019, the country boasted about 203 public tertiary institutions,[51] 24 technical schools, and 6 higher institutes for teacher training.[52] Notably, 44 percent of tertiary education graduates hold degrees in science and engineering.[53] To further promote education and skills development, in 2015, Tunisia's Ministry of Education launched a digital school program to work with 2 million students and 150,000 primary and secondary teachers. The program promotes digital tools in the learning process, expands access to digital resources for all students, and uses digital technology to support academic success and pedagogical innovation.[54] These initiatives may help Tunisia continue to improve the quality of its education system and better match the skills taught in schools to those desired by industry.

The availability of developed infrastructure and the quality of local human resources has attracted several international companies and partners to locate R&D activities in Tunisia. In 2012, nearly 80 percent of the country's exports were from foreign or foreign-owned companies in Tunisia. Although much foreign investment in Tunisia is in low value-added and labor-intensive sectors, such as textiles and clothing, a significant share of investments targets the offshore industry. A growing number are targeting higher-technology sectors.[55] Tunisia and China, for example, recently signed a partnership

---

[49] Ben-Hassine (2019)   [50] Latif Dahir and Kazeem (2018)
[51] Statista (2021)   [52] Oxford Business Group (2017a)
[53] Cornell University, INSEAD, and WIPO (2018, p. 332)   [54] Yarrow (2017)
[55] El Elj (2012, pp. 183–197)

agreement on developing the digital economy, which will offer opportunities for young Tunisians in the areas of telecommunications, fiber optics, network computing, and e-commerce.[56] Another example is creating a digital transformation center sponsored by the German Corporation for International Cooperation (GIZ) to help prepare Tunisia for the 4IR.[57] The growth of investment and foreign-led R&D in Tunisia may lead to technology spillovers in the rest of the economy.

Despite the strengths of the sector, most ICT companies in Tunisia remain small. According to a World Bank report, approximately 80 percent of ICT-industry firms have fewer than fifty employees, a significant disadvantage for the sector in Tunisia. Most of the demand for ICT services in Tunisia comes from large orders from the public sector. Larger, foreign firms then have a competitive advantage over small, local firms.[58] Local firms also face the challenge of growing in a relatively small market. In 2017, Tunisia only had 11 million people and $40 billion GDP, and altogether limited angel and venture capital funding. Tunisia's well-trained entrepreneurs and dynamic firms can mitigate some of these challenges by expanding to neighboring countries – helped along by 4IR technologies in themselves.[59]

Tunisia is taking a leading position among African countries in boosting its burgeoning entrepreneurial and innovative ecosystem. Tunisia is ideally positioned as a hub to access neighboring markets, such as Algeria and Libya, and other African and Middle Eastern markets. The country has excellent potential to position itself as a regional leader in ICT, thanks to a business environment that encourages investment and forward-looking government policies.[60] To fully prepare for the 4IR, however, Tunisia must continue to enact policies supporting local firms and further develop the capacities of its universities and academic centers.

7.3 Mauritius

Mauritius is ranked as one of the most competitive and innovative economies in Africa consistently. On the GII, the country is powerful in the

[56] Xinhua (2018)   [57] African News Agency (2020)
[58] Oxford Business Group (2020)   [59] Schultz (2018)
[60] Oxford Business Group (2020)

Table 7.5 *Mauritius GII and GCI scores*

Category	Ranking
GII score (among African countries)	3
GII score (among all countries)	75
GCI score (among African countries)	1
GCI score (among all countries)	49

following areas: institutions, reflecting its political stability, government effectiveness, and business environment; infrastructure, including ICT infrastructure and e-governance; market sophistication, mainly due to the availability of credit and good investment environment; and creative outputs, including those that incorporate ICTs. On the GCI, Mauritius is relatively competitive in eight of the twelve pillars; the country received its highest rankings in product market, business dynamism, and institutions. The pillars in which Mauritius received lower scores are related to human capital and include the labor market, skills, and health (Table 7.5).[61]

The World Bank consistently ranks Mauritius as the easiest African country to do business,[62] and the country's infrastructure is on par with international standards. Broadband penetration in the country stands at 78 percent, and mobile phone penetration is over 100 percent.[63] There are over 860,000 active internet users in the country or 68 percent of the population.[64] In the World Economic Forum's Global Information Technology Report 2015, Mauritius ranked as the third-best country globally in terms of the affordability of connectivity. It was the only African country to rank in the top fifty overall.[65]

The country also has high-quality business and industrial parks in strategic locations and at competitive prices. These physical infrastructure projects, coupled with financial incentives provided by the government, have attracted many international banks and companies to choose Mauritius as a regional hub.[66] Mauritius is now an attractive outsourcing destination and has seen rapid growth in many multinational firms operating on the island. For example, between

---

[61] World Economic Forum (2018e)   [62] Bastos de Morais (2017)
[63] Mauritius Ministry of Technology, Communication, and Innovation (2018, p. 19)
[64] Kemp (2020)   [65] Banda (2015)   [66] Bastos de Morais (2017)

October 2006 and March 2007, over forty-one international ICT companies began working in Mauritius, including Oracle, Microsoft, IBM, HP, Cisco, and Accenture.[67] Mauritius has also hosted several extensive technology and innovation conferences. These include the Africa Peering and Interconnection Forum, held in August 2019, and the World AI Show and World Blockchain Summit, inaugurated in 2018.

Mauritius has developed into a well-known financial center, and the country has now begun to embrace blockchain technologies and cryptocurrencies, seeking to become a fintech hub for Africa. The government considers innovations in AI and fintech, particularly blockchain, to be a critical method to increase private investment and employment.[68] The ICT sector, which was nascent less than a decade ago, had a growth rate of 3.9 percent in 2020, despite the disruptions brought on by COVID-19, and now contributes 7 percent of Mauritius's GDP, with over 850 businesses.[69]

7.3.1 Noteworthy Innovations

Mauritius has a robust financial service outsourcing sector that relies upon the country's strong ICT infrastructure. While much of the finance sector is traditional, Mauritius has also embraced innovations in blockchain and cryptocurrencies. It has recently established regulations to improve safety for users of cryptocurrency custodian services – the first nation in the world to offer this regulatory framework for digital assets.[70] The Mauritius-based International Derivatives and Commodities Exchange also provides digitized gold buying and selling underpinned by blockchain technology.[71] The Mauritian government has embraced the use of other innovative technologies, launching over 100 e-services, including a Smart Traffic app to reduce road congestion, an Emergency Alert System app, and a Domestic Violence and Child Abuse app.[72] In the agriculture industry, research institutions and private companies utilize biotechnology for micropropagation, crop breeding, disease diagnosis, and waste treatment.[73]

---

[67] Tanner (2009, pp. 57–86)   [68] "Mauritius Is Willing" (2018)
[69] Economic Development Board of Mauritius (2021)
[70] "Mauritius' Financial Sector" (2019)   [71] MINDEX (2018)
[72] Government of the Republic of Mauritius (2018)   [73] Puchooa (2004)

The Ministry of Technology, Communication and Innovation announced, in 2019, the Digital Mauritius 2030 Strategic Plan. This plan outlined the role of 4IR technologies, which promote digitalization, e-governance, and higher levels of trust among citizens.[74] This will benefit the growing internet users in Mauritius, which saw a 40 percent increase from 2019 to 2020 and had 1.91 million mobile connections in January 2020.[75] Ultimately, government-sponsored incentives and policies will continue to advance programs such as the Ebene Cyber-City to offer basic business processing services and create value in the private sector.[76]

7.3.2 Strengths and Challenges

Mauritius's development plan focuses heavily on the digital economy and on innovation, creativity, and high-value addition. Mauritius adopted a National Information Technology Strategy Plan relatively early in the country's development. This plan also created a special ministry to promote ICT applications in different sectors.[77] Mauritius's current digital strategy consists of five pillars: ICT infrastructure, e-government and business facilitation, cybersecurity, innovation and emerging technologies, and talent management. In 2021, Mauritius spent an estimated $3.9 trillion in 2021 on IT, an increase from 6.2 percent from 2020.[78] The government focuses on improving the availability, accessibility, and affordability of ICTs to lead to innovation.[79]

These strategies have resulted in a significant number of technology-related projects and relatively high funding levels for innovation. Mauritius's 2015 budget included funding for eight smart cities and five "technoparks" meant to boost the economy and drive the country's regional and international competitiveness. These innovation areas focus on a range of sectors, including air transport, tourism and hospitality, ICT, health, agriculture, and government administration.[80] Additionally, the Mauritian government dedicated $4.3 million to promote innovation in 2017. In the same year, the Mauritius Research Council received a budget increase from around $1 million to $2.5 million after receiving over 130 proposals for innovative research projects.[81]

---

[74] Ministry of Technology, Communication, and Innovation (2018)
[75] Kemp (2020)   [76] ITU News (2019)   [77] Wijkman and Afifi (2002)
[78] Bholanauth (2021)   [79] "Digital Mauritius 2030 Strategy" (2018)
[80] Sahadut, Bundhoo, and Catherine (2015)   [81] Hamuth (2017)

Mauritius's National Computer Board (NCB) has partnered with the Community Empowerment Program, a citizens' outreach initiative meant to enable the creation and sharing of information and knowledge for community development, improve digital literacy, and build an inclusive information society. The NCB has set up more than 270 computer clubs in social welfare and community centers and manages 100 public internet access points in all postal offices across Mauritius.[82] Furthermore, in cybersecurity, Mauritius is one of few African countries with a National Computer Emergency Response Team, which provides information and assistance to help users implement proactive measures that reduce the risks of information security incidents.[83]

Mauritius's Financial Services Commission has made significant progress in establishing the Mauritius International Financial Center as a fintech hub for Africa.[84] The high occurrence of outsourcing in Mauritius has helped the country benefit from the technology and knowledge transfer that multinational companies provide. Innovation is not limited to large international companies. However, due to the government's efforts, Mauritius has attracted many small- and medium-sized ICT companies[85] and the country is now aiming to develop emerging tech entrepreneurs through ICT incubators.[86]

Mauritius needs to improve its infrastructure and educate its labor force for high-skill jobs to prepare for the 4IR fully.[87] Human capital, as discussed above, remains a significant challenge with no short-term solution. Training Mauritian workers for 4IR jobs is expected to take between five and ten years.[88] Due to the structural changes over the past decade in the country, with the economy shifting from traditional, low-skill sectors to high-skill services, the demand for skilled labor has outpaced the increase in supply. This impacted the country's ranking in digital competitiveness between 2017 and 2019 due to the regression of digital skills among the population and attitudes toward entrepreneurial risk.[89] The Mauritian labor market is also increasingly characterized by a skills mismatch and unemployment among highly educated youth. In a survey conducted by the World Economic Forum

[82] National Computer Board (2020)
[83] Oolun, Ramgolam, and Dorasami (2012, pp. 161–168)
[84] Financial Services Commission of Mauritius (2018, pp. 1–2)
[85] Wijkman and Afifi (2002)   [86] Hamuth (2017)   [87] Singh (2018)
[88] Banda (2015)   [89] Aufait Team (2020)

in 2017, employers reported educational inadequacy as the third most problematic factor in doing business on the island.[90]

Equitable access to fast internet is another main challenge that may reduce Mauritius's ability to ensure that citizens benefit from the 4IR.[91] Additionally, new financial structures will be required to boost innovation and entrepreneurship in the country. Mauritius, for example, lacks angel investors to invest in startups. As the country becomes more expensive, Mauritian operators find it more challenging to compete with low-cost call center operators due to rising labor costs. Many Mauritian companies in the business processing sector are beginning to search for opportunities elsewhere in Africa.[92] By investing in human capital and strengthening the business environment, Mauritius can ensure that the country's private sector can continue innovating and remain competitive as the 4IR unfolds.

Mauritius's highly competitive business environment has helped transform the country into a services-based economy that is an attractive destination for outsourcing. This strength has led to the increasing adoption of ICTs and innovation, particularly in the finance sector. Human capital development remains a challenge for Mauritius. However, overall, the country is well poised to take advantage of the 4IR. For example, during the COVID-19 pandemic, the development of digital platforms increased in Mauritius due to work-from-home mandates and online shopping.[93] Continued efforts to decrease the costs of international connectivity, improve the quality of the workforce, and promote a business-friendly environment will further ensure that Mauritius becomes a preferred provider for the areas in which it has a comparative advantage during the 4IR.[94]

7.4 Morocco

Since the 1990s, Morocco has been one of Africa's frontrunners in using ICT to boost social and economic development. Notably, Morocco performs best on the GII's infrastructure pillar, where it ranks 50th of all 126 GII countries. The country also performs well in creative output, driven by its strengths in industrial design,

---

[90] World Bank (2018a)   [91] Hamuth (2017)   [92] Banda (2015)
[93] IBL Group (2020)
[94] Oolun, Ramgolam, and Dorasami (2012, pp. 161–168)

Table 7.6 *Morocco GII and GCI scores*

Category	Ranking
GII score (among African countries)	4
GII score (among all countries)	76
GCI score (among African countries)	3
GCI score (among all countries)	75

trademark application, and cultural and creative services exports, and institutions, with a healthy political environment, high government effectiveness, and excellent ease of starting a business score. By contrast, Morocco performs particularly poorly in terms of business sophistication.[95] It ranks in the bottom 11 of all 126 countries; this score is partly dragged down by low degrees of knowledge-intensive employment, accounting for only 6.9 percent of total employment.[96]

On the GCI, Morocco's strong performance is driven by the country's macroeconomic stability, financial system, infrastructure, and institutions. Government policies have had a substantial effect on Morocco's 4IR preparedness, with high levels of support for R&D compared to other African countries. The government's involvement and that of Morocco's leading universities and businesses have led Morocco to rank among the top African countries on the Africa Capacity Report, which examines the status of and capacity for science, technology, and innovation in African countries.[97] It has also led to annual growth in the ICT sector of more than 10 percent during the past five years and a robust technology export sector, with 45 percent of technology experts in the MENA region originating from Morocco (Table 7.6).[98]

Morocco's robust infrastructure has also enabled innovative activities and prepared the country for the 4IR. Access to electricity is 100 percent, and mobile phone subscription rates are greater than 100 percent.[99] The government has supported ambitious public infrastructure projects,

---

[95] Business sophistication includes indicators such as employment in knowledge-intensive services, firms offering formal training, innovation linkages between universities and industries, and knowledge absorption.
[96] Cornell University, INSEAD, and WIPO (2018, p. 294)
[97] El Masaiti (2017)   [98] Ismaili (2018)
[99] World Bank (2016b); World Bank (2016c)

including constructing a massive solar farm in the Sahara Desert covering 1.4 million square meters.[100] Internet usage rates in Morocco have steadily grown, rising from 33 percent of the population in 2008 to almost 85 percent in 2020.[101] Moroccan internet usage is above the MENA region average but below the OECD average, demonstrating Morocco's potential for further improvement.[102]

There is a large pool of talented labor in Morocco, and as a result, Moroccan companies and entrepreneurs are innovating and finding success in 4IR sectors. Moroccan tech startups raised $3.9 million in venture capital funding in 2017, the ninth-largest figure among all African countries and a fourfold increase from 2016.[103] Morocco is also home to thirty-four tech hubs, the sixth-highest number on the continent,[104] and three "technoparks" hosting startups and small and medium enterprises specializing in ICTs, green technologies, and cultural industries in Tangiers Casablanca, and Rabat.

7.4.1 Noteworthy Innovations

Morocco's investments in technology and innovation have begun to drive a digital transformation in the country and position it as a leading African tech hub. Three Moroccan startups were included on the World Economic Forum's list of Arab startups shaping the 4IR: Education Media Company, which produces educational websites for Moroccan secondary and postsecondary school students to facilitate their transition to university; Elum, which developed software that optimizes energy between solar panels, batteries, and the grid to reduce energy bills and increase energy reliability in industrial and commercial buildings; and Ma Navette, which offers technology-enabled private car and staff transportation services.[105]

Established companies have also embraced the role of innovation in growth. S2M, a financial services company founded in 1983, has used innovation as a driver of continued growth by developing mobile payment and instant card issuance systems. They have also entered the software-as-a-service market in Europe while increasing their penetration in African and Middle Eastern markets.[106] In the public sector, some of

---

[100] Jezard (2018)   [101] World Bank (2020)   [102] OECD (2018, pp. 35–36)
[103] Collon (2018)   [104] Norbrook et al. (2020)
[105] World Economic Forum (2017d)   [106] Casey (2015)

the government's most important 4IR achievements have been establishing electronic tax reporting for large and medium businesses, digitizing customs procedures, and mobile payments through a public–private partnership.[107] As the second-fastest in digital transformation, it will be critical for Morocco to continue advancing digital innovation in fields such as engineering, business, and ICT.[108]

Morocco is also an African leader in the production and use of 4IR infrastructure. The country has invested significantly in renewable energy technologies, and the Moroccan energy strategy aims to use 50 percent renewable energy for electricity needs by 2030 and 100 percent by 2050.[109] Tangiers, in 2018, launched the first fiber-optic manufacturing plant in Africa and the Middle East in the field of online connectivity.[110] Inwi, a Moroccan telecommunications company, has a data center in Rabat that offers Moroccan companies hosting services and solutions to international standards of availability, security, and connectivity.[111] In 2019, Morocco joined the Smart Africa Alliance to help in Africa's digitalization and market growth.[112]

Morocco is also one of few African countries with its own satellites. Satellites Mohammed VI-A and B are used for cartographic and cadastral surveys, spatial planning, monitoring of agricultural activities, prevention and management of natural disasters, and monitoring of environmental trends and desertification, among other purposes.[113] In addition, Mohammed VI Polytechnic University launched a power supercomputer center in partnership with Cambridge University, Dell, and Intel to gather research in Africa about 4IR technologies. This computer has 69,000 processing units and can hold more than 8,000 terabytes of storage, ranking 98th on the Top 500 List of Supercomputers globally.[114] As one of the first supercomputers in Africa, Morocco is pioneering the way for the 4IR in Africa.

7.4.2 Strengths and Challenges

Morocco's government has played a significant role in creating the enabling conditions needed for success in the 4IR. It launched the Moroccan Innovation Strategy in 2009 to guide its decision-making process in

---

[107] "Morocco Seeks" (2019) [108] Hamann (2021) [109] Shahan (2021)
[110] Abjiou (2018) [111] Pape (2019) [112] Trade Commissioner (2021)
[113] Zaari Jabiri (2017) [114] Sawahel (2021)

strengthening the country as a regional digital hub, establishing universal digital access, and addressing current gaps in governance and digital skills.[115] To help achieve these goals, the Ministry of Industry, Investment, Trade, and the Digital Economy and the Moroccan Office of Industrial and Commercial Property created the Moroccan Club of Innovation in 2011 to create a network of innovators, including researchers, entrepreneurs, and students, and help them develop innovative projects. The ministry additionally supports research in advanced technologies and the development of innovative cities in Fez, Rabat, and Marrakesh.[116] The Digital Development Agency, another key government agency, is mandated to coordinate the efforts of the public and private sectors, be a primary reference for foreign investors, accelerate the implementation of facilitating policies, and energize the Moroccan digital ecosystem.[117]

Concurrently with these efforts, between 2006 and 2010, Morocco increased its percentage of GDP dedicated to research from 0.64 percent to 0.73 percent, one of the highest ratios in the Arab world, although still below the global average for research spending (1.7 percent of GDP).[118] In October 2017, the Moroccan government also launched a $32 million project to support 300 innovative projects over five years.[119] Additionally, through the National Fund for Scientific Research and Technological Development, the government has encouraged companies to support research in their sector. Moroccan telecom operators, for instance, now dedicate 0.25 percent of their turnover to research; today, they finance about 80 percent of all public research projects in telecommunications through this fund.[120]

The World Bank praised Morocco for its COVID-19 pandemic response, which was considered swift and necessary. The Kingdom of Morocco embedded social protection measures in the spring of 2021 and gradually digitalized public services.[121] Businesses aided in Morocco's response. For example, the startup Dakibot created a free chatbot to answer questions about the virus; the Moroccan Ministry of Health and the WHO also launched an app for medical providers and staff to communicate strategies to combat the pandemic better.[122] The partnerships formed among the different sectors in Morocco during the pandemic will help fuel the country's competitive advantage in

[115] UNESCO (2017a)   [116] UNESCO (2016)   [117] Mellah (2018)
[118] UNESCO (2016)   [119] Caisse Centrale de Garantie (2017)
[120] UNESCO (2016)   [121] Deloitte (2021)
[122] Baumann and Hoffmann (2020)

global markets. Collaborations will be vital in developing successful economies in the digital world.[123]

Outside of the government, Moroccan universities and businesses play a key role in innovation. The business enterprise sector currently contributes 30 percent of Morocco's funding for research and development.[124] Mobile operators such as Maroc Telecom, Orange, and Inwi have partnered with local entrepreneurs to promote tech sector development.[125] Several competitive funds, such as the Moroccan Spin-off and Incubation Network, are also fostering business-university partnerships and providing startups with pre-seed capital to help them develop business plans. The network, coordinated by the National Center for Scientific and Technical Research, currently supports fourteen incubators at top Moroccan universities. Another program, the Moroccan Research Association's InnovAct, provides companies with logistical support and the financial means to recruit university graduates to work on research projects, covering 40 to 50 percent of costs for SMEs and 20 percent for consortia of enterprises. The program aims to support up to thirty enterprises each year in mostly high-technology fields.[126] As a result of these and similar initiatives, only South Africa and Tunisia outperform Morocco in investment for education, knowledge creation, and ICT-related business.[127]

Morocco's weaknesses on the GII are in business sophistication, market sophistication, and human capital and research. This suggests that despite efforts to modernize the country's industrial and information sectors, the country still needs further investments to generate high-impact R&D.[128] Furthermore, the country has the second-highest potential for automation in Africa, according to McKinsey, with 50.5 percent of work activities at risk of automation.[129] Morocco's labor force will need to be prepared for a future competing against robots, both domestically and in the countries of its important trade partners such as the European Union. Risks of noninclusive growth pose a challenge for Morocco. They could potentially lose up to 2 percent of GDP if they do not embrace the 4IR.[130] Currently, Morocco lags in the skills and the labor market; one major issue is that the skillsets of university graduates do not match the needs of employers, driving high

[123] Hatim (2020)   [124] Hatim (2020)   [125] Bayen (2018b)
[126] UNESCO (2016)   [127] Koundouno (2018)   [128] Koundouno (2018)
[129] "Morocco Has Second" (2017)   [130] Lou, Sadeski, and Lacave (2019)

levels of unemployment among educated youth and reducing the country's capacity for innovation.

The Moroccan government has provided the foundational elements needed for the digital economy to take hold, but further advances are necessary to make the country a global leader in the 4IR. Reforming the educational system to better fit the evolving needs of the labor market and create graduates capable of undertaking cutting-edge research and technology projects should be a priority. Overall, opportunities abound for Morocco to take advantage of the 4IR and position itself as Francophone Africa's first digital hub. Public–private partnerships, particularly with mobile operators, appear to be a window of opportunity for Morocco to enhance its knowledge-based community in the context of the 4IR. To reach the status of global innovation leader, Morocco must create the conditions for sustainable economic growth in which investment acts as a catalyst. The country's future progress may depend on continued infrastructure achievement alongside efforts to support its burgeoning startup community and promote skilled employment.

7.5 Kenya

Kenya significantly outperforms other countries at its income level and is best known for its mobile money innovations, an area in which it is a global leader. The country is also a hotbed for innovation in various 4IR-relevant sectors, not just mobile money. According to the 2018 GII report, Kenya's strong innovation environment is supported in part by its high levels of business and market sophistication. Furthermore, on the GII, Kenya's efficiency ratio of 0.69 ranks 41st out of 126 countries, illustrating that the country is generating a relatively high return on its efforts to spur innovation.[131]

On the GCI, Kenya particularly excels in the labor market, business dynamism, institutions, and innovation capability. A clear source of Kenya's strong business dynamism is the country's entrepreneurial culture, with rankings of twenty-eighth and eighteenth in the world on the sub-indicators of entrepreneurship and attitudes toward entrepreneurial risk, respectively. Kenya's government has also played a leading role in enabling innovation and preparing the country for the

---

[131] Cornell University, INSEAD, and WIPO (2018, p. 276)

Table 7.7 *Kenya GII and GCI scores*

Category	Ranking
GII score (among African countries)	5
GII score (among all countries)	78
GCI score (among African countries)	7
GCI score (among all countries)	93

4IR and ranks highly in terms of long-term vision, responsiveness to change, legal adaptability to digital business models, and future-oriented decision-making (Table 7.7).

Over the past decade, Kenya has experienced a rapid and widespread increase in digitalization, reaching, in 2021, 59.24 million phone subscriptions, 21.75 million internet users,[132] and 67.8 million mobile money accounts.[133] Mobile penetration among Kenya's 54.38 million people, which started at almost 0 percent in 2000, is up to 108.9 percent as of January 2021. The country has one of the fastest mobile internet speeds in the world.[134] The laying of the first fiber-optic cable on the eastern seaboard of Africa in 2009 has led to cheaper and more widespread telecommunications and internet access.[135] Access to electricity has also rapidly improved, from 24.7 percent of the population in 2005 to 69.7 percent in 2019, though much of the rural population still lack access.[136]

The ICT sector has been the main driver of Kenya's economic growth over the past decade, growing at an average of nearly 20 percent per year from 1999 to 2009. Since 2000, Kenya's economy has increased at an average rate of 3.7 percent; without growth in the ICT sector, this rate would have been a lackluster 2.8 percent, similar to the population growth rate of 2.7 percent and insufficient to raise GDP per capita.[137]

Nairobi – the "Silicon Savannah" – is the center of technological innovation in Kenya. Most innovation spaces, incubation centers, accelerators, and maker labs are concentrated in the city, making it an attractive area for those looking to reap the benefits of agglomeration.

[132] Kemp (2021)   [133] Faria (2021)   [134] Kemp (2021)
[135] Ndemo (2016)   [136] World Bank (2019)   [137] World Bank (2010, p. vi)

In fact, one Nairobi innovation space, iHub, founded in 2010, has launched as many as 170 startups. However, the innovation landscape has begun decentralizing in recent years due to Nairobi's high cost of living and market saturation. New tech hubs, both independent and within academic institutions, are sprouting up in cities across Kenya.[138] Further decentralization may help ensure that 4IR-related opportunities are available across Kenya, not just in the capital.

7.5.1 Noteworthy Innovations

Kenya's most well-known tech success story is the e-finance startup M-Pesa, a mobile banking and payment service launched by network operator Safaricom in 2007 (see Section 6.1.1, for more details). The application evolved from a simple cash transfer system to a mobile provider of various financial services including international transfers, loans, and health payments. M-Pesa now serves over 30 million users in ten countries, most of whom would otherwise be unbanked, and an estimated 2 percent of Kenyan households have escaped extreme poverty, thanks to mobile money services.[139] The success of M-Pesa has also inspired multiple operators across Africa and the world to develop similar services.

But Kenya's achievements do not end at M-Pesa: The "Silicon Savannah" tech hub has become a host to a wide range of innovative startups and services. It is a leader, particularly in the area of open data. The Kenya Open Data Initiative has become a platform to empower firms and entrepreneurs to develop new apps and services.[140] Building on this, the Code4Kenya initiative places fellows in media and civil society organizations to help them create open data applications that provide easy-to-access information to citizens on health, education, and development. Kenya is also a leader in the development of e-government innovations. A service called "I Paid a Bribe" allows Kenyans to report bribery cases online or over SMS, while the Ushahidi platform provides election monitoring through information gathering, visualization, and mapping, and is now used across the globe, including in the United States.[141]

---

[138] Latif Dahir (2017)   [139] Monks (2017)   [140] Ndemo (2016, p. 2)
[141] Fengler (2013)

7.5.2 Strengths and Challenges

Kenya has embraced technology and innovation as drivers of socio-economic growth. The government has employed a combination of innovation-focused strategies that incorporate public–private partnerships, ICT infrastructure development, human resource capacity building, and job creation efforts.[142] Kenya's development plan also sets out goals related to the ICT sector, including enacting enabling policy, legal, and institutional reforms; upgrading ICT capacity and infrastructure; developing ICT industries, including a Technology City and digital villages for business process outsourcing; and improving public service delivery through e-government and other innovations.[143] Alongside this policy framework, Kenya's government, legal institutions, and central bank have taken concrete steps to prepare for the 4IR, with, for example, the government adopting open data and e-government solutions, increasing funding for R&D, and proactively playing a role in the introduction of M-Pesa.

Academic institutions and public institutions with a history of R&D, such as the Kenya Agricultural Research Institute and the Kenya Medical Research Institute, have also played a role in the growth of innovation and research in Kenya. In line with national policy, all public Kenyan universities have a senior staff member in charge of research. Universities across the country have set up software and hardware incubation centers with links to industry and international academic and private sector partners. Multinational companies, such as Google, IBM, and Microsoft, also have regional headquarters and research labs in Kenya.[144]

Despite the strength of academic institutions in research, however, Kenya has a very low degree of tertiary enrollment at 4 percent.[145] Expanding access to higher levels of education will be critical for preparing the Kenyan labor force to be resilient against 4IR disruptions, especially as 52 percent of the country's jobs are automatable and Kenyan employers continue to identify an inadequately skilled workforce as a constraint to their industry.[146] A continued priority on ICT access, improving the quality of education, and expanding

---

[142] Ndemo (2016, pp. 2–3)   [143] Government of Kenya (2008)
[144] Ndemo (2015)   [145] Ndemo (2015)
[146] World Economic Forum (2017a, p. iii)

enrollment for tertiary education appears necessary for Kenya to solidify its role as a regional 4IR hub.

The fact that Kenya has developed a robust tech ecosystem despite low tertiary education rates may be a testament to the ingenuity of the country's entrepreneurial community. The most dominant drivers of innovation thus far have been Kenyan technology companies and individual entrepreneurs. Official innovation policy, while effective, has mostly been designed in response to innovative activities, rather than proactively. The success of technologies such as Safaricom's M-Pesa and entrepreneur-developed Ushahidi has encouraged a culture of innovation and entrepreneurship, which has resulted in communities of innovators who have created and gathered in tech hubs to share knowledge and skills. These communities have been supported by corporate and development aid financing, as well as the forward-thinking actions of the government.[147]

Notably, while Kenya's ICT industry has quickly grown as an export sector, domestic access to ICT appears to lag: The country ranks 19th out of all 126 countries in terms of ICT service exports as percentage of total trade, yet in the bottom 25 on indexes of ICT access and use.[148] In other words, rapid growth has translated to growing disparities in technology use and access, including a gender gap, poverty gap, and urban-rural gap. This discrepancy underscores the necessity of continued investment for internet access even with the relatively strong growth of the mobile sector. Overall, however, Kenya's main challenges – human capital and infrastructure – are also areas in which it is trending toward improved access and better outcomes, and the expansion of the country's ICT sector and the government's policy responsiveness to disruptive innovations are encouraging signs of preparedness for the 4IR.

---

[147] World Economic Forum (2017a, p. iii)
[148] Cornell University, INSEAD, and WIPO (2018, p. 276)

8 | Emerging Leaders in the Fourth Industrial Revolution on the African Continent

Three emerging leaders in 4IR innovation on the continent are now analyzed. These three countries – Egypt, Rwanda, and Nigeria – are ranked lower than Africa's innovation leaders on the GII (Table 8.1) and GCI (Table 8.2) but have either made consistent and significant gains in recent years (in the case of Rwanda) or have become major sources of innovation despite significant challenges (in the case of Egypt and Nigeria). The three countries have diverse strengths and weaknesses; Rwanda, for example, has a small market size and strong institutions, while Nigeria and Egypt have large markets but score relatively poorly on indicators for institutions.

Table 8.1 *2018 GII scores and rankings for leading African countries*[1]

Country	2018 GII score/ ranking	Strongest GII subcategory (rank)	Weakest GII subcategory (rank)
Egypt	25.1/94	Knowledge & technology outputs (70)	Institutions (114)
Rwanda*	23.9/102	Institutions (54)	Creative outputs (117)
Nigeria	20.1/118	Business sophistication (76)	Knowledge and technology outputs (123)

* Indicates that a country performs better on the 2018 GII rankings than other countries at a similar level of economic development.[2] (This is still accurate for Rwanda.)

[1] Cornell University, INSEAD, and WIPO (2018, p. xx); see pp. 251, 314, and 301 for each country's respective profile in the order presented in Table 8.1.
[2] Following the methodology described in Cornell University, INSEAD, and WIPO (2018, p. 36), a curve is fit for the relationship between GII scores and GDP per capita (PPP). Countries whose plotted GII score and GDP per capita fall above

Table 8.2 *2018 GCI scores and rankings for leading African countries*[3]

Country	2018 GCI score/ranking	Strongest GCI subcategory (rank)	Weakest GCI subcategory (rank)
Egypt	53.6/94	Market size (24)	Macroeconomic stability (135)
Rwanda	50.9/108	Institutions (29)	Market size (128)
Nigeria	47.5/115	Market size (30)	Financial system (131)

Table 8.3 *2018 Egypt GII[4] and GCI[5] rankings*

Category	Ranking
GII score (among African countries)	9
GII score (among all countries)	95
GCI score (among African countries)	8
GCI score (among all countries)	94

Analysis of these countries can thus guide stakeholders in a diverse range of African countries looking to improve their ability to capitalize on the 4IR.

8.1 Egypt

Egypt is becoming a key hub for technology and innovation in Africa and, on the GII, significantly outperforms in terms of innovation output relative to its input score: Egypt ranks 95th overall on the 2018 GII, but its efficiency ratio of 0.66 ranks 45th of 126 countries.[6] This performance is due in part to Egypt's rank of 66th in terms of knowledge and technology outputs, with top fifty performances in indicators such as computer software spending, intellectual property receipts, and citable documents. The country has achieved these high marks while remaining in the bottom

this curve have a greater-than-expected GII score for their level of GDP per capita and thus outperform other countries at a similar level of economic development.
[3] Schwab (2018)
[4] Cornell University, INSEAD, and WIPO (2018, p. xx); see p. 251, for country's respective profile presented in Table 8.3.
[5] Schwab (2018)   [6] Cornell University, INSEAD, and WIPO (2018, p. 251)

7 of 126 countries for both its overall institutions pillar and on index indicators for political stability.[7]

On the GCI, Egypt's primary strengths include its large market size; infrastructure, including strong air, land, and sea connectivity; and innovation capability, including the quality of its research institutions, number of scientific publications, and the government's responsiveness to change. However, low scores in macroeconomic stability, the labor market, and the product market detract from Egypt's overall competitiveness. High levels of youth unemployment and political instability present further challenges and may be exacerbated by the Fourth Industrial Revolution.

Egypt has some of the most widespread and advanced technology infrastructure on the continent. The country, as of 2021, has 60 million internet users, 93 percent mobile penetration, and 57 percent internet penetration.[8] Egypt has also seen enormous growth in international internet connectivity in recent years. From January 2019 to January 2020, Egypt reported an increase in international internet bandwidth of nearly 36 percent;[9] the country is now connected to twelve of the eighteen fiber-optic cables that pass through the Mediterranean Sea and into the Red Sea through ducts buried underground in the TE Transit Corridor.[10]

Egypt hosts fifty-six tech hubs identified by GSMA. The city of Cairo, in particular, is a critical tech ecosystem that hosts many hubs and startups.[11] The GrEEK Campus, a tech park, is located in the heart of Cairo and hosts different local, regional, and international firms and innovators, including startups. From RiseUp and Udacity to MO4 and Flat6Labs, the hub is home to some of the most influential players in Egypt's startup ecosystem.[12]

Both within these tech hubs and across the nation, information technology has been a steady source of economic growth, especially with the recent introduction of 4G systems, and has become a particularly important contributor to the economy. Egypt's ICT export industry was worth over $3.6 billion in 2019 and grew to $4.1 billion in 2020.[13] More than 500,000 Egyptians are employed in ICT-related occupations, and the sector's contribution to national employment is continuing to expand.[14] Egypt is a regional leader in ICT outsourcing, and the outsourcing sector directly

---

[7] Cornell University, INSEAD, and WIPO (2018, p. 251)   [8] Kemp (2021)
[9] Oxford Business Group (2021)   [10] Qui (2020)
[11] Giuliani and Ajadi (2019)   [12] Paracha (2018)
[13] Ministry of Communications and Information Technology (2020)
[14] Oxford Business Group (2018a)

employs 90,000 and, since 2014, is growing at 7.5 percent annually.[15] The ICT sector expanded even during the volatile period surrounding the 2011 Arab Spring, with several major companies, including Dell EMC, Vodafone, and Teleperformance, experiencing growth between 2011 and 2014.[16] This trend of expansion continued once again despite the devastating impact of COVID-19, growing by 15.2 percent in 2020.[17]

8.1.1 Noteworthy Innovations

Seventeen out of the 100 startups featured in the 2019 "100 Arab startups shaping the Fourth Industrial Revolution" by the WEF – in partnership with the Bahrain Economic Development Board (EDB) – were based in Egypt.[18] Many of these companies offer digital platforms and analytics in domains such as finance, retail, educational services, and entrepreneurship. Since 2011, for example, Egyptian company Yaoota was created to compare online shopping prices, ElWafeyat to digitize death and obituary services, and Nafham to provide free crowdsourced Arabic-language online education.[19]

Notably, Egyptian startups and established companies are also venturing into more complex industrial technologies associated with the 4IR. For example, D-Kimia is an Egyptian health-tech firm that uses nanotechnology to detect a broad range of diseases. Simplex is a startup specializing in advanced robotics and machinery for Egyptian manufacturers.[20] Startup Affectiva, which uses AI to recognize human emotions in real-time, raised $34 million in venture capital from 2014 to 2016.[21] MISC is an Egyptian company and Siemens Solution Partner that designs and installs industrial automation systems and has over 100 projects across Egypt.[22] Research institutions have also taken a leading role in innovation in some sectors; the Central Metallurgical Research and Development Institute, for example, is a leader in Egypt in the field of advanced manufacturing technologies, including additive manufacturing and nanotechnologies.[23]

---

[15] World Economic Forum (2017d)   [16] Oxford Business Group (2018a)
[17] Ministry of Communications and Information Technology (2020)
[18] World Economic Forum (2019)   [19] Alley (2017)
[20] World Economic Forum (2017d)   [21] Affectiva (2016)   [22] MISC (2018)
[23] Sher (2014)

8.1.2 Strengths and Challenges

The Egyptian development strategy launched in 2016 enshrined knowledge, innovation, and scientific research as a key pillar, with the goal of developing a knowledge-based society and a strong digital economy.[24] In fact, much of the growth of the ICT industry in recent years can be attributed to programs initiated and developed by the government through agencies including the MCIT, the Information Technology Industry Development Agency (ITIDA), and the public sector internet service provider, TE Data. To achieve these goals, the government's initiatives include running educational programs to build the capacity of youth to use new technologies; supporting industry development programs; and creating the Technology Innovation and Entrepreneurship Center (TIEC). Technology Innovation and Entrepreneurship Center runs technology incubation centers across Egypt, assists startups with technical, financial, and support issues, and provides training courses in conjunction with local universities.[25] The government itself has also taken steps to embrace technology. The "Digital Egypt Project" aims to supply all government entities with fiber-optic cable connection, completed in 5,300 government buildings.[26] In addition, the central bank of Egypt is conducting feasibility studies into the issuance of a blockchain-based digital currency.[27] There is scope for further improvement; however, the Egyptian government spent only $6.4 million, or 0.7 percent of GDP, on R&D in 2018,[28] one of the lowest levels of R&D spending in the world.[29]

Egypt's thriving startup culture is partly due to community initiatives such as the GrEEK Campus and government-led efforts to encourage entrepreneurship among the nation's youth. A rapid expansion in access to funding through venture capital firms and partnerships between the public and private sector has also enabled the growth of the startup scene.[30] However, local ICT startups and businesses currently face many hurdles, ranging from importing high-quality ICT equipment to dealing with inadequate intellectual property regulations. Many firms and research institutions have also faced challenges in securing adequate financing for R&D projects due to

[24] Oxford Business Group (2017b)	[25] Oxford Business Group (2018b)
[26] Ministry of Communications and Information Technology (2021)
[27] Suberg (2018)	[28] World Bank (2021)	[29] El-Behary (2016)
[30] Vithani (2017)

low government expenditure.[31] One way to combat this challenge is the newly developed national strategy for artificial intelligence, which is being used to push AI reliance in the country to assist with Egypt's development goals. This new strategy has been named "Artificial Intelligence for Development and Prosperity."[32]

Egypt's strong research community, with around 100,000 researchers and scientists at over 200 universities and research institutions, has also driven innovation and technology development.[33] On the continent, the country's research output was second only to South Africa.[34] Egypt's number of patent applications and grants is among the highest of any African country,[35] and Egyptian researchers published 163 peer-reviewed academic articles in 2018. However, low government expenditure on R&D has had detrimental effects on research institutions, as researchers are often underpaid and do not have sufficient funding to equip laboratories with the technologies needed to conduct advanced research.

The proportion of working-age adults with tertiary qualifications in Egypt is nearly 20 percent higher than the global average, and 81 percent of Egypt's jobs are classified as either high- or medium-skilled. However, the overall quality of Egypt's education system is the second lowest in the MENA region. Employers report difficulty finding appropriately skilled labor, indicating a significant skills mismatch between graduates and employers, with academic institutions failing to prepare students for the modern workplace effectively.[36] This skills mismatch is also one factor contributing to Egypt's high level of youth unemployment. Over 26 percent of youth (15–24) in the country are unemployed,[37] and the highest rates of unemployment are for university-educated youth, at 36 percent.[38] Youth unemployment will continue to be a primary concern for Egypt, particularly given the significant skills mismatch. It is estimated that 48 percent of all work activities in Egypt are susceptible to automation, which is likely to displace unskilled workers further.[39]

Furthermore, given the disruptive and unpredictable nature of the 4IR, international investors may become increasingly concerned with the costs generated by political uncertainties already high in the

[31] Oxford Business Group (2017b)   [32] Alaa El-Din (2021)
[33] Bond et al. (2012, p. 14)   [34] Nature Index (2018)
[35] Bond et al. (2012, p. 25)   [36] World Economic Forum (2017d, p. 6)
[37] World Bank (2021)   [38] Zawya (2020)
[39] Moore, Chandran, and Schubert (2018)

Table 8.4 *2018 Rwanda GII[41] and GCI[42] rankings*

Category	Ranking
GII score (among African countries)	10
GII score (among all countries)	99
GCI score (among African countries)	11
GCI score (among all countries)	108

country. Moreover, Egypt continues to rank in the bottom half of GII countries on indexes measuring the ease of starting a business and resolving insolvency. However, Egypt's success in the face of political challenges may be a model for other African nations seeking to overcome political barriers to innovation. Focusing on specific cluster development, as Egypt has in the Cairo region, can allow even relatively unstable states to concentrate resources, encourage investment, and develop a knowledge-based economy. Egypt has also made strides to limit uncertainty in the ICT sector through targeted reforms at cybersecurity; the Egyptian parliament passed a comprehensive cyber-crime law in July 2018 to mitigate cyber threats and align Egyptian standards with the EU's GDPR cyber regulations.[40]

8.2 Rwanda

Rwanda is an upcoming leader in innovation in Africa, particularly for its income level. The country significantly outperforms other countries at its income level, with a GII score more than four standard deviations above the score predicted for a country with the same GDP per capita PPP. Rwanda particularly excels in the areas of institutions due to its political stability, government effectiveness, and strong business environment; market sophistication, due to its high scores on ease of doing business-related indicators; and business sophistication.

These strengths are also evident in Rwanda's performance on the Global Competitiveness Index, where the country scores highly in the

[40] Africa Business (2018)
[41] Cornell University, INSEAD, and WIPO (2018, p. xx); see p. 314 for country's respective profile presented in Table 8.4.
[42] Schwab (2018)

areas of institutions, product market, labor market, and business dynamism. However, weak scores in the areas of workforce education and skills, innovation capability, infrastructure, and ICT adoption lower Rwanda's overall GCI ranking. But the government's policy decisions reflect an understanding of the country's comparative advantages and the need to strengthen areas including education and infrastructure, and a growing community of entrepreneurs and innovators suggests that Rwanda has great potential to take advantage of the opportunities presented in the 4IR.

Few would have guessed that Rwanda would become one of Africa's leaders in innovation and smart city technology two decades ago. In 2000, the country had a GDP per capita of $216. Only 5.2 percent of Rwandans over the age of twenty-five had any secondary education. The vast majority of the population – 88.6 percent – was employed in agriculture, and only 2 percent of Rwanda's exports were classified as high technology. Access to technology and the inputs needed for advanced innovation was very low – electricity access was limited to 6.2 percent of the population, there were 0.5 mobile subscriptions per 100 people, and only a minority of Rwandans had access to the Internet.[43]

Today, Rwanda is in the midst of a transformation driven by the goal of becoming a knowledge-based economy. Since 2000, sustained high GDP growth rates have increased the country's GDP per capita to $798 as of 2020.[44] The expected years of schooling for a child have increased by four years, to 13.3 years.[45] The government has allocated a significant portion of its budget to improve the quality of learning and ICT education.[46] Access to electricity has increased significantly from almost zero to 66.8 percent, as of 2021, as has access to technology[47] – Rwanda has a 31.4 percent internet penetration rate and 9.69 million mobile connections as of January 2021.[48]

Rwanda is consistently trending toward better access to higher-quality infrastructure and education, which will allow the country to further capitalize on the opportunities of the 4IR. Rwanda may also be able to take advantage of 4IR technologies to accelerate improvements and mitigate challenges in these areas. Technology-enabled learning

---

[43] World Bank (2018c); UNDP (2018)   [44] World Bank (2021)
[45] UNDP (2020)   [46] UNICEF (2017)   [47] Rwanda Energy Group (2021)
[48] Kemp (2021)

platforms, for example, can minimize the negative impacts of high student-to-teacher ratios while preparing students for computer-based work environments. Rwanda's lack of legacy infrastructure, while currently presenting a challenge to innovation, also means that the country can build the infrastructure needed for the 4IR without needing to undergo costly conversion processes. Rwanda's strong *Ease of Doing Business* scores will also help the country attract external investors and multinational firms, bringing with them the opportunity for technology transfer.

8.2.1 Noteworthy Innovations

Rwanda is now becoming a hub for ICT activity. A series of public programs, from innovation camps run by the country's Workforce Development Agency to international partnerships such as the kLab and FabLab incubator projects, are driving the development of a knowledge-based economy.[49] The country has begun to leapfrog developed countries in areas such as smart city infrastructure, vocational training, and strategic foreign investment. More than 95 percent of the country has 4G/LTE coverage, and public and private investors are working toward a national roll-out of fiber-optic broadband.[50] Kigali's smart bus network lets users to tap on and off with a contactless card and connect to a free 4G network. A fleet of drones owned by social entrepreneur Keller Rinaudo's Zipline company delivers blood at high speed to a network of twenty-one remote transfusion clinics in the country.[51] The Rwandan government has partnered with Nokia and SRG to improve urban network connectivity and deploy sensor technology to enhance public safety and utility management, among other goals.[52] Alongside public–private partnerships, Rwanda has benefited from a longstanding investment in fostering a culture of entrepreneurship. In 2009, Rwanda became one of the only countries in the world to require entrepreneurship classes in secondary school.[53]

In 2017, the World Economic Forum collaborated with the state to develop the Center for the 4IR, which helped establish drone-governing safety requirements.[54] With the help of this framework, manufacturers were given the freedom to innovate new designs that

[49] Root (2016)   [50] Razavi (2018)   [51] Fleming (2018)
[52] Siba and Sow (2017)   [53] Root (2016)   [54] Abusalem et al. (2021)

have enabled Rwanda to deliver COVID-19 vaccines, conduct land surveys, and inspect infrastructure.[55] Rwanda also deployed humanoid robots during the COVID-19 pandemic to help with food delivery and temperature screens and limit the exposure of health care workers.[56] These achievements serve as inspiration and motivation for Rwanda's youth, who are distinguishing themselves as entrepreneurs within the country's ICT sector.[57]

8.2.2 Strengths and Challenges

Thus far, Rwanda's growth has been mainly due to structural transformation, rather than productivity growth, and has been driven by public investments. The country aims to become a hub for financial, ICT, transport, and logistic services in the region[58] – sectors whose ability to employ a large portion of the labor force will be largely resilient to the disruption of the 4IR. Growth has been guided by Rwanda's development plan, which is based around six pillars for improvement – good governance, human resources, the private sector, infrastructure, productive agriculture, and regional and international integration – and three cross-cutting issues – gender equality, natural resources and the environment, and ICT. The ICT component recognizes that innovations in science and technology that complement Rwanda's cultural strengths will be necessary for the development process to succeed. It emphasizes the need for high-skilled scientists and technicians and provides a framework for Rwanda to achieve its objectives by developing the teaching of science and technology at secondary and university levels, facilitating the creation of high and intermediate technology enterprises, and improving ICT access down to the administrative sector level.[59] An example of this is the Digital Opportunity Trust, which was launched out of a partnership with the World Economic Forum to employ 5,000 youth to aid in the digital training of 5 million citizens in an effort to propel the country into the 4IR.[60]

Rwanda's current growth through structural transformation, particularly its increasing employment within the service sector, suggests

[55] Abusalem et al. (2021)   [56] Brown (2020)   [57] JICA (2019)
[58] World Bank (2018c)
[59] Republic of Rwanda Ministry of Finance and Economic Planning (2000)
[60] Adhikari (2019)

that the country may be able to take advantage of 4IR-driven disruption more so than countries with a large or growing share of the population in manufacturing, which are likely to be heavily affected by automation and related technological innovations. The government's forward-thinking work toward transforming Rwanda into a knowledge-based economy may enable the country to use disruptive technologies to overcome inherent economic growth constraints, such as its landlocked geography and lack of natural resources.

Several priority areas for improvement emerge from the analysis of both indexes. As discussed above, Rwanda's human capital scores remain low despite significant gains over the past two decades. Challenges include high student-to-teacher ratios; limited numbers of qualified teachers, particularly in science, technology, and engineering; an education system that is not tailored to the needs of the labor market; and a low proportion of girls studying science and technology.[61] Similarly, infrastructure, though improving, remains limited, particularly in rural areas.

Furthermore, within its component GII scores, there is a large discrepancy between Rwanda's innovation "inputs" and "outputs" – factors that enable innovation versus the actual impact and products of innovation. While Rwanda has relatively strong marks for its institutions and its business and market sophistication, its score for knowledge and technology outputs ranks in the bottom three of all 126 GII countries.[62] Overall, its innovation input rank is sixty-three places above its innovation output rank, reflecting a lag between the government's policy

Table 8.5 *2018 Nigeria GII[63] and GCI[64] rankings*

Category	Ranking
GII score (among African countries)	21
GII score (among all countries)	118
GCI score (among African countries)	13
GCI score (among all countries)	115

---

[61] UNESCO (2017b)
[62] Cornell University, INSEAD, and WIPO (2018, p. 314)
[63] Cornell University, INSEAD, and WIPO (2018, p. xx); see p. 301 for country's respective profile presented in Table 8.5.
[64] Schwab (2018)

intentions and the innovative activities of entrepreneurs and companies. Furthermore, government agencies have been active in helping to build innovation hubs and train entrepreneurs, but these initiatives have not always been inclusive or efficient, as they have generally targeted Rwanda's highly educated population. Deeper scrutiny at the scale and effectiveness of both public and private projects may be key to enhancing the impact of innovation in Rwanda.

8.3 Nigeria

As the largest economy in sub-Saharan Africa, with a population of 190 million and a growing ecosystem of tech startups, Nigeria has the potential to play a central role in bringing the 4IR to Africa. But despite the successes of Nigerian entrepreneurs and the growth of tech hubs, Nigeria performs poorly on the GII and underperforms, given its income level.[65] Nigeria's weak performance may reflect that even successful Nigerian entrepreneurs face significant obstacles to innovation in the form of infrastructure deficits, weak educational support, and political inefficiencies. The country underperforms relative to other lower-middle-income countries on indexes of ICT use and access, government effectiveness, and the rule of law; low scores for university-industry collaboration and tertiary school enrollment also drag down Nigeria's GII ranking.[66]

While Nigeria ranks slightly better on the GCI, it still underperforms relative to other economies at similar income levels. Nigeria's slightly stronger performance on the GCI is driven by its market size, large labor market, and business dynamism, particularly in entrepreneurship. Nigeria also outperforms on the innovation capability indicator, with relatively high-quality research institutions and levels of R&D as well as large numbers of scientific publications. However, Nigeria's academic institutions and individual innovators and entrepreneurs are, for the most part, not integrated with nor effectively supported by the public or private sector. This imbalance is one of the primary reasons for the country's underperformance on the GII and GCI and may hinder Nigeria's ability to take advantage of the 4IR.

Nigeria's economy has been volatile and slow growing in recent years, partially due to changing oil prices, which dominate the country's

---

[65] Schwab (2018, p. 301)   [66] Schwab (2018, p. 301)

growth pattern. This volatility has imposed significant negative impacts on the welfare of households; as a result, the government has prioritized economic diversification and growth in the private sector.[67] The country's ICT and telecoms sector has performed well in recent years and currently contributes about 18 percent of Nigeria's GDP,[68] up from only about 0.6 percent of GDP in 2001. The telecoms sector is currently valued at over $75 billion.[69]

Innovative activities are generally geographically restrained to major cities, which serve as hubs for entrepreneurs, researchers, and ICT-related businesses. Afrilabs and Briter Bridges have identified, in 2019, ninety tech hubs in Nigeria, making it home to the most hubs per country.[70] The cities of Lagos and Abuja in particular have grown into robust ecosystems for innovation and entrepreneurship initiatives. Tech startups regularly generate large amounts of investment; Nigeria is the second-most popular investment destination in sub-Saharan Africa, following Kenya, with $150.4 million in investment.[71]

8.3.1 Noteworthy Innovations

Despite the country's overall underperformance, many of Nigeria's innovators have successfully introduced new technologies and platforms to serve the needs of the country's large, often underserved population, and in doing so have attracted large amounts of investment, often from foreign sources interested in capitalizing on Nigeria's market size. From 2012 to 2016, Nigeria hosted its first three tech startups valued at over $100 million: Andela, a company that invests in software developers; Konga, an online shopping platform; and Jumia, an online marketplace, which became part of the African continent's first $1 billion company in 2019.[72] In addition to these large startups, Nigeria is host to a variety of innovations that target its large populations of agriculturalists, small and informal business owners, and students. For example, Farmcrowdy, a digital agriculture platform launched in 2016, connects farmers' groups to provide them with improved seeds, farm inputs, and training on modern farming techniques, in addition to providing a market for the sale of farm produce.[73]

---

[67] World Bank (2018e)   [68] Osuagwu (2021)   [69] Adepetun (2020)
[70] Shapshak (2019)   [71] Kene-Okafor (2021)   [72] OC&C (2018, p. 10)
[73] Farmcrowdy (2022)

Piggybank.ng (now PiggyVest), which attracted $1.1 million in seed funding in 2018, is an online savings platform that allows users to deposit as little as $1 a day into their account.[74] PrepClass, a tutoring marketplace that connects students and tutors through an online platform, is improving access to and quality of education and generating employment for tutors.[75] As the ICT sector is growing, and in need of employees, the Global Skill Partnership between Nigeria and the European Union was created to help with digitalization skill training and migration landscapes across countries.[76] However, while Nigeria is host to successful innovations such as these, the country still lags behind in its use of more advanced 4IR technologies, such as the Internet of Things, additive manufacturing, blockchain, and nanotechnology. Artificial Intelligence has the potential to help in collaborative efforts between industries and the government, civil society and AI experts will also play a critical role in helping advance AI in Nigeria policies and regulations in order to help advance economic development.[77]

8.3.2 Strengths and Challenges

Nigeria's growth in 4IR-related areas thus far has been primarily driven by entrepreneurs and startups. Nigeria's large population in particular offers an attractive market. However, large Nigerian firms have generally not had many incentives to innovate, as they are often able to accrue large profits due to the structure of the Nigerian economy. Nigerian companies have generated few patents, and scientific research in the country generally has a low level of sophistication. The country also remains fairly isolated from major international centers of research and development. Despite this, relatively high levels of private sector spending on R&D indicate interest in innovation – although possibly spurred by low levels of government funding – and may provide a good springboard for Nigeria to capitalize on the 4IR.[78]

Across the country, access to technology is improving: Nigeria had 187.9 million mobile subscriptions in 2021, equivalent to 90 percent of the total population, and 50 percent internet penetration,[79] compared

---

[74] Nsehe (2018)   [75] GSMA (2018b, p. 37)   [76] Adhikari et al. (2021)
[77] Heldreth et al. (2019)   [78] Radwan and Pellegrini (2010, pp. 95–100)
[79] Kemp (2021)

to access near zero for both mobile and Internet in 2000.[80] But although the improvements to ICT access and growth of the ICT sector, tech hubs, and tech startups are encouraging signs of Nigeria's preparedness for the 4IR, many development challenges remain which, if not addressed, will prevent Nigeria from taking advantage of the opportunities presented by the 4IR. Access to education remains low at all levels, as does the quality of education. Access to electricity has consistently trended upward and now reaches about 60 percent of the population, but the supply of electricity is inconsistent.[81] Inequality of income and opportunities, particularly between the north and south of the country, may also be exacerbated by the disruptions of the 4IR. Political, cultural, and economic factors must be taken into consideration by public and private leaders when determining the strategy used in advancing into the Fourth Industrial Revolution.[82]

Nigeria's major expansion in telecom access has been largely limited to mobile access. Government policy has been effective in this area, with the Nigerian Communications Act of 2003, which liberalized the sector, contributing to the development of one of the most competitive telecom sectors in Africa. The government should now consider increasing ICT spending, promoting e-government services, subsidizing ICT training for government employees, and promoting ICT literacy in schools to move Nigeria to the next frontier.[83] Steps must also be taken to improve the business environment, which suffers from poor infrastructure, low access to finance, an unstable macroeconomic environment, and high levels of corruption, and thus stifles innovation and entrepreneurship. A recent report from OC&C Strategy consultants commissioned by Google identified these as key challenges, stating that Nigeria has "a vibrant entrepreneurial culture fueled by abundant activity" but also "infrastructure challenges" and "gaps which need to be addressed" in internet infrastructure, education spending, and capital financing.[84] The Nigerian government echoed the importance of ICT development when they called for increased regional collaboration within the West African economy during the West Africa Telecommunications Regulators Assembly general meeting in 2021.[85]

---

[80] Freedom House (2017)   [81] World Bank (2018e)   [82] Ladimeji (2020)
[83] Radwan and Pellegrini (2010, pp. 85–87)   [84] OC&C (2018, p. 10)
[85] Nigeria Communications Commission (2021)

Nigeria's large English-speaking population and cheap labor may allow it to be competitive in the global ICT services outsourcing industry, in a process similar to that in India. For this process to succeed, however, Nigeria needs to strengthen the collaboration between its universities and the private sector; higher education institutions currently have few formal linkages to industry, and the knowledge and training provided to students at academic institutions often do not match the needs of the job market.[86] Further support should also be given to universities to improve the quality of education and research productivity, which is currently constrained by inadequate funding, poor research infrastructure, and excessive workloads for professors driven by high student-to-teacher ratios.[87] By improving government support for research institutions and academic-private sector linkages, Nigeria can better position itself to generate innovation at the institutional and firm levels, rather than primarily through the efforts of individual entrepreneurs.

Nigeria's large market presents many opportunities for innovation, entrepreneurship, and the 4IR. To date, these opportunities have been seized primarily by a small community of forward-thinking individuals whose startups and technologies have attracted a great deal of interest and investment from domestic and foreign sources. But with sufficient support from and collaboration between the government, private sector, and research institutions, Nigeria could quickly become a leader in the 4IR in Africa. Continued focus on building human capital and improving infrastructure and the business environment are key priority areas to strengthen the country's performance in innovation and global competitiveness and take advantage of the 4IR.

---

[86] Radwan and Pellegrini (2010, p. 6)   [87] Yusuf (2012, p. 1)

9 | The Imperative of Cybersecurity during the Fourth Industrial Revolution

Though the 4IR is engendering innovation, optimizing costs, and creating new opportunities, its opportunities are accompanied by evolved threats to states, firms, and individuals. Unfortunately, African countries rank relatively low in cybersecurity resilience: According to the 2018 International Telecommunication Union's Global Cybersecurity Index (ITU-GCI), thirty-two of the fifty-two African countries evaluated were ranked in the bottom two quintiles in the world in terms of cybersecurity.[1] Africa, as a whole, scores the lowest of all regions on the ITU-GCI's five pillars: legal, technical, organizational, capacity building, and cooperation.[2]

As technologies increasingly underlie national infrastructure, the critical infrastructure of states has often become the target of cyber-attacks that can disrupt whole sectors, such as energy, water, transportation, and heavy industry. In smart cities, massive real-time data exchanges, integration among IoT devices, and dynamically changing processes, compounded by complexities and lack of standards in data governance, collection, and management in poorly designed ones, make these cities easy targets.[3]

---

[1] ITU (2018)

[2] "Legal" includes cybercriminal legislation, cybersecurity regulation, and cybersecurity training on regulation and laws. "Technical" includes national, government, and sectoral cyber incident response teams; standards implementation frameworks for organizations; and standard and certifications for professionals. "Organizational" includes strategy, designation of responsible agencies, and cybersecurity metrics. "Capacity building" includes standardization bodies, best practices, R&D programs, public awareness campaigns, professional training courses, national education programs and academic curricula, incentive mechanisms, and home-grown cybersecurity industries. "Cooperation" includes bilateral and multilateral agreements, international fora participation, public–private partnerships, and interagency partnerships.

[3] Pandey et al. (2019)

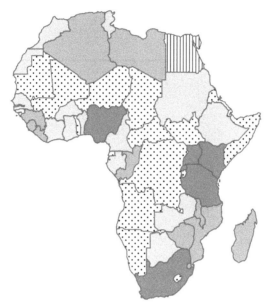

Figure 9.1 2018 Global Cybersecurity Index heat map for Africa.
Note: Scale indicates level of commitment to cybersecurity by quantile compared to global standards (dotted area = lowest quantile; area marked using vertical lines = highest quantile).
Source: ITU (2018)

Attacks using technological means are progressing in terms of occurrence, complexity, and operational and financial impact for individuals, firms, and states.[4] Although Africa is relatively limited in communications infrastructure, due to the high penetration rate of new technologies and low levels of legal, technical, organizational, capacity building, and cooperative commitment to cybersecurity (Figure 9.1), it is increasingly a target for cybercriminals.

Five African countries are in the top ten in the world for ransomware threats – Botswana, Malawi, Namibia, Uganda, and the Democratic Republic of Congo – and analysts estimate that as many as 80 percent of computers in Africa are currently infected with viruses or malware.[5] Africa is particularly vulnerable to cyberattacks due to the high

---

[4] PwC (2015); Symantec (2017)
[5] UNECA (2014, p. 2) referencing recent reports from Symantec Corporation (2013) and Norton (Kshetri 2019).

number of domains in the region, relatively weak network and information security, a lax regulatory climate, and the prevalence of pirated software.[6] Moreover, with higher mobile penetration rates than anywhere else in the world, since many Africans have multiple mobile phones, rather than personal computers or tablets, malware attacks targeted at mobile phones are increasing exponentially each year.[7]

Corporations working in Africa are, in many ways, even more vulnerable than individuals. A recent survey of Kenyan businesses found that all 275 had been exposed to malicious software. More than two-thirds of the malware discovered had been uniquely designed for the African market.[8] While the financial sector is a particularly prime target – East Africa's banking sector, for instance, lost roughly $245 million to cyber fraud in 2011 – the shift to e-government and the relative deficiency of technical expertise in state administration has put Africa's public sector at an even higher cyber security risk according to recent reports.[9] In recent years, South Africa, Kenya, Angola, Ghana, and Senegal have all had to remove government-related websites due to hacking.

Thus, businesses and governments on the continent must strengthen their cyber-risk protection systems to avoid damaging effects on their finances, reputation, employees, customers, and, more generally, on the local and regional economy. Cybersecurity can be addressed within both the public and private sectors; a harmonized approach in both areas will help coordinate efforts to combat cybercrime and ensure the safety of individuals' and companies' data.

9.1 Cybersecurity in African Business

Cyberattacks targeting companies involved in new technologies, advanced services, media, and software development cause leaks or destruction of data and are often motivated by industrial espionage. A loss of classified data such as commercial plans, patents, and state security data, among other sensitive items, can compromise years of labor and research. This problem is particularly acute in Africa, as legal standards for curbing the theft of intellectual property are generally not

---

[6] Asongu (2014, pp. 527–528); "Software piracy" (2011)
[7] Lotz (2015); "The battle" (2017)   [8] Kigen et al. (2015, p. 28)
[9] Quarshie and Martin-Odoom (2012, p. 98)

aligned with international standards. Furthermore, a lack of licensed and updated software in Africa exacerbates the problem: In a 2016 study, the Business Software Alliance (BSA) announced that 57 percent of software – with $3.7 billion worth of commercial value – installed in Africa and the Middle East was pirated, enabling cyberattacks.[10] This is why the African Development Bank has extended a $2 million grant to help strengthen cybersecurity measures and inclusivity measures across the continent. By creating the African Digital Financial Inclusion Facility (ADFI), this grant will help advance digital equality with the help of the French Development Agency and the French Treasury's Ministry of Economy and Finance.[11]

In Africa, the sectors most affected by cybercrime include banking and financial services, government, e-commerce, mobile transactions, and telecommunications.[12] Loss or theft of data through cyberattacks also hampers productivity as companies recovering from a cyberattack often have to delay essential daily activities. For example, the 2017 WannaCry attack forced companies around the world to shut down their systems to stop the spread of the malicious code, immobilizing banks, hospitals, and government agencies in dozens of countries. In Africa, Kenya's financial institutions were hit particularly hard, and the Renault Tanger-Méditerranée automobile plant in Morocco closed for a full day, causing a loss of production of a thousand cars. Region-wide, the extent of the damages is unknown due to companies' failures to report these attacks to the national authorities due to weak reporting structures.

While many financial impacts are obvious, such as production stop costs, penalties, legal costs, and compensation, many are less direct, including increased operational costs, loss of customer confidence, and cancellation of contracts. In the 2017 cybercrime case involving BGFIBank Group in Gabon – the largest financial holding company in the Central African region – customers experienced massive fraud of more than $2.8 million on its prepaid card service. While the company reimbursed its customers, the loss of customer confidence was severe.[13]

---

[10] Business Software Alliance (2016)   [11] AfDB (2021)
[12] For example, in Africa cybercrime cost the following sectors the most in 2017: banking and financial services, $248 million; government, $204 million; E-commerce, $173 million; mobile transactions/e-payment, $140 million; telecommunications, $119 million (*Source*: Serianu 2017).
[13] "Gabon: La BGFI-Bank" (2017)

9.2 Cybersecurity in Governance

The cost of cyberattacks to African organizations and the local economy, including direct damage and postattack disruption, has been estimated to be around $3.5 billion, with South Africa holding $573 million and Nigeria holding $500 million of this cost burden.[14] In 2017, public institutions represented 12 percent of declared global data leaked, in the third position behind financial institutions (24 percent) and health organizations (15 percent).[15] Losses primarily result from tax fraud, benefits fraud, local government fraud, website defacements, and ransom demands.[16] Losses in Cameroon[17] of more than $80 million in 2015, particularly due to fraud in the banking and telecom systems, generated a shortfall of $7.5 million for the Cameroon state in terms of taxes not collected.[18] Governments rely heavily on foreign actors for data management and cloud infrastructure. Their limited control over African data makes it vulnerable to targeted risks. An example of this was the high-profile attack of North Korea's 2017 WannaCry Ransomware.[19]

The high cost of this insecurity has resounding effects on the ability of the state to re-secure its systems and data and to rebound after attacks. A lack of cybersecurity has implications for democracy and stability too. During the controversial presidential election of August 2016 in Gabon, the Gabonese government denounced the interference of foreign powers in the electoral process after the adviser to the Ivorian president encouraged hackers to broadcast foreign reports and hack Gabonese government data to influence the election.[20]

An additional risk of cyberattacks is leaks of personal data. Breaches to privacy can have significant personal consequences. To date, only companies have faced lawsuits filed by their clients or employees for insufficient data protection. Governments should recognize their roles and responsibilities to protect individual data and ensure privacy rights are absolute. Governments and civil society organizations have the purview to investigate and adjudicate instances of data misuse or privacy breaches. In South Africa, for example, the Information Regulatory Authority is currently investigating the cause of the country's largest-

---

[14] Kodjani (2021)   [15] IDG (2013)   [16] Serianu (2017)
[17] "Cameroon" (2016)   [18] Necdem (2015)
[19] Nathaniel and van der Waag-Cowling (2021)
[20] "Gabon-Côte d'Ivoire" (2016)

known data leak in history – a 2017 leak during which the personal data of more than 30 million citizens was stolen – and has made formal requests for explanations from the companies concerned.

9.3 Challenges and Risks

The common perception that Africa lacks the legal framework to respond to and prosecute cybercrime is not entirely accurate.[21] Thirty of the fifty-four African Union member states still lack cybercrime legislation, which points to a glaring gap across the region and severely limits the potential for an effective continent- or regional-level policy coordination.[22] In many places, such as South Africa, relevant policies on issues related to property rights are decades old.[23] On the other hand, many countries have passed policies specifically addressing the threat in recent years, including South Africa, Ethiopia, Kenya, Nigeria, Angola, Madagascar, and Zimbabwe. For example, in June 2020, the Ethiopian Information Security Agency partially stopped an Egyptian cyber-attacker from a large breach; tensions overfilling the Nile River's Grand Ethiopian Renaissance Dam (GERD) led to this attempt, raising concerns over national security issues.[24]

However, even where legal and regulatory frameworks are written in a way that is rational, progressive, and based on best practices in the sector, implementation is often hindered by the realities on the ground. For one thing, there is a clear disconnect between the Western, capitalist-based norms of privacy and individualism and the overriding cultural primacy of community, reciprocity, and openness in Africa, which results in gaps in awareness and in political will.[25] Victims are often unaware or unwilling to report cyberattacks to relevant bodies, undermining prosecution; internet property rights are barely enforced or complied with, even when legal protection exists, allowing unsafe and unreliable pirated software to dominate the market.[26] Internet cafes and mobile phones – the most common modes of access for Africa's internet users – lack antivirus software and malware protection, making them highly vulnerable to attacks.[27] Meanwhile, the majority of the African population continues to lack even basic

---

[21] Rowe et al. (2010); Akuta, Ong'oa, and Jones (2011)   [22] Terebey (2016)
[23] Heuler (2014)   [24] Nathaniel and van der Waag-Cowling (2021)
[25] Kritzinger and von Solms (2011)   [26] Heuler (2014)
[27] Kumar (2010); Kritzinger and von Solms (2012, pp. 2–3)

knowledge of computers and the Internet. Thus, the absence of technical expertise and training among both the workforce and the civil service makes enforcement of cybercrime legislation nearly impossible.[28] On the other hand, from individual users' perspectives, the primary hurdle to cybersecurity is cost. The vast majority of African consumers cannot afford software licenses, so a focus on law enforcement would have little impact on Africa's piracy market compared to Russia, where piracy rates fell from 73 percent to 63 percent of all software between just 2007 and 2011.[29]

Moreover, several "loopholes" exist among the different stakeholders in the fight against cybercrime.[30] In particular, there is a glaring gap between the public and the private sector in Africa's approach to cybersecurity, even though most government agencies are forced to rely on private security companies in their day-to-day operations. The process of drafting the African Union Convention on the Confidence and Security in Cyberspace, which formally began in 2009, took place behind closed doors and involved only government stakeholders, excluding civil society organizations or business advocates. This resulted in a range of criticisms to its formal release in 2013–2014, focusing mainly on the infringement of privacy rights, freedom of speech, and judicial overreach.[31] While the Draft Convention went through a revision process, this too lacked transparency or involvement from nongovernment stakeholders. Even so, only a handful of countries ultimately signed the Convention – Benin, Guinea-Bissau, Mauritania, Congo, Cape Verde, Sierra Leone, Sao Tome and Principe, and Zambia – and none have ratified it, signaling a lack of political will among government leaders.

African governments have themselves come under criticism for passing flawed policies at the national level, which will have little hope of sufficiently addressing online threats while potentially stifling entrepreneurship and investment. In 2016, South Africa was accused of proposing "Africa's worst new internet censorship law" with a bill aimed at online entertainment, while Ethiopia's new cybercrime law criminalizes defamatory language, spam advertising, and pornography with up to ten years' jail time. In Nigeria, Kenya, Tanzania, Zimbabwe, and elsewhere, cybercrime legislation has been used to justify the arrest of

---

[28] Terebey (2016)　　[29] Heuler (2014)
[30] Kritzinger and von Solms (2012, pp. 2–3)　　[31] Terebey (2016)

journalists, political bloggers, and government critics, as well as to shut down social media, especially in the run-up to national elections.[32] Rather than proposing technocratic solutions to the existing vulnerabilities to online threats, Africa's cybersecurity laws are often perceived as political tools to silence opposition and manipulate electoral outcomes. Increased digitalization and current struggles with extremism in Africa challenge lawmakers to formalize their cyber defenses because, without a framework, vulnerable areas and populations are prone to cyberattacks.[33] As a result, approaches to improving the legal and regulatory framework relevant to the Internet often conflict with human rights groups, resulting in a normative battle that makes progressive and effective reform even more difficult.

9.4 Strategies to Improve Cybersecurity

Strategies for African businesses. African businesses must implement strategies to protect their clients, their data, and themselves from a cyberattack. Given the regional context, this can be achieved through four key initiatives: implementing cyber-resilience strategies, developing cybersecurity skills, protecting data integrity, and integrating cyber-risk protection in decision-making processes throughout all levels of management.

9.4.1 Design and Deploy Cyber-Resilience Strategies

Companies must prepare for cyberattacks and improve cyber-resilience as threats increase with the inception of the 4IR. Cyber-resilience strategies should begin at the board or executive level of a company, which can prioritize and enact procedures that will protect valuable assets and integrate them as requirements into all business processes. Companies can then build their cyber capabilities by raising awareness of and building employees' skills in information security, securing configurations, and regularly updating infrastructure and software systems, using technologies for active surveillance, implementing proactive detection and rapid response technologies to respond to security breaches and incidents, and performing regular security audits and

---

[32] Kihara and Njeri (2016); Mourdoukoutas (2017)
[33] Van der Waag-Cowling (2020)

penetration testing. Certification processes can be useful resources for businesses seeking a baseline to address cybersecurity from a management system perspective. Technologies such as AI, data analytics, and automation can help manage the costs of discovering potential attacks.[34] Building cyber-resilience will help with preventative measures and collaboration to form protective measures.[35]

Creating resilience goes beyond constructing walls to prevent attacks; it also involves setting up dedicated processes for managing cyber-crises within the company and collaboration at the sectoral, national, and international levels for exchanges of information and experience. Already, many African companies are taking these steps: In 2016, ISO reported a 73 percent increase in Information Security Management System-certified companies, from 129 in 2015 to 224 in 2016, with the majority of companies located in South Africa, Nigeria, and Morocco.[36] ISO documented another significant increase again from 2019 to 2020 of 18 percent.[37] Despite this significant growth, the number of companies exposed remains large.

9.4.2 Develop Cybersecurity Skills

Experienced and qualified cybersecurity and risk management personnel are essential for ensuring cybersecurity but are rare on the continent. African companies must develop skills-building and retention strategies to attract and maintain the relevant talented professionals, a particular challenge for businesses in Africa. As the need for information security and cybersecurity specialists rises around the world, many specialists may choose to relocate to developed economies in Europe and North America. Strategies to mitigate brain drain are essential for African cybersecurity.

9.4.3 Protect Data Integrity

Data integrity – the maintenance and assurance of the accuracy and consistency of data – could supplant confidentiality as the primary goal of cybersecurity. The resurgence of attacks aimed at manipulating or destroying data has highlighted the importance of data integrity and the

---

[34] Bissel, Lassale, and Dal Cin (2019)   [35] Mathe (2019)   [36] ISO (2017)
[37] ISO (2020)

impact of breached data on organizations and citizens.[38] Companies must strengthen their measures to prevent and recover from an incident of massive data corruption. For this purpose, conventional means such as backups and regular restoration of critical systems are important steps. In addition, innovative technologies such as blockchain can be useful to protect data integrity if companies can mitigate the adverse risks of using a nascent technology. Some African companies – especially in North Africa – are already investing in new technologies to address security threats: In the Middle East and North Africa, information security spending on both conventional and new processes reached $1.8 billion in 2017.[39]

9.4.4 Integrate Cyber-Risk Awareness into the Decision Process

The best way to involve top management of organizations in cybersecurity is to relay risks to all levels of the decision-making system. This process involves aligning cybersecurity objectives with the company's strategic ambitions and defining the essential systems and assets that should be prioritized for protection. These objectives can then be appropriately budgeted for and addressed at the tactical and operational levels to spread cyber-risk awareness at all levels of the company.

Companies' boards and executive management must be aware of their accountability to those affected in case of a cyberattack and recognize the need for skilled managers to identify and act against potential cyber threats. Globally, just 22 percent of chief information security officers (CISOs) report to the chief executive officer (CEO) or the board, while 40 percent report through the chief information officer (CIO).[40] This reporting structure, which is even more common in Africa, positions security as a technical issue rather than a business concern, reducing any cybersecurity initiatives' scope of action and effectiveness.

Regional approaches. To date, just a handful of African countries have established Computer Emergency Response Teams (CERTs): Tunisia, Morocco, Egypt, South Africa, Nigeria, and Kenya.[41] A lack of both technical expertise and political will to divert scarce resources

---

[38] Richards (2017)   [39] Olyaei (2017)   [40] Westby (2015, p. 6)
[41] Morel (2016)

toward averting future losses has contributed to the deficiency of national bureaucratic infrastructures working on cybersecurity, particularly in smaller and poorer countries. However, in light of the borderless nature of cybercrime and the increasing interconnectivity of African countries, there is potential for the continent to undertake an innovative approach to overcome the hurdles to national-level approaches by building regional arrangements, thereby reducing the financial and technical resource burden on each country. Governments should use holistic approaches to develop strategies and implementation plans for cybersecurity initiatives.[42] Regional organizations already exist that could help to channel and coordinate such efforts. They include the Common Market for Eastern and Southern Africa (COMESA), the Economic Community of West African States (ECOWAS), the East African Community (EAC), and the Southern African Development Community (SADC).

Cybercrime has become a notable problem in West Africa, both as a source and as a target, and ECOWAS has already shown some indications that it could serve as an example to the rest of the continent on regional approaches to cybersecurity. An agenda on "Enhancing Cybersecurity in the ECOWAS Region" has existed since 2015, which aims to support member states in building capacities, improving responses to threats, and protecting national internet and data infrastructures. The official view from ECOWAS is that cybersecurity is a shared responsibility that mandates regional cooperation, information sharing, and the dissemination of best practices via partnerships with international and private sector experts. For instance, a number of workshops have been held to train and educate national policymakers in West Africa, aided by new partnerships between ECOWAS and the Global Forum on Cyber Expertise (GFCE), the Cybersecurity Alliance for Mutual Progress (CAMP), the UN Conference on Trade and Development, governments of Europe and the United States, and others.[43]

Education, training, and awareness. Pooling resources at the regional level could also help channel resources toward research into Africa-specific threats, such as mobile money services and other innovative initiatives that can help Africa "leapfrog" past existing technology and infrastructure gaps. However, it also has the potential

---

[42] Jansen van Vuuren and Leenen (2019)   [43] Oyelola (2016)

to create new vulnerabilities for cybercriminals. In particular, regional organizations should invest in creating academic degree programs in cybersecurity at the top universities in the region.

It will also be crucial for organizations working in Africa – especially those relying on a bring-your-own-device policy – to recognize the potential loss to investment returns caused by the insider threat and how employee training programs can offset this. Topics to be covered include email and password "hygiene," protection of personal data, detection of phishing scams, and internet best practices. Ideally, organizations should invest in a technical team to manage ongoing security issues and threats, and conduct technical training exercises for the broader workforce. Given the typical deficiency of in-house expertise and resources in African organizations, however, it is likely that such exercises will need to be outsourced. As a result, an assessment should be conducted in order to identify the specific needs and vulnerabilities of the organization before adopting an employee training program.[44] Where resources are even more scarce, online programs exist that provide periodic training and workshops to keep employees updated on the latest threats. These could potentially be shared across similar organizations, if necessary, to save money.

Beyond organizations, it will be vital that African society develops a culture of cybersecurity awareness. This requires ensuring that home users are made aware of potential threats and provided access to information about information security best practices.[45] According to pessimistic perspectives, it is unrealistic to expect home users, who generally have low expertise and little interest in increasing their knowledge, to be responsible for their online security.[46] Yet, incorporating regulating bodies such as ISPs can help protect users from the threats introduced to a network by a compromised user by identifying and blocking malicious incoming and outgoing internet traffic.[47]

Monitoring and assessment. The constantly adapting nature of cybercrime means that African organizations will need to implement ongoing monitoring and risk assessment programs. In addition to antivirus software, automated vulnerability scanners exist to identify network vulnerabilities, such as open ports, firewall gaps, missing patches,

---

[44] Serianu (2016, pp. 39–40)
[45] Kumar, Mohan, and Holowczak (2008); Kramer, Starr, and Wentz (2009)
[46] Schneier (2007)   [47] Kritzinger and von Solms (2011); Rowe et al. (2010)

and systems needing updates.[48] Obviously, these kinds of products will need to be adapted to the African market to ensure uptake, which means – among other things – addressing the issue of affordability, or else risk falling into the software piracy trap.

Harmonizing cybersecurity initiatives. Cybersecurity is a chain whose links must all be robust for the global system to be resilient. The cybersecurity of a state is ensured by both the government and private institutions. Still, it is the government's responsibility to support the implementation of regulatory directives that align the levels of security of each link of this chain. This approach results in centralized and specific definitions and publications of fundamental security measures.

A national strategy for cybersecurity is necessary to protect governance structures and services. Some states may find it appropriate to adopt a national entity responsible for defining, implementing, and overseeing the national cybersecurity strategy. One of the priority actions of this entity or key cybersecurity decisionmaker should be to define a national standard for cybersecurity and identify the critical national infrastructure that will have to completely conform to this standard to increase resilience in the case of cyberattacks. Additionally, the entity or decisionmaker must ensure that all stakeholders are involved, including private actors, state entities, and the general public. The overseeing entity must also have the mechanisms, resources, and authority to conduct its mission and report to the highest level of decision-making. The entity may take the form of an independent national agency tied to a ministry or one that is tied to the national defense services. Regardless of the exact structure, there must be information sharing between different ministries and the defense services because cyber threats require coordination among all levels of national, local, and municipal governance.

Given the proliferation of cyberattacks, an increased number of African countries have adopted and implemented laws to protect the privacy and personal information of their citizens. In Morocco, for example, companies are required to comply with a set of laws on cybercrime, electronic exchanges, and personal data protection; the country also has a national cybersecurity directive issued by the National Defense Administration to protect critical infrastructure all

---

[48] Serianu (2016, pp. 39–40)

over the country. Furthermore, the Moroccan Central Bank published a 2016 directive requiring credit establishments to perform intrusion tests on their information systems.[49] This directive followed a 2015 directive from the Central Bank of West African States related to the cybersecurity of the West African Monetary Union's banks.[50]

The European Union's General Data Protection Regulation (GDPR), which entered into force in early May 2018, is an additional obligation for African companies to maintain their commercial relations with Europe. Companies that are unable to comply with the mandated standards are subject not only to proceedings but also to penalties, fines, and loss of reputation, among other consequences. General Data Protection Regulation thus makes improving the cybersecurity of African businesses even more consequential for the continent's continued economic growth in the 4IR.

Thus, new technology has the potential not only to transform lives but also to create significant harm. Cybersecurity represents a prerequisite for the digital transformation, improvement of growth potential, and reinforcement of national security of every African nation.

---

[49] "Une directive" (2016)   [50] BCEAO (2015)

10 | *The Importance of Health Care and Technological Innovations during the Fourth Industrial Revolution*

Continued investment in health care across the African continent has contributed to improving health outcomes. Still, the high incidence of mortality rates for infectious and noncommunicable diseases plagues the continent. The 4IR offers Africa's health care sector immense potential to benefit through investments and innovations to bridge the gap between health care promise and delivery. The 4IR offers efficient and effective ways to carry out public health measures to improve health care outcomes and overcome crises such as COVID-19, Ebola, and other widespread diseases at various levels of cost, scope, and scalability. This chapter will explore recurring challenges and policy constraints to effective health care and highlight trends and illustrations of emerging technologies and innovation of the 4IR in health care in Africa. This will set the stage to present effective strategies and policy options for bridging the gap between promise and delivery in Africa's health care with the 4IR.[1]

Recent studies have demonstrated the positive relationship between improved health care and economic performance,[2] including the importance of the 4IR in transforming health care, human capital, and economic development.[3] Indeed, experts estimate that additional investments in health care in Africa (an average of $21 to $36 per capita per year over the next five years) could save 3.1 million lives and generate economic gains of more than $100 billion over that time.[4]

Improved health leads to longer life expectancy, better educational performance, increased savings and investment, decreased debt and health care expenditure, and increased productivity. In fact, the

---

[1] Signé (2021)

[2] Weil (2014); Bloom et al. (2019); UNECA, GBC Health, and Aliko Dangote Foundation (2019)

[3] Ndung'u and Signé (2020)

[4] UNECA, GBC Health, and Aliko Dangote Foundation (2019) referring to WHO work.

WHO estimates that for every 10 percent increase in life expectancy at birth, annual economic growth increases by 0.4 percent.[5] Thus, investing in a healthy population is also critical for Africa's development beyond enhancing human life.

10.1 Recent Trends in Health Care in Africa

Efforts to improve health outcomes and respond to health crises in Africa have increasingly regionalized. In 2017, as a response to the Ebola epidemic, the African Union launched the Africa Centers for Disease Control and Prevention (Africa CDC) for member states to coordinate strategic public health initiatives, including emergency preparedness and response, disease surveillance, and technical support. Since the beginning of the COVID-19 pandemic, the Africa CDC's COVID-19 task force has led the region's response to the crisis by creating a response fund, providing testing and research capacity, spearheading education and prevention campaigns, deploying health workers, and procuring donations from international partners. The COVID-19 pandemic also accelerated the adoption of 4IR technologies to help address the challenges brought on by the virus. The rapid expansion of innovative and agile framework models such as Rwanda's adoption of drones for vaccine deployment helped combat Africa's limited vaccine manufacturing capacity on the continent. The African Union partnered with the Africa CDC and the African Export-Import Bank to establish the African Vaccine Acquisition Trust initiative, which sources the majority of Africa's vaccines bilaterally or through COVAX, a global multilateral partnership.[6] The Africa CDC and the African Union created an initiative to foster the development of manufacturing hubs to help lift Africa's overdependence on vaccine imports.[7] However, the Africa CDC needs more autonomy to fully carry out its mission, as well as the cooperation of member states to fulfill national budget obligations.[8] More than fifteen years ago, in the Abuja Declaration, African Union member states committed themselves to raise government spending on health to 15 percent of the national budget. However, most countries still fall short of this target,

[5] World Health Organization (2014, p. 6)
[6] World Health Organization (2021e)   [7] Africa CDC (2021)
[8] Uche Ordu (2020)

with many allocating less than 5 percent before the pandemic. As a result, health care access in Africa is heavily dependent on assistance from international donors and aid agencies, along with out-of-pocket payments for services, which places significant strain on low-income households.

Meanwhile, nearly half of the population in sub-Saharan Africa lacks access to clean water or sanitation services – a pressing concern, especially considering the rapidly expanding population in the region's slums. New solutions and methods to address health concerns will be a key challenge Africa will need to address in the 4IR. African health care can only improve throughout the next digital wave with many new technologies aiding in disease prevention, agro-processing, and information management.

Furthermore, Africa's burgeoning health sector hosts too few medical professionals, proportional to the size of the population in most countries. As of 2015, the African region had an average of 1.3 health workers per 1,000 people, far fewer than the Sustainable Development Goal target of 4.5 per 1,000 people.[9] Relatedly, many African countries are also susceptible to the "brain drain" of medical professionals, a trend in which African-trained health professionals move abroad, leaving African countries with a shortage of qualified health care workers.

Then again, despite these challenges and common perceptions about health outcomes in Africa, the region has made substantial progress on many health indicators over the past fifty years. For example, the World Bank reports that, between 2005 and 2012, the number of hospital beds in Africa increased by 7.1 percent, the number of doctors by 3.3 percent, and the number of nurses by 5.1 percent. The infant and under-five mortality rates in sub-Saharan Africa decreased by more than half between 1990 and 2019 (Figure 10.1).[10]

The burden of communicable diseases in the region has similarly dropped. For example, there has been substantial progress in combatting the HIV/AIDS epidemic over the past decade. There was a 42 percent decrease in AIDS-related deaths in the WHO's Africa region from 2010 to 2017.[11] By 2019, at least nine sub-Saharan African countries

---

[9] World Health Organization (2017a)
[10] World Bank (2019a); World Bank (2019b)
[11] WHO Regional Office for Africa (2019)

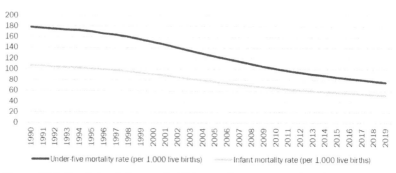

Figure 10.1 Declining infant and child mortality rates in sub-Saharan Africa.
Data source: World Bank (2019a, 2019b)

had achieved more than 80 percent coverage in antiretroviral treatment,[12] with the region exhibiting a 20 percent reduction in disease prevalence from 2000 to 2019.[13]

The average life expectancy at birth in Africa is now 64.5 years,[14] an increase from just thirty-eight years in 1950 and fifty years in 1990[15] – yet significantly lower than the global mean of 73.3 years.[16] Notably, most improvements in Africa's life expectancy rates over the past fifty years are attributed to improvements in infant and childhood mortality ratios.[17]

Much of the global comparison masks variation within Africa. Regional averages tend to be pulled down by poor performers, where mortality rates are actually increasing and places where progress has lagged substantially due to the heavy disease burden.[18] For example, the region's adult female mortality rate is roughly double the world average. Still, the rate is over three times as high in some countries – such as Lesotho and the Central African Republic.[19] Africa also exhibits some of the lowest numbers in the world regarding life expectancy: just fifty-three years in the Central African Republic, fifty-four in Chad, fifty-five in Nigeria, and fifty-nine in Cameroon.[20] In contrast,

---

[12] World Bank (2019h)   [13] World Bank (2019i)
[14] World Health Organization (2019a, p. 16)
[15] World Health Organization (2016, p. 9); World Health Organization (2019a, p. 6)
[16] World Health Organization (2021c, p. 16)
[17] World Health Organization (2016, p. 26)
[18] World Health Organization (2016, p. 44)   [19] World Bank (2019e)
[20] World Bank (2019f)

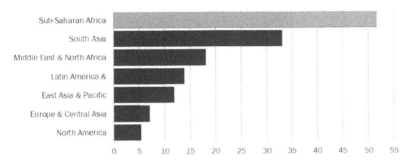

Figure 10.2 Infant mortality rates (per 1,000 live births), 2019.
Source: World Health Organization, extracted from World Bank data

people born in North Africa and the island nations of Mauritius, Seychelles, and Cabo Verde can expect to live more than seventy years – approximately equal to the global average.[21]

In fact, within Africa, the most significant progress in health to date has been made in North Africa. Over the past two decades, North Africa's maternal mortality rate has decreased by 54 percent, compared to a 39 percent decrease in sub-Saharan Africa,[22] while the under-five mortality rate has decreased by about 50 percent.[23] Several North African countries have also exhibited the continent's most impressive reduction in infant mortality since 2000: 53 percent in Egypt, 42 percent in Tunisia, 59 percent in Libya, and 57 percent in Morocco.[24]

Other impressive performers in Africa include Sierra Leone, where the maternal mortality rate decreased by more than half between 2000 and 2017, from 2,480 per 100,000 live births to 1,120; and Eritrea and Mozambique, where maternal mortality declined by roughly 63 percent over the same period.[25] In Angola, the maternal mortality rate has fallen by almost 71 percent since 2000, from 827 deaths per 100,000 live births to 241.[26]

Despite the overall progress in health care outcomes, sub-Saharan Africa still underperforms compared to the rest of the world in major indicators such as infant mortality, the number of physicians, or the number of nurses and midwives (per 1,000 people), as illustrated in

[21] World Bank (2019f)   [22] UNFPA et al. (2019); Borgen Project (2020)
[23] World Bank (2019a)   [24] World Bank (2019b)   [25] UNFPA et al. (2019)
[26] UNFPA et al. (2019)

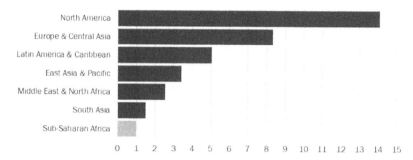

Figure 10.3 Nurses and midwives (per 1,000 people), 2018.
Source: World Health Organization, extracted from World Bank data

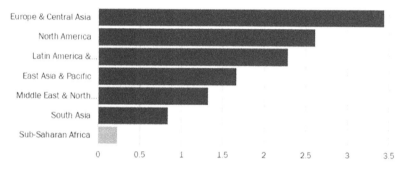

Figure 10.4 Physicians (per 1,000 people), 2017.
Source: World Health Organization, extracted from World Bank data

Figures 10.2, 10.3, and 10.4. The following section discusses some of the recurrent challenges and policy constraints responsible for Africa's health care system.

10.2 Recurrent Challenges and Policy Constraints to Health Care in Africa

African citizens have some of the lowest satisfaction rates with their health care systems of any region in the world.[27] Despite heavy investment by foreign donors and local governments over the past two decades, the sector is still characterized by a lack of access and infrastructural gaps,

---

[27] Deaton and Tortora (2015)

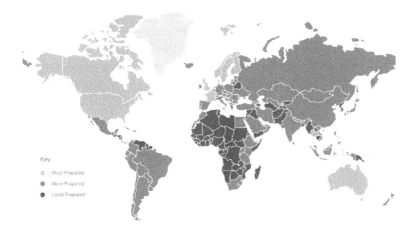

Figure 10.5 "Preventing the emergence or release of pathogens" indicator from the Global Health Security Index 2019.
Source: Global Health Security Index (2019)

shortages of medications and medical staff, and corruption. In combination with poor access to clean water and sanitation, as a result, health outcomes on the continent are dire. Furthermore, many African policymakers have not succeeded in prioritizing health care and do not devote sufficient resources. The implementation of 4IR technologies is critical in boosting the state of health care around the continent. With many of these challenges not being adequately addressed, increased participation of the private sector in the health sector is needed, especially with the involvement of technology.

10.2.1 Limited Preparedness for Epidemics and Pandemics

Africa is the least-prepared region when it comes to preventing the emergence or release of pathogens, according to the Global Health Security Index 2019 (Figure 10.5), meaning its ability to detect and respond to epidemics is very low. A series of challenges can explain this low performance. The first challenge is the limited disease detection ability, given the lack of qualified personnel and quality laboratories, timely surveillance and reporting, and effective data sharing among stakeholders. The second challenge is the weak preparedness and, consequently, often slow response and mitigation in case of epidemic take-off. Contributing factors include the scarcity of trained health care professionals (including epidemiologists to investigate when the outbreak occurs) combined with the limited availability of equipment and medication, whether for detection, prevention, deployment, or treatment. And even when countries have the resources, they are not necessarily effectively prepared to face disruptive epidemics and pandemics. Finally, limited social protection initiatives for the most vulnerable complicate the ability to contain any disease. In the quest for economic survival, citizens may adopt behaviors that contribute to worsening epidemics.

10.2.2 Human Capital and Brain Drain

Africa's shortage of trained medical professionals is a significant contributor to the gap between supply and demand in the health sector, and the poor management of health care facilities. The WHO estimates that Africa will have a shortage of 6.1 million health workers by 2030, a 45 percent increase from the estimated 2013 shortage of 4.2 million.[28] In twenty African countries,[29] there is fewer than one doctor for every 10,000 people. In fact, the sub-Saharan African region as a whole has just 2.1 physicians per 10,000 people (less than 12 percent of the world average) – the lowest ratio in the world.[30] Similarly, the average sub-Saharan African country has just 9.94 nurses and midwives per 10,000 people (less than one-third of the world average) – and in twelve countries,[31] fewer than five.[32] Figure 10.6 illustrates the low density of skilled health professionals by sub-region, showing not only the overall low performance of African countries but also the disparities within and across sub-regions.

[28] World Health Organization (2020b, p. 44)
[29] Malawi, Liberia, Niger, Chad, United Republic of Tanzania, Benin, Lesotho, Central African Republic, Sierra Leone, Ethiopia, Togo, Eritrea, Guinea, Mozambique, Senegal, Cameroon, DRC, Zambia, Burkina Faso, and Eswatini.
[30] World Health Organization Global Health Observatory data (various years), www.who.int/data/gho/data/indicators/indicator-details/GHO/medical-doctors-(per-10-000-population)
[31] Cameroon, Guinea, Chad, Central African Republic, Niger, Madagascar, Benin, Angola, Malawi, Mali, Togo, and Mozambique.
[32] World Health Organization Global Health Observatory data (various years), www.who.int/data/gho/data/indicators/indicator-details/GHO/nursing-and-midwifery-personnel-(per-10-000-population)

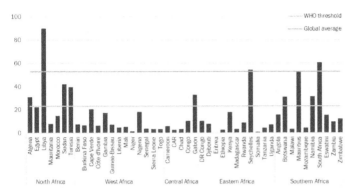

Figure 10.6 Skilled health professional density (per 10,000) by African sub-region, various years.
Note: The WHO threshold is the minimum density of skilled health professional per 10,000 people required to provide the most basic health coverage.
Source: World Health Organization, Global Health Observatory data repository (2018)

Due to limited domestic capacity for medical education and training, many African countries pay for doctors and nurses to be trained abroad. However, once accredited, better working conditions and higher salaries abroad incentivize those newly trained professionals to stay there – resulting in a "brain drain" away from Africa's health sector.[33] In fact, according to data collected by the Center for Global Development, Liberia, Angola, and Mozambique have more doctors working in foreign countries than in their home countries. In fact, in 2008, two doctors were working abroad for every one working at home in Liberia.[34]

While there is no doubt Africa desperately needs more trained providers, technology itself can also be part of the solution. In 2015, for example, Uganda had only twelve technicians in ten locations certified to make plaster prostheses, a job in which it takes at least three years to become certified. Demand for such medical equipment and specialized care far outstrips the supply, as children outgrow prosthetics in six months. The traditional process to properly design, produce, and fit the prosthetic takes weeks and multiple patient visits. That year, Comprehensive Rehabilitation Services Uganda partnered with the University of Toronto to make 3D-printed prosthetics. The 3D printing process they used cut the time to complete the process by 75 percent

[33] Oxford Business Group (2017)   [34] Clemens and Pettersson (2008)

and allowed technicians to see five more patients per week.[35] In addition to the lower cost, that efficiency drastically increased accessibility of prostheses for poor, rural patients.

10.2.3 Weak Infrastructure

One of the greatest current challenges to health care delivery in Africa is access, primarily due to the low numbers of health facilities and gaps in pharmaceutical availability and affordability. The hospital-to-patient ratio is exceptionally low in sub-Saharan Africa, where fewer than 50 percent of people have access to a quality health facility. The existing health facilities tend to lack diagnostic equipment – such as X-ray machines, ultrasounds, and chemistry analyzers – causing medical staff to rely on alternative diagnostics and often delaying diagnosis until diseases are more advanced and challenging to treat. Similarly, in April 2020, *The New York Times* reported that the CAR, DRC, Liberia, Mali, Madagascar, and South Sudan all had fewer than ten ventilators each; Somalia had none.[36] Where such technologies exist, they have usually been donated by an NGO for communities that lack skilled technicians for maintenance and upgrading. Moreover, many vital preventative medications are not available in numerous health centers, including dispensaries and government clinics. Given there are few pharmaceutical manufacturing facilities in sub-Saharan Africa, most countries import 70 to 90 percent of their drugs, resulting in high prices and low preparedness.[37]

Beyond the deficiency of staff, facilities, and equipment, the health system is threatened by broader infrastructural gaps that threaten all economic sectors in Africa, such as those in basic utilities and ICTs, further complicating and even hindering potential uptake of 4IR technologies. For example, only 28 percent of the rural population in sub-Saharan Africa has access to electricity. Hospitals and clinics – particularly those in rural areas – often face power outages, which pose a significant risk to surgical patients and limit clinics' ability to store vaccines and other pharmaceuticals.[38,39] Roughly two-thirds of the

---

[35] Burpee (2015)   [36] Maclean and Marks (2020)   [37] Conway et al. (2019)
[38] Today, utility infrastructure must not only be reliable and sustainable but also invulnerable to cybersecurity breaches, which are becoming increasingly common in Africa and globally (Power Africa 2020).
[39] World Bank (2019d)

population lack access to basic sanitation services. Nearly 40 percent lack basic drinking water services,[40] exacerbating the incidence of communicable diseases that have been all but eradicated in other regions, especially cholera and dysentery.[41]

Finally, the absence of mass internet connectivity severely limits the capacity of national health management and information systems to generate, coordinate, store, analyze, and disseminate data relevant to health crises, as well as data relevant to patients' long-term health.[42] Providers and patients need access to a reliable internet connection to benefit from various digital health solutions, from cloud-based electronic medical records to telemedicine to IoT devices. While most African countries have been trying to solve some of the challenges mentioned above, the continent still lags in terms of the quality of health care systems and overall health care outcomes.

10.2.4 Investment Gaps in Health Care

Feeding into the challenges listed above is a lack of financing for improved health outcomes. UNECA, GBCHealth, and Aliko Dangote Foundation (2019) estimate Africa's health financing gap at $66 billion per year, as the required financing is at about $114 billion.[43] By combining indicators such as the "domestic government health expenditure, out-of-pocket expenditure, density of skilled health workers, average disease burden, government debt, and the annual GDP growth rate" among others, the authors posit that a total of twenty countries are either very health-stressed[44] (Benin, Cameroon, Central African Republic, Democratic Republic of the Congo, Republic of the Congo, Côte d'Ivoire, Guinea, Guinea-Bissau, Mali, Mozambique, Niger, and Zambia) or severely health-stressed (Angola, Chad, Mauritania, Nigeria, Sierra Leone, South Sudan, Togo, and Zimbabwe), given their vulnerability.[45]

---

[40] World Bank (2017c and 2017d)
[41] World Health Organization (2014, p. 94)   [42] Kirigia and Barry (2008)
[43] UNECA, GBCHealth, and Aliko Dangote Foundation (2019, p. vi)
[44] The report determines health-stress by evaluating the thresholds of domestic government health expenditure, out-of-pocket expenditure, density of skilled health workers, average disease burden, government debt, and the annual GDP growth rate indicators.
[45] UNECA, GBCHealth and Aliko Dangote Foundation (2019, p. xvi)

The limited investment in health care on the continent also contributes to other problems, for example, the widespread circulation of counterfeit drugs. Between 2013 and 2017, 40 percent of reported fake medicine seizures in the world were in Africa,[46] and fake medication in circulation could represent up to 70 percent of the total pharmaceuticals on the continent.[47] Counterfeit pills are estimated to result in about 450,000 preventable malaria deaths globally[48] and disproportionately affect Africa, which accounted for 94 percent of malaria deaths worldwide in 2019.[49] Without investment in quality and affordable drug production and technology such as mPedigree (Ghana) for the detection of fake pharmaceuticals, the continent will be left behind, especially its poorest citizens.

10.2.5 Low Government Spending

As noted above, in the Abuja Declaration in 2001, leaders of African Union member states committed to increasing health-related spending to 15 percent of their national budgets.[50] However, while the average share of government expenditure on health increased markedly between 1995 and 2004, it has remained relatively constant at around 11 percent since then.[51] Just seven countries – Uganda, Rwanda, eSwatini, Ethiopia, Malawi, Central African Republic, and Togo – currently meet the 15 percent benchmark, while ten countries allocate less than half that amount.[52] However, in per capita terms government health expenditure has continued to increase steadily since the mid-1990s, with the average African country now spending roughly $110 per person every year, compared to just $40 in 1995 (considering purchasing power parity) (Figures 10.7 and 10.8). Some countries spend $400 per capita or more, as shown in Table 10.1. Although out-of-pocket expenditure as a percentage of current health expenditure decreased by nearly 7 percent from 2000 to 2018 in all of Africa, sub-Saharan African countries still have the highest out-of-pocket expenditure per capita globally (Figure 10.9), resulting in a significant financial burden on their citizens.[53]

---

[46] World Health Organization (2017b)   [47] PwC (2017)   [48] PwC (2017)
[49] World Health Organization (2020c, p. xiv)   [50] Kaseje (2006, p. 4)
[51] It is worth noting that this ratio is higher than some other WHO developing regions, including Southeast Asia and Eastern Mediterranean.
[52] World Health Organization (2016, p. 62)
[53] World Health Organization (2021b)

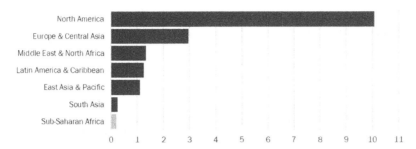

Figure 10.7 Current health expenditure per capita, PPP (current international $) in 2018.
Source: World Health Organization, extracted from World Bank data

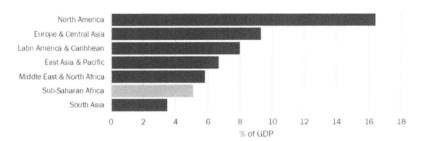

Figure 10.8 Current health expenditure (% of GDP), 2018.
Source: World Health Organization, extracted from World Bank data

10.2.6 Regulatory Environment and Public Inefficiencies

The public regulatory environment facing the health sector also tends to lack resources and coordination. Public inspectors often go unpaid in the DRC and Madagascar, and private clinics report not being inspected for years. Furthermore, only one in five African countries have education requirements for medical staff working in private facilities.[54]

Moreover, corruption in the public health sector has led to inefficiencies and a loss of resources, reducing access and affordability for patients more broadly and creating uncertainty in the sector overall. With bilateral

---

[54] African Development Bank (2013, p. 14). According to the African Development Bank's 2013 report *Health in Africa over the Next 50 Years*, only 20 percent of African countries explicitly mandate Continuing Medical Education requirements for privately practicing health care workers.

Table 10.1 *Per capita government health expenditure in the WHO Africa Region*

Domestic general government health expenditure (GGHE-D) per capita, 2018	African countries
High (> $100)	Mauritius, Namibia, Botswana, South Africa, Algeria, Seychelles, Gabon, Cape Verde
Medium-high (between $30 and $100)	Eswatini, Equatorial Guinea, São Tomé and Principe, Ghana, Lesotho, Angola, Kenya, Zimbabwe
Medium-low (between $10 and $30)	Niger, Malawi, Liberia, Nigeria, Senegal, Tanzania, Burkina Faso, Congo, Rwanda, Mauritania, Côte d'Ivoire, Zambia
Low (<$10)	Democratic Republic of the Congo, South Sudan, Cameroon, Central African Republic, Eritrea, Guinea-Bissau, Chad, Ethiopia, Burundi, Comoros, Benin, Guinea, Gambia, Uganda, Togo, Madagascar, Sierra Leone, Mozambique, Mali

Source: The Global Health Observatory (World Health Organization) 2018

and multilateral assistance flowing into Africa in an attempt to reduce the out-of-pocket payments facing households seeking health care, reports of public officials and medical staff directly diverting aid money, trading bribes for drug registration or health inspections, or selling medications meant to be provided for free have amassed over the past decades. In some countries, the tenure of health ministers has averaged just six months due to mismanagement of resources; in 2009 alone, Gambia had four health ministers in office.[55] Some countries are taking action: For example, health ministers in the DRC[56] have been jailed for misappropriation of health financial resources.

---

[55] African Development Bank (2013, p. 14)   [56] Alfa Shaban (2020)

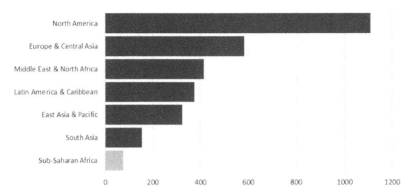

Figure 10.9 Out-of-pocket expenditure per capita, PPP (current international $), 2018.
Source: World Health Organization, extracted from World Bank data

10.3 Emerging Technologies and Innovation of the 4IR in Africa

The World Economic Forum's Insight Report[57] on health and health care in the 4IR identifies three broad key drivers of innovation in health care: the unsustainable rise of costs, digitalization of health and health care, and rapid evolution of science and medicine.[58] In the African context, given the gap between health care professionals, infrastructure, equipment, facilities, spending, investment, and enabling policies, among others, "necessity is the mother of invention" in increasing health care effectiveness through the 4IR.[59] Numerous African entrepreneurs and innovators, including dynamic youth, are exploring affordable technological solutions to address their immediate health care challenges, benefiting from technology diffusion, transfer, adoption, adaptation, and, when possible, innovation. This emerging dynamism offers the opportunity to African innovators, often in partnership with their international counterparts, to leapfrog in addressing some of the continent's persisting critical health care challenges. However, success can only occur if they can scale up, something that remains a true challenge. Therefore, it is important to

[57] World Economic Forum (2019)   [58] World Economic Forum (2019)
[59] Schwab (2016)

explore some of the health care solutions associated with the 4IR technologies in Africa, discussing their relevance in addressing the continent's current health care challenges. In so doing, we are building on the classification of WEF's Insight Report,[60] adapting it to the African context.

10.3.1 Trends in "Analytics and Computing" That Seek to Improve Diagnostics, Treatment, Storage, and Security: Artificial Intelligence (AI), Machine Learning, Big Data, and Blockchain Technology

Artificial intelligence systems are programmed using algorithms that allow for the practice of machine learning, which enables the system to recognize patterns and make predictions using data collection and analysis.[61] In health care, AI is often used for diagnostics and accelerated treatment strategies. Ilara Health, founded in Kenya, produces affordable diagnostic equipment using AI, including a portable ultrasound device and a diagnostic app that detects respiratory infections from the sound of a cough.[62] Artificial Intelligence is often paired with blockchain, a secure transaction ledger database shared by a decentralized network of computers.[63] Blockchain is instrumental in health document verification, secure data storage systems, and digital identification. PanaBIOS (Kenya), Econet Group, the African Union, and the Africa CDC launched the Trusted Travel digital platform in a public–private partnership. This platform uses blockchain to facilitate cross-border health certificate verification (and prevent the use of false documents) between travelers, laboratories, and border agents and immigration officers.[64] Zimbabwean digital identity firm FlexFinTx provides a platform for medical providers to store licenses and credentials. License portability could be particularly useful in allowing health care workers to cross borders during a pandemic and work in areas with doctor shortages. Other companies integrating AI, blockchain, sensors, and machine learning include Afya Rekod (Kenya), which equips patients and providers with a decentralized, user-generated medical data storage platform, and mPedigree (Ghana), which

[60] World Economic Forum (2019)   [61] World Economic Forum (2019)
[62] Jackson (2020a)   [63] Kaushal and Tyle (2015)
[64] African Union and Africa CDC (2021)

prevents and detects counterfeit medicine, and other products, within supply chains.[65]

10.3.2 Trends in "Modern Machines" Addressing the Gap in Infrastructure, Equipment, and Facilities in Health Care in Africa: 3D Printing and Drones

In the context of infrastructure deficits or medical supply scarcity, where traditional options are unavailable or too costly, African firms have pivoted to adopting, adapting, or innovating modern machines. 3D printing, also known as additive manufacturing, enables a computer to use a digital design to produce a 3D object layer by layer, using materials such as plastics, metal, nylon, and ceramic. For example, when medical equipment was in high demand but supply was low during the height of the pandemic, Kenyan 3D printing company Ultra Red Technologies printed face masks and ventilator components. Despite the extremely limited resources in Sierra Leone, a Dutch organization has established a 3D printing lab and training center to manufacture prosthetic limbs.[66] Drones, or unmanned aerial vehicles (UAVs), provide life-saving solutions through on-demand last-mile delivery of crucial medical supplies. In cold chain supply cases, health centers cannot store blood or vaccines at the proper temperature. This is primarily due to unreliable electricity, poor road conditions inhibiting timely delivery, lack of access to cold chain supply trucks, or other factors that result in wastage. Therefore, companies such as Zipline (highlighted below) and Nigerian logistics and supply chain company Lifebank have had an important impact. Lifebank has saved 14,000 lives in Nigeria and Kenya using UAVs, among other transport methods; data analytics; AI; and blockchain to safely deliver over 40,000 affordable and trackable medical supplies such as blood, oxygen, COVID-19 tests, and medications.[67] Johnson & Johnson has started using drones to transport lab samples and HIV medication to 2,700 people per day on remote islands on Lake Victoria, where weather conditions have made boat deliveries difficult.[68] The project will allow the existing health workers more time to treat patients and create jobs for local Ugandans.

---

[65] Salient (2021)   [66] Van der Stelt et al. (2020)   [67] Retief (2021)
[68] Goad (2021)

10.3.3 Trends in the Capitalization of Digitalization to Address the Shortage in Human Capital and Limited Access to Financing of Health Care: Telemedicine, the Internet of Things (IoT), Cloud Computing, and Fintech

The digital health industry leverages the high mobile penetration in many African markets to facilitate telemedicine, including remote doctor consultations and inventory shortages. Mobile health (mHealth) companies such as Zuri Health, whose offerings include SMS-based telehealth services to patients who lack access to the Internet, address the gap in digital infrastructure. In Uganda, where many patients had previously traveled long distances to reach clinics only to find that the needed medications were unavailable, a mobile health (m-health) system called mTRAC now provides information about medicine stocks in clinics across the country.

Telemedicine platforms are adding direct-to-consumer product distribution services and vice versa, often through partnerships with other startups.[69] A 2021 Salient study of over sixty health tech companies showed that nearly half are actively targeting markets in both urban and rural areas, and some are even pursuing strategies to facilitate cost-savings at pharmacies in low-income communities.[70] The eHealth company mPharma (Ghana) has branched beyond pharmacy inventory and operational software to several other sectors, including fintech (technology-driven financial services). mPharma's newest product in Ethiopia is Mutti, a mobile money membership program that offers health care financing services to help patients, especially uninsured patients, pay for health care costs.[71] Maisha Meds, a point-of-sale and operations management software used by over 300 pharmacies in East Africa, has built a digital reimbursement feature that utilizes mobile money to lower drug costs for patients. These patients often cannot afford to buy the quantity or quality of medicine their doctor has prescribed.[72] Innovative fintech companies such as MicroEnsure, Jamii Africa, and M-Tiba are bringing affordable health insurance policies to Africans as well, including microinsurance and cellular plan add-ons.[73]

Specific devices utilizing sensors, the Internet of Things, and other 4IR technologies facilitate diagnoses of specific health conditions. For

---

[69] Mureithi (2021b) [70] Salient (2021, p. 20) [71] Jackson (2021)
[72] Maisha Meds (2020) [73] Signé (2021)

example, the Matiscope is a tool created by the Ugandan company Matibabu that fits onto the index finger and, without drawing blood, can detect the presence of malaria-causing parasites. The Matiscope determines the results and sends them to a user-friendly smartphone or computer application in just a few minutes.[74] Many digital health applications and devices use cloud computing to store and manage data on a network of remote servers. Such is the case with RxAll's RxScanner, a device that uses AI and cloud computing to detect counterfeit drugs rapidly.[75]

However, there are immense challenges when integrating emerging technologies into health care systems, particularly when firms pursue new markets across borders. For example, African telemedicine start-ups have incredible momentum. Still, expansion across borders requires adapting to a country's unique regulatory policies internally as well as demonstrating that understanding and preparedness to investors.[76]

10.3.4 Medical Discoveries and Biotechnologies Providing Innovative Treatments, Preparedness, and Responses in the African Context

Biotechnology has been recognized as contributing to medical break-throughs, and although breakthroughs do not happen often, even incremental discoveries can make a difference. Despite the challenges in human resources and infrastructure on the continent, Africa has been home to some discoveries. It hosts small yet evolving genetic engineering activities that can reshape global public health and reduce the burden of disease. Early in the pandemic, scientists at the Africa Higher Education Center of Excellence for Genomics of Infectious Diseases (ACEGID), in partnership with the Nigerian Center for Disease Control, contributed to understanding SARS-CoV-2 by iden-tifying multiple viral lineages through genome sequencing.[77] The Africa Higher Education Center of Excellence for Genomics of Infectious Diseases, with funding from the World Bank, USAID, pri-vate foundations, and others, trains hundreds of students in genomics and has COVID-19 knowledge-sharing and skill-transfer programs for

---

[74] Lewis (2019) [75] Kene-Okafor (2021) [76] Mureithi (2021b)
[77] Happi (2020); World Bank (2021)

established scientists.[78] Other active biotechnology hubs exist in Mauritius, Kenya, Uganda, and South Africa.[79]

Biotechnology has a fundamental role in driving malaria research.[80] The Target Malaria research alliance had encouraging results from releasing genetically modified mosquitos in 2019 in Burkina Faso. However, to drive forward their goal of bioengineering to eradicate the disease,[81] CRISPR, a gene-editing tool, is recommended by scholars for use in pursuing the development of a malaria vaccine, or outright malaria eradication, in Sub-Saharan mosquito populations. Furthermore, CRISPR application has been identified as a tool to correct the genetic mutation that causes sickle-cell anemia, for which eight out of ten cases occur in sub-Saharan Africa.[82]

Africans are drastically underrepresented in the data that fuels genomics research and is used for precision medicine. This medical model provides individual patient treatment based on genetics, environment, and lifestyle.[83] The mission of Nigerian company 54Gene is to close that data gap by building a biobank through global partnerships with public and private institutions and glean insights that positively impact the future accessibility and equity of precision medicine.[84] Similarly, Kenya-based IndyGenUS uses partnerships to build a blockchain-enabled indigenous and diasporic genomics database for disease and drug research use.[85] These examples demonstrate that major investment in African biotechnology initiatives can lead to discoveries that drastically reduce the burden of diseases and improve lives on both the continent and globally.

10.3.5 Agile Governance and Policy: The Experience of Rwanda

Agile governance is integral to the optimization of life-saving technologies for improved health outcomes. In 2016, Rwanda faced a major barrier to reducing maternal mortality: rural hospitals had poor access to cold chain blood supply.[86] Capitalizing on drone technology, the

---

[78] World Bank (2021); Ikegbune (2021)   [79] Bitok (2016)
[80] According to the WHO, 94 percent of 2019 malaria cases occurred in Africa (World Health Organization 2020c)
[81] Diabaté (2021)   [82] Ogaugwu, Agbo, and Adekoya (2019)
[83] World Economic Forum (2019)   [84] Jackson (2020b)
[85] IndyGeneUS AI (2021)   [86] Russo and Wolf (2019)

government worked with Zipline, then a US startup, to implement a
blood delivery program that has since scaled across Rwanda and into
Ghana, Nigeria, and other areas. Rwanda's approach to drone regulation provides a rich case study of the benefits of agile frameworks
through mechanisms such as regulatory sandboxes, stakeholder engagement, and cross-sectoral partnerships.

Approaching the project holistically, Rwanda's Ministry of Health
created the Drone Advisory Council, a task force that included repre-
sentatives from the ICT, agriculture, and transportation ministries,
among others. Zipline forged partnerships with local and global institutions, such as Rwanda's Civil Aviation Authority and the World
Economic Forum, fostering knowledge sharing, mutual understanding,
and training opportunities.[87] Both Rwanda and Zipline prioritized
continuous stakeholder engagement in capacity building and market
research, approaching the project from a health care delivery perspective, rather than the common association of drones as a military or
surveillance tool.[88] Instead of spending years building a complex and
comprehensive air traffic control system before launching the program,
Rwanda used a regulatory sandbox to test a basic, functional, and
flexible framework. Regulations were built on a mission-based use of
airspace, with scalability in mind, requiring operators to prove they
meet safety and quality-control standards before receiving clearance to
fly.[89]

The program was successful and scaled nationally, and today
Zipline's drones provide the majority of blood supply outside of
Rwanda's capital city. They are delivering life-saving medical supplies,
including COVID-19 vaccines, in several countries, reaching a population of 25 million, with a plan to serve 40 million people by the end of
2021.[90] Other African countries have replicated Rwanda's use of
drones: Ghana and Nigeria have contracts with Zipline. Notably,
Zipline's CEO says the business model is proving to be self-sustaining,
attracting investors, and accelerating expansion.[91]

Despite some efforts, such as those of Rwanda explained here,
African governments and regional institutions continue to face similar
challenges, such as those discussed in WEF's Insight report: "workforce," "regulation," "ethics, equity, and social considerations,"

[87] World Economic Forum (2018)   [88] World Economic Forum (2018)
[89] World Economic Forum (2018)   [90] Duffy (2021)   [91] Duffy (2021)

"norms, standards, responsible conduct," "data ownership, privacy, and sharing," "biosecurity and biosafety," and "cybersecurity."[92] It is critical for such governments and regional institutions to adopt a broader and cohesive digital and 4IR strategy that confronts the barriers to scale both nationally and regionally, such as poor infrastructure (internet connection and electricity), financial access, technology adoption, and regulation of the broader business environment. The following section discusses more comprehensive strategies and recommendations to address those challenges and capitalize on the 4IR in health care.

10.4 Strategy for Effective Health Care in Africa with the 4IR

Given these challenges, African governments should capitalize on the 4IR in the health care sector and facilitate the development and adoption of disruptive and scalable innovations capable of addressing the obstacles discussed above – leading to better health service delivery more broadly. This section discusses some of the strategies necessary for bridging the gap between the promise and delivery in Africa's health care during the 4IR. Although several countries are making progress in specific areas, an intentional, coordinated, and systematic approach or strategy to the entire health care system, combining vertical and horizontal approaches would greatly multiply the benefits of the 4IR. Even as 4IR technologies are increasingly adopted, they are not sufficiently scaled across the continent. For the continent to reap the full benefits, additional investment will be needed in the most effective innovations, as well as Africa's human capital and infrastructure. One opportunity that may benefit Africa in the coming years is the $400 million health care fund established by Quantum Global Group to invest in private medical centers, pharmaceuticals, biotechnology, medical equipment, and medical support services across the continent. Over forty African e-health startups received funding in 2020, compared to seven in 2015.[93]

Commission a national 4IR or Digital Health Strategy task force that will develop (and help successfully implement) vertical and horizontal strategies

---

[92] World Economic Forum (2019)   [93] Disrupt Africa (2020)

and mechanisms adapted to local and national contexts while benefiting from international innovations and experiences to deliver on health care promises

A dedicated section of the national government should focus directly on improving country readiness and proactivity for implementing 4IR technologies in the health sector, including timely adoption of the most effective tools during crises such as COVID-19. A task force could build on multi-stakeholder collaboration (public and private sectors, academia, civil society, etc.) and agile governance (including flexibility, rapidity, adaptability, inclusiveness). To face the complexity of disruptive challenges such as COVID-19, simplify emergency regulatory processes, and capitalize on the strengths of key actors that could react quickly and with agility, innovate, and test and implement timely, effective options, whether originating from local, national, continental, or global spheres.

Regulatory issues such as data privacy, cybersecurity, unregulated airspace (drones), and health system integration and interoperability will need to be evaluated, as will workforce capacity, emergency response systems, and budget constraints so that the overall strategy is adapted to the local reality. Such an approach will help policymakers better bridge the gap between the promise and delivery. The task force will need to identify gaps in digital infrastructure and health care delivery, and opportunities to partner with international organizations and the private sector for financing and scaling.[94] Most importantly, it will need to design a sustainable digital health strategy framework with a roadmap outlining timelines and goals, including monitoring mechanisms. There should be dedicated government officials engaging with the private sector throughout the process. As well as official liaisons to work with lawmakers on potential policy initiatives that attract local and regional tech entrepreneurs and innovators, educate and retain health professionals (reverse brain drain), and provide an incentive for foreign investors.[95]

Engage in "public-private-philanthropic partnerships" (4P) to foster risk pooling and increase access to capital for smaller, local health organizations and innovators

[94] Knapp, Richardson and Viranna (2010)
[95] Stroetmann (2018, pp. 19 and 27); Akileswaran and Hutchinson (2019, pp. 42–43)

Several African countries are beginning to offer incentives for private investment in health, as well as vital sectors that bolster the health system, such as infrastructure and education.[96] While ministries of health are likely to maintain their central role in managing and coordinating health policy, the need for funding signals an opportunity for private industry to use its expertise to assist African governments in areas such as facilities, logistics, and distribution and production of pharmaceutical products. That way, prioritized programs can best reach target populations, especially in rural and remote locations.[97] From a risk management perspective, public–private coordination through government national payment schemes or commercial insurance can foster higher-quality health care and better organization among private health actors.

Investments are critical to the emergence and scaling up of disruptive innovations. Support of public initiatives as local businesses often have a wealth of knowledge about specific patients, public, or private needs and demands, as well as existing recognition and development opportunities, but tend to lack technical capacity and capital.[98] Some health-industry companies in Africa have already used this strategy. For example, in Nigeria and Kenya, GSK works with pharmaceutical production and packaging companies to offer products that range in size and price to be competitive in a wide variety of markets. In partnership with the Africa CDC, the Mastercard Foundation committed over 1 billion dollars toward initiatives including the development of the vaccine manufacturing sector as well as human capital.[99] Along with Zain Verjee Group and NAMU Communications, both organizations launched the COVIDHQ digital platform, attracting users through storytelling while also serving as a COVID-19 public health resource with accurate information and data from the WHO and Africa CDC.[100]

Most of the 4IR innovations addressing Africa's health care challenges are driven by SMEs, if not individual entrepreneurs, and are often not scaled enough, suggesting the need for improved access to capital for small entrepreneurs and businesses in sub-Saharan Africa that are often unable to innovate and scale due to limited financing

[96] Bastos de Morais (2017)
  Breedon and Brufal (2016)   [97] Kaseje (2006, pp. 10–11)
[98] Breedon and Brufal (2016)   [99] Mastercard Foundation (2021a)
[100] Mastercard Foundation (2021b)

opportunities. Governments can support this effort by providing local banks with more information on the risks involved with the health sector or by developing equity-based financing mechanisms for health care SMEs.[101]

Capitalize on e-learning strategies to train both clinical and managerial medical personnel and prepare them to properly use more complex technologies

E-learning strategies for medical personnel foster collaboration across the world. In this way, improving physical and digital infrastructure will allow Africa to confront another major challenge accompanying the eHealth transition: the shortage of medical personnel and skilled health care workers. There is an urgent need to increase access to medical education to grow the health care workforce.

Many of the existing eLearning programs serve existing networks of community health workers, a crucial part of health systems. As of February 2021, Amref Health Africa had used its mobile learning platform to deliver free COVID-19 training to 60,000 community health workers in forty-seven Kenyan counties.[102] Early in the pandemic, UNICEF's Somalia nutrition and health sections generated learning materials in less than a week and leveraged their existing networks to deliver COVID-19 training webinars to hundreds of Somalia's community health workers.[103] Nigeria's health ministry trained thousands of its program managers on COVID-19 using e-learning, reducing costs by over 80 percent and equipping them to transfer knowledge to health workers they manage.[104] While this training is crucial, especially in the short term, to prevent COVID-19 cases and deaths, more can be done to use e-learning more effectively to grow the workforce beyond the community level, particularly skilled health professionals.

While there is enormous potential for success, e-learning medical education programs in sub-Saharan Africa have repeatedly failed to move beyond the pilot stage due to scope, scalability, and structural flaws. Furthermore, academia has not produced a widely accepted framework for evaluating the effectiveness of medical e-learning programs in low-to-middle income countries. Most publications attempting to evaluate

---

[101] International Finance Corporation (2008, p. 33)
[102] Amref Health Africa (2021)   [103] UNICEF (2020)
[104] Dele-Olowu et al. (2020)

effectiveness conclude with mixed or unclear results, leaving e-learning advocates without the scientific body of knowledge they need to incentivize investment in new programs.[105] To achieve an optimal outcome, experts must play a role in developing the pedagogy to adopt a digital training strategy rooted in local universities and driven by national governments.

Furthermore, health care providers may find ICT solutions overly expensive or complicated or may have liability concerns regarding the use of new technologies. As eHealth systems are implemented, and the sector becomes more reliant on technology, existing workers must be equipped with e-learning platforms to improve their digital competencies.[106] A Finnish study on Tanzanian private sector urban health care workers, published in the *Journal of Health Informatics in Developing Countries*, found that although many workers lacked the necessary level of digital literacy to successfully transition to an eHealth system, most personnel had positive attitudes toward job training for eHealth technologies.[107] Therefore, the public and private sectors should seize this opportunity to increase the e-learning offering for the medical personnel, whether for clinical, managerial, and digital training or to prepare them to properly use technologies for remote health care delivery, among others. Special attention should be paid to rural health care workers, who are likely to be less digitally literate and perhaps even less comfortable with the concept of e-learning.

Leverage technological platforms and networks to face the shortage of human capital through a "digital brain gain" from the diaspora and friends of Africa

To address brain drain in the health sector, African countries could develop a more effective digital strategy to use their large medical diaspora better. About one-fifth of all African-born physicians practice outside of Africa in developed countries.[108] In numerous advanced economies such as the United States, the United Kingdom, and Canada, the African medical diaspora (Nigeria, Egypt, Sudan, Cameroon, etc.) is already organized, including with the goal of supporting their home countries through health care services and training, including distance learning, but remains under-utilized.[109]

---

[105] Barteit et al. (2019)   [106] Stroetmann (2018, p. 16)
[107] Laitinen et al. (2019, p. 16)   [108] Duvivier, Burch and Boulet (2017, p. 2)
[109] Frehywot, Park and Infanzon (2019)

Digital innovations could help build communities of knowledge, consisting of professional Africans at home and abroad, as well as provide critical channels through which African professionals abroad can contribute more directly to the growth of the health and science ecosystem in Africa. These interdisciplinary knowledge communities can span multiple countries and regions, thereby contributing more effectively to regional integration and building knowledge-based economies in Africa. This is, for example, the case of Nexakili, a network of African and African diaspora health professionals, scientists, and engineers, which aims to promote the global collaboration of African professionals and the transfer of knowledge to Africa; promote the circulation of scientific and medical knowledge in Africa; take advantage of the latest digital and technological innovations to develop innovative algorithms that mobilize the collective intelligence of medical and scientific experts; and to accelerate the availability of innovative medicine in Africa. Governments and the private sector should scale up such types of initiatives, including in the case of epidemics and pandemics such as COVID-19.

10.4.1 Leverage Fintech and Digital Health Innovations to Improve Financial Access to Care and so Achieve Universal Health Coverage

Out-of-pocket expenditures represent about 36 percent of Africa's health care spending, putting a considerable burden on the people living below the poverty line.[110] One study found that as many as 38 percent of low-income Kenyan households will delay or refuse health care treatments due to the unbearable cost.[111] Innovations to increase financial access are critical for improving health care access and coverage, especially for those working in the informal economy and often not participating in the formal banking system. Some of the most prominent solutions could facilitate savings for health, contribute to voluntary pooling of resources or insurance, or in some cases facilitate participation in the broader mandatory universal health coverage. Health-specific mobile or online payment platforms can encourage patients and caretakers to save up for health care expenses. For example, M-TIBA in Kenya[112] is a mobile health payment platform that enables its members to save money for

---

[110] UNECA, GBCHealth, and Aliko Dangote Foundation (2019)
[111] Ogbuoji et al. (2019)   [112] Seo (2019)

health care or collect it from others, constituting a medical savings account. People can contribute money for their children, siblings, or extended family members without handling cash or having formal bank operations. Funds can also be deposited from abroad, facilitating the mobilization of remittances for health purposes. M-TIBA has over 4 million users, more than 1,200 active providers, and has handled 1.5 million transactions.[113]

Other solutions involving the pooling of funds include mobile or online platforms offering voluntary insurance packages to households. For example, Jamii[114] is a human-centered innovation offering mobile micro-health insurance products, especially for the informal sector in Tanzania. Mobile health-saving and mobile or online micro-health insurance are not mutually exclusive. Still, they are both limited as not mandatory and universal, resulting in a significant number of people without coverage. Digital technologies provide sufficient innovations to facilitate the achievement of universal health coverage, from patient identification and public health data management to the facilitation of targeted interventions, effective health service delivery, quick reimbursement, and evaluation of the patient's experience.

10.4.2 Engage Local Communities and "Community Health Care Leaders" to Accelerate 4IR Technology Adoption, Usage, and Efficiency

One of the primary criticisms of previous health interventions in Africa is the failure to incorporate local communities in the processes of implementation, monitoring, and evaluation. The success and sustainability of all health programs are intrinsically tied to local ownership, such as through local volunteers and community health workers but also through specialized training to build the supply of medical staff at the local level.[115] Pharmaceutical companies, for example, can work to overcome the deficiency of skilled and educated workers in Africa by building in-house, mobile, and online training capabilities.

For example, in Uganda, Kenya, and Zambia, Living Goods is a network of health entrepreneurs that leverage social capital from their local communities. Through the help of local female leaders, Living Goods facilitates the provision of collateral and technical training on

---

[113] Seo (2019)   [114] Jamii Africa (2017)   [115] Kaseje (2006, p. 11)

health and business to develop local product distribution chains and channels for knowledge sharing. Over time, this work has reached approximately 5 million people. An evaluation of the program found that its community relationship-building approach was associated with a 27 percent decrease in child mortality in the regions of interest.[116] Living Goods demonstrates how micro-engagement through training and dissemination of information to local people and communities can greatly affect health outcomes, access, and innovation across Africa. Such initiatives could be supported and replicated across the continent.

Moreover, trust and uptake of health programs, especially in remote villages, are often dependent on the incorporation of "community health care leaders," who are integral to many African cultures in various ways. Since these community health care leaders are often more available in rural areas than most health care professionals, policymakers should encourage capacity building, possibly through e-learning, if available. That way, they could be tapped for non-vital, preventative procedures in areas where there is a shortage of doctors,[117] provided that they receive the appropriate training and resources, and would immediately refer to the closest doctor when the situation imposes. This strategy could also result in better regulation of community health care leader activities, helping to distinguish between the accredited or recognized community health care leaders that could serve as health auxiliaries while ending unauthorized local practices. For example, the engagement of "community health care leaders" for preventive procedures has proven highly effective in combatting Uganda's HIV/AIDS epidemic in Uganda. Where trained "community health care leaders" proved willing to translate and implement national-level health policies in ways that included local beliefs and practices. Similarly, the Bajenu Gox Initiative in Senegal has contributed to maternal and child health by creating community support for women, training women to be leaders in reproductive health, and providing advice from the prenatal period until the children reach the age of five.[118] Ethiopia has recruited a "health army" network of community leaders and respected mothers trained with basic information to improve maternal and child health.[119]

---

[116] McHugh (2017)
[117] Chatora (2003); Kasilo (2003); Kaseje (2006, pp. 10–11) [118] IDRC (2022)
[119] VOA (2011)

10.4.3 Invest in Health Facility Electrification, Developing Digital Infrastructure, and Universal Access to Broadband Internet

For any of the above strategies to be successful, bottlenecks to the 4IR must be addressed by encouraging substantial investments in electrification, digital infrastructure, and universal access to broadband internet, as well as a systematic and synergistic integration of digital technologies across actors and sectors beyond health (as they are mutually reinforcing).

To take advantage of the many health care solutions the 4IR offers, national governments must capitalize on existing multilateral initiatives and public–private partnerships to accelerate powering health facilities with reliable energy. In many cases, off-grid, renewable energy resources are being used to provide power to the three-fifths of sub-Saharan health care facilities that currently lack reliable access to electricity.[120]

Since nearly all 4IR technologies rely on internet access, investment in the development of physical and digital infrastructure and universal and affordable access to broadband internet is critical for the broader adoption of 4IR for health care in Africa. Indeed, in Africa, although the number of broadband connections exceeded 400 million in 2018, the average broadband penetration was only about 25 percent.[121] Internet penetration varies wildly among countries – from (as of 2017) 4 percent of the population in the CAR, 6 percent in Chad, and 8 percent in South Sudan to 56 percent in South Africa, and (as of 2019) 59 percent in the Seychelles, 59 percent in Mauritius, 67 percent in Tunisia, and 74 percent in Morocco.[122] The Broadband Commission Working Group on Broadband for All published a report estimating that to achieve affordable and universal broadband in Africa by 2030,[123] investments of $100 billion are required. Such investments will help achieve affordable and

---

[120] Sustainable Energy for All (2021)

[121] Broadband Commission Working Group on Broadband for All (2019)

[122] World Bank (2017–2018). In sub-Saharan Africa, approximately 25 percent of individuals used Internet in 2017.

[123] About 80 percent of the investments are related to infrastructure (about 250,000 new 4G base stations and at least 250,000 kilometers of fiber, Wi-Fi based solutions for remote rural areas, etc.), about 20 percent related to building skills and local content, and 2–4 percent for policy framework.

universal broadband in Africa by 2030, connecting an additional 1.1 billion people.

Closing the current internet gap will empower Africa to find sustainable 4IR solutions to its health care (and other) challenges,[124] fostering engagements among governments, the private sector, civil society, and individual citizens. Once connected, existing technologies can be implemented to address the lack of access to health care providers, limited preparedness for emergency health situations, and insufficient medical equipment and supplies, among others.

Additional challenges may result from patient's apprehensiveness to use ICT-enabled health care platforms. Most ICT platforms, particularly those that improve the provision of information, still require patients to engage with the technology proactively, but many patients are unfamiliar, distrustful, or untrained. Civil society groups with the appropriate resources can position themselves to help ease the digital transition through localized support and training. Without investment in digital infrastructure, the Fourth Industrial Revolution may be limited in ushering in more efficient, effective health care.

10.5 Final Considerations: Reinforcing Preparedness and Capacity Building for Effective Health Care Delivery in the Fourth Industrial Revolution Context

In the aftermath of the Ebola crisis and in the midst of the COVID-19 pandemic, African countries must integrate digital health into their preparedness strategy while prioritizing investments in local scientific and medical research, technological innovation, and regional collaboration. COVID-19 has shown Africa's overreliance on external scientific production and medical equipment, and pharmaceutical products. Although international cooperation is extremely important, the persistence of low local capacity highlights its limits. Therefore, African leaders should act boldly to unlock the local preparedness potential at the continental level with the strengthening of institutions such as the Africa Center for Disease Control,[125] and, most importantly, at the regional, national, and local levels.

---

[124] Broadband Commission Working Group on Broadband for All (2019)

[125] Specialized technical institution of the African Union which aims at creating "a safer, healthier, integrated and prosperous Africa, in which Member States can efficiently prevent disease transmission, implement surveillance and detection,

Health ministries can use a plethora of 4IR tools to stay prepared and to react quickly in an emergency. Disaster-preparedness strategies should incorporate mHealth applications for nationwide alerts and information sharing. The strategic incorporation of these tools requires a focus on local and national needs to build resilience, agile governance, capable administration for quick deployment, and the creation of well-endowed specific emergency funds to support preparedness and response operations. Perhaps most importantly, African countries should incorporate an interoperable health information system across public and private health facilities that use digital health apps and big data analytics for routine data collection. These 4IR technologies provide the resources for efficient disease reporting and data analysis, which would help increase accuracy and strengthen decision-making, especially in times of crisis. For example, in 2015 and 2016, Sierra Leone built its Electronic Integrated Disease Surveillance and Response (eIDSR) application in under a year. Over 95 percent of health facilities participated in weekly reporting after the implementation, instead of about a third of facilities when reporting was paper-based.[126]

Additionally, blockchain for personal medical records would protect a patient's information while still providing accessibility to doctors in any health care facility, provided it is integrated into the national health information systems. This will help facilitate more efficient and effective treatment no matter the patient's location, especially when health systems are overwhelmed during a public health crisis. Furthermore, if medical professionals' licensing were stored on blockchain, the medical workforce would be freer to move across borders if needed during a disaster (assuming license portability). When clinics and hospitals are over capacity and experiencing shortages during a public health crisis, the government should have an existing implementation strategy that utilizes drones and 3D printing for crucial medical supplies. During shortages, they should also focus on building up local medical supply and pharmaceutical manufacturing that can scale up and distribute across the continent. The African Continental Free Trade Area (AfCFTA) will make this easier by removing tariffs on intra-African trade, which is expected to increase by 52.3 percent once

and always be prepared to respond effectively to health threats and outbreaks."
Africa CDC (2022)
[126] Stroetmann (2018, p. 11)

the AfCFTA goes into effect.[127] The AfCFTA will empower local SMEs to grow their businesses as supply chains develop and infrastructure improves.

Africa's health challenges require a coordinated approach by policy-makers, business leaders, international institutional investors, philanthropists, local actors, and civil society. The strategies discussed in this chapter will be necessary to create a sustainable health care system with the capacity to handle both long-term illnesses and short-term disease outbreaks. An increase in technology available on the continent will only facilitate the expansion of health solutions to rural communities and regions still facing infrastructure challenges. Each stakeholder in the sector must tackle the technology, policy, institutional, and investment challenges that remain to create a sustainable health sector that can facilitate economic growth, encourage innovation, and contribute to Africa's achievement of the Sustainable Development Goals and the African Union's Agenda 2063.

[127] UNECA (2020); Signé and van der Ven (2019)

11 | *Conclusion*

4IR in Africa: Strategies for a Better Future

The 4IR presents states in Africa and across the world with both intense challenges and immense opportunities. The wide scope and rapid pace of technological growth offer the potential for unprecedented growth and exacerbated inequality, enhanced governance, and increased insecurity. Artificial Intelligence, additive manufacturing, the Internet of Things, robotics, blockchain, and other innovations will disrupt global systems of production and modern industry. They likely will have as-yet-unforeseen implications for countries around the world.

Governments, firms, and individuals cannot afford to be passive observers of the next phase of the 4IR: Efforts to shape technological growth to maximize benefits and minimize risks conscientiously will be crucial for success in the 4IR. As discussed in Chapter 2, key themes related to the 4IR include *productivity and sustainability*, which refer to the ability to harness new technologies to increase energy-efficient production and foster sustainability while also augmenting growth; *disruption and structural transformation*, which will make it vital to manage rapid and massive changes to industry by preparing the workforce with new education systems and securing databases across the globe to combat challenges to governance and security; *cooperation and inclusivity*, which refer to ensuring the broad distribution of benefits by fostering diverse input and engagement with technological growth; and, finally, *cybersecurity and integrity*, which will be needed to complement innovation with a strong regulatory framework and encryption technology to ensure consumer protection and a stable transition into the 4IR.

To make the most of the 4IR, African governments must exploit the momentum of innovations already occurring across the continent and remove the barriers to growth and development that remain. They must improve access to new technologies through mechanisms such as trade and FDI, and their country's capacity to use these new technologies through mechanisms such as education, financing, and high-quality regulations. Specifically, Africa should adopt nine strategies to navigate the 4IR:

First, African countries must develop inclusive national and continental strategies to drive and manage the 4IR, soliciting input from diverse stakeholders to accelerate growth that leaves no one behind. Inclusive prosperity requires diverse stakeholders, including firms, government agencies, nonprofits, and individuals of various backgrounds, to check against organizational and group biases.[1] States must adopt proactive strategies to drive and manage the impacts that balance the interests of potential winners and losers. Without preparation, a 4IR led exclusively by tech capitalists and top firms could mean that the benefits of new technologies are narrowly distributed. In contrast, a revolution led by tech skeptics and wary governments could mean heavy-handed regulation that hinders potential growth. A model that includes the voices of diverse special interests, however, might be able to strike a balance between competing interests and reach an optimal outcome. Public–private partnerships that have succeeded in Kenya and Rwanda should not only be replicated elsewhere but enhanced with input from local communities targeted by 4IR development.

Second, national institutions and policies should be created to manage the disruption of the 4IR, encourage innovation, and ensure security. The creation of a department or ministry for ICT and the 4IR can help signal the importance placed by the government on the role of technology and innovation in economic growth and development. These institutions can also help ensure that consumers are protected from practices such as overpricing, poor quality, and privacy violations and can foster a fair and competitive ICT market. Industrial policy should be developed under the specific economic conditions of the country adopting the policy to ensure that firms can learn and adapt in the 4IR.[2] These may include tariffs, subsidies, incentives to businesses, infrastructure investments, and other measures aimed at improving the competitiveness of domestic firms and promoting structural transformation.[3] Additionally, regional organizations should create frameworks to help address youth unemployment challenges

---

[1] Schwab and Davis (2018, pp. 48–50)
[2] Akileswaran and Hutchinson (2019, p. 38)   [3] UNCTAD and UNIDO (2011)

around the continent[4] to help other areas of expansion. In line with successful examples seen in countries such as Mauritius and Rwanda, countries can also establish science parks and technology hubs to encourage innovation. Another successful example is the creation of the Smart Africa Alliance, a collaboration between Smart Africa, the Digital Impact Alliance, and the Kenyan government to create a framework used for developing and achieving a digital economy.[5] With digital innovation comes risk threatening privacy and security worldwide, so domestic policies and international cooperation can play a critical role in creating a more inclusive future.[6] Thus, establishing a data privacy act and a national cybersecurity plan and identifying and addressing regulatory gaps related to new technologies can mitigate some of the risks presented by the 4IR.[7]

Third, governments should steer investment toward high-productivity and labor-intensive industries and inclusive technologies such as blockchain and 3D printing. States will need to take proactive measures to identify and exploit comparative advantages in the new industrial niches presented by the latest technology. The Moroccan government's work to create networks of innovators in key industries, support research in advanced technologies, coordinate the efforts of the public and private sectors in innovation, and provide information for foreign investors can serve as a model for African countries, which are still exploring ways to encourage productive investment in new technologies. Prioritizing the growth of labor-intensive industries is particularly important for ensuring employment among Africa's growing youth population. Another key step will be fostering competition between firms by reducing barriers to entry.

Fourth, CEOs and firms should develop comprehensive corporate 4IR strategies for the sensible and efficient application of 4IR technology. African firms need to think strategically about how the 4IR will impact their business and determine which technologies will drive the most growth in their industry. Though most innovations from the 4IR have a wide scope of applications, not all technologies can be applied to every business and context. African firms such as Jumia have demonstrated how the "creative imitation" model can generate powerful returns by modifying best practices and technology from the Western

---

[4] Pharatlhatlhe and Byiers (2019)   [5] Nyakanini et al. (2020)
[6] WTO (2021)   [7] Dadios et al. (2018)

world to fit the African market. Firms should closely examine how new technologies can shore up key weaknesses in their business models and allow them to fill currently unmet demand in their industry. The most successful firms will carefully analyze how technologies can help them address internal and external challenges to find ways they can both expand profits and achieve transformative results.

Fifth, the private sector should invest with an eye for both scale and impact. Some of the most rewarding gains will lie in industrial sectors with the most transformation and growth potential, including online work, tourism, the creative industries,[8] and banking and finance. The explosion of mobile financial services across the continent provides a concrete example of the potential for investment in technologies tailored to the needs of African consumers and markets. In the future, investments may have high yields in, for example, providing robust ICT services and IoT products to Africa's burgeoning urban population; extending credit access to informal sectors with verifiable, low-risk transactions through blockchain and mobile payment; and spurring innovation in cheap and efficient manufacturing methods that incorporate 3D printing. Many of these 4IR initiatives have already begun to capture the gains that Africa's growing consumer market has to offer, and investors would be wise to take advantage of these opportunities while they remain in their infancy. Supporting recovery programs such as the Global Health Platform sponsored by the World Bank and IFC efforts will also provide investors with the necessary leverage to help with the economic and financial recovery, which is crucial as the private sector navigates the COVID-19 pandemic.[9]

Sixth, governments should continue to invest in ICT and infrastructure development. Internet expansion will be key to long-term innovation and adoption of more advanced technology, from IoT to AI and beyond. Although COVID-19 has delayed investment in numerous countries, it has also presented new opportunities for innovation.[10] While the ICT and mobile sectors have grown in recent years, millions in Africa still lack connectivity. Gaps in internet access slow economic growth; limit Africa's potential to trade and interact with the world; cause inaccurate, biased data collection; and prevent citizens from accessing the full scope of internet services. If African countries want

---

[8] Akileswaran and Hutchinson (2019, p. 43)   [9] World Bank (2021)
[10] Abdella (2020)

to advance technologies such as electricity and broadband, they must better their access to physical and digital infrastructure.[11] On top of efforts to invest in ICTs, commitment to energy and transportation projects will be necessary for African countries to attract greater amounts of venture capital and investment. Completing major projects such as Ethiopia's Grand Renaissance hydroelectric dam, the North-South Rail and Road Corridor in Southern Africa, and South Africa's Jasper Solar Farm will be a key step in signaling Africa's modernization to firms and investors from around the globe.[12] African countries can learn from Morocco, whose robust infrastructure development has succeeded, in part, by incorporating multiple public and private sector partners under regional initiatives. For example, the country's high-speed rail project was built by French engineering company Alstom and received joint funding from France, Kuwait, Saudi Arabia, and Abu Dhabi.[13] African countries can do this by improving their infrastructure and making faster progress by courting regional and international partners, rather than by working alone.

Seventh, intra-regional trade and investment should be expanded. Lowering trade barriers within Africa can spur industrial growth and innovation. It can allow African countries to compete globally with the advanced economies that are currently dominating the 4IR. Some African countries are already benefiting from their participation in trade. Tunisia, for example, has gained technical capacity from facilitating the import and export of high-tech goods. The AfCFTA now represents a key stepping stone toward building a robust, competitive market for goods across Africa. Further cooperation among African states using existing multilateral arrangements such as the African Union and African Development Bank is a vital way for African states to pool their resources efficiently and reduce regional deficits in trade and infrastructure. The East African Northern Corridor Agreement, for example, could be a potential starting point for larger agreements extending into North and sub-Saharan Africa incorporating ICT integration and other infrastructure development.[14] Greater collaboration holds the key to expansion. The African Continental Free Trade Area agreement is an example of the national government taking proactive steps to accelerate development across the continent.[15]

[11] Madden (2020)   [12] Ichikowitz (2017)   [13] Wood (2018)
[14] Meads (2017)   [15] World Bank (2020b)

Eighth, access to education, learning, and skills must be modernized and expanded. Training workers and entrepreneurs with a diverse set of skills are critical in the context of a rapidly changing global economy with quick-paced disruption. The structure of markets in the 4IR will be difficult to predict as systems of production and distribution shift quickly. Key policy areas to target for Africa's digital transformation include bridging the digital divide, supporting local innovation, empowering own-account workers, and harmonizing, implementing, and monitoring digital strategies.[16] Africa's workforce will need to be literate in a range of soft and hard skills to be flexible and dynamic. Fostering productive, inclusive growth in the context of automation will require that workers are complements, not substitutes, with new technology. Education spending and curriculum reform should be prioritized to train workers for high-skill, high-productivity jobs in the 4IR, such as those in STEM fields. African states could benefit greatly from the further development of business schools and technical vocational colleges to support industrial growth and create models of training based on the changing needs of the private sector.[17] Additionally, African countries should explore the use of 4IR technologies to improve learning outcomes through adaptive and collaborative learning platforms, distance learning, increasing the availability of learning materials, and disseminating advanced pedagogies.[18] Tunisia's successful educational reform efforts have demonstrated that countries should not be satisfied with high levels of education spending, literacy, or enrollment. Developing real skills to adapt to 4IR disruption requires that states pay attention to the quality of education and the ability of tertiary school and technical and vocational school graduates to find meaningful employment. On top of these efforts, continued support of mobile banking and financial development will be an important part of expanding educational access since savings are often a critical source for financing education.[19]

Ninth, the capacity of research institutions to participate in research and development (R&D) activities should be increased. R&D investments, including in the public and private sectors and universities, positively affect economic growth by encouraging the development of

[16] AUC/OECD (2021)   [17] Naudé (2017, p. 17)
[18] Akileswaran and Hutchinson (2019, p. 42)
[19] Akileswaran and Hutchinson (2019, p. 17)

new knowledge, techniques, and technologies that improve productivity.[20] In the context of the 4IR, R&D will continue to increase in importance due to the need for countries to adopt new technologies and innovate to compete globally. An increase in R&D will be critical for a continent such as Africa. Currently, South America and Africa are responsible for less than 5 percent of the total global R&D spent while they have more than 20 percent of the world's population.[21] An urgent cry has been called out to African political and research leaders to help streamline research programs since Africa falls short of the 1.7 percent R&D global average, with many African countries only investing 0.42 percent of their total GDP.[22] To improve participation in R&D, governments can provide incentives to research organizations by allowing companies to exploit technology developments arising from government-funded research commercially; building pools of researchers and innovators by providing scholarships and investing in human capital and education; increasing the capacity of research institutions to undertake quality research by providing funding; and encouraging diaspora scientists, engineers, and innovators to return.[23] Innovation is the vital ingredient for economic transformation, so African governments need to learn to digitalize, establish governance structures that support innovation, build local capacity in manufacturing, and increase innovation investments[24] to succeed in the 4IR.

This book contributes directly to policy discussions on the 4IR through the above-proposed strategies. However, it also makes a broader contribution to the academic discourse on Africa and innovation in three ways. First, the book provides a comprehensive discussion of the potential impact of the 4IR in Africa in five domains: economic growth and structural transformation; labor, skills, and production; poverty and inequality; power and governance; and peace and security. It explores the trends, transformations, implications, and opportunities of the 4IR in the primary, secondary, and tertiary sectors. This academic analysis can be seen as an extension of works analyzing the effects of major disruptions – technological or otherwise – on countries' functioning and their populations. Second, the book takes an in-depth look at critical topics such as the importance of cybersecurity for Africa's developing nations but also the importance

---

[20] Yazgan and Yalcinkaya (2018, p. 3)   [21] Heney (2020)
[22] The Conversation (2021)   [23] Dadios et al. (2018)   [24] Yawson (2021)

of healthcare and technological innovations during the 4IR, expanding upon literature that generally focuses primarily on developed countries. Third, by analyzing a diverse range of Africa's leading and emerging innovators, with a focus on explaining why some countries are outperforming others, and how to bridge the gap between the outperformers and other countries, the book provides a framework for further analysis of the evolution, strengths, and weaknesses of developing and developed countries in the context of the 4IR.

To make the most out of the 4IR, it will be incumbent upon African governments and entrepreneurs to recognize new niches for industry and leverage uniquely African advantages to achieve sustainable, inclusive growth. It will be difficult to avoid asymmetric growth between Africa and the rest of the world, especially due to considerable gaps in infrastructure and R&D output. However, that does not mean that Africa should sit on the sidelines during a global period of structural transformation: Conscientious efforts by African stakeholders to engage and grapple with new technology can push the continent in the right direction.

The 4IR will be a global reality that impacts states and industries across the globe, whether they choose to be active players in technology or not. The future of Africa will depend on whether its governments and industries can seize the windows of opportunity offered by the 4IR while balancing against new threats to growth.

References

Abdella, Amrote. 2020. "How Investing in Digital Infrastructure Can Make the Difference to Africa's Economic Recovery." *Microsoft News Center.* https://news.microsoft.com/en-xm/2020/09/02/how-investing-in-digital-infrastructure-can-make-the-difference-to-africas-economic-recovery/

Abjiou, Ali. 2018. "Technologie: Le Maroc, un champion régional." *L'Economiste.* www.leconomiste.com/article/1028598-technologie-le-maroc-un-champion-regional

Abusalem, Khaled, Mansour Alsaleh, Timothy Reuter, and Talal Alsedairy. 2021. "Why the Future Is Bright for Drone Technology." *World Economic Forum.* https://www.weforum.org/agenda/2021/07/the-bright-future-for-drones/

Access to Medicine Foundation. 2016. *Access to Medicine Index 2016.* https://accesstomedicineindex.org/media/atmi/Access-to-Medicine-Index-2016.pdf

Ackerman, Evan, and Michael Koziol. 2019. "The Blood Is Here: Zipline's Medical Delivery Drones Are Changing the Game in Rwanda." *IEEE Spectrum* 56(5): 24–31.

ACT-IAC Emerging Technology COI and Management Concepts. 2021. "RPA in Federal Agencies: How Federal Agencies Achieve More through Robotic Process Automation." https://www.actiac.org/documents/rpa-federal-agencies-how-federal-agencies-achieve-more-through-robotic-process-automation

Adegoke, Y. 2018. "Africa's Startup Funding Deals Are Entering the Million-Dollar Era." *Quartz.* https://qz.com/africa/1264614/africas-venture-capital-deals-are-entering-the-1-million-era/

Adepetun, Adeyemi. 2020. "Policies Shaping Telecoms Sector's Growth, Contributions." *The Guardian Nigeria.* https://guardian.ng/technology/policies-shaping-telecoms-sectors-growth-contributions/

Adepoju, Paul. 2017. "This Nigerian AI Health Startup Wants to Save Thousands of Babies' Lives with a Simple App." *Quartz.* https://qz.com/africa/1158185/nigerian-ai-health-startup-ubenwa-hopes-to-save-thousands-of-babies-lives-every-year/

Adhikari, Ratnakar. 2019. "Six Ways the Least Developed Countries Can Participate in the Fourth Industrial Revolution." https://trade4devnews .enhancedif.org/en/op-ed/6-ways-least-developed-countries-can-par ticipate-fourth-industrial-revolution

Adhikari, Ratnakar, and Fabrice Lehmann. 2020. "Least Developed Countries Can Become Authors of Their Technological Revolution." *OECD Development Matters.* https://oecd-development-matters.org/ 2020/02/05/least-developed-countries-can-become-authors-of-their-technological-revolution/

Adhikari, Samik, Michael Clemens, Helen Dempster, and Linda Ekeator Nkechi. 2021. "A Global Skill Partnership in Information, Communications, and Technology (ICT) between Nigeria and Europe." *Center for Global Development.* https://www.cgdev.org/sites/default/files/Global-Ski ll-Partnership-ICT-Nigeria-Europe.pdf

AfDB. 2016. *Africa Tourism Monitor: Sustainable Tourism through Innovation, Entrepreneurship, and Technology.* https://www.afdb.org/ fileadmin/uploads/afdb/Documents/Publications/Africa_Tourism_ Monitor_2016.pdf

2018. *African Economic Outlook 2018.* www.afdb.org/fileadmin/ uploads/afdb/Documents/Publications/African_Economic_Outlook_ 2018_-_EN.pdf

2021a. "Strengthening Food Systems Must Be at the Centre of Africa's COVID-19 Recovery, Says African Bank Group." https://www.afdb .org/en/news-and-events/strengthening-food-systems-must-be-centre-africas-covid-19-recovery-says-african-development-bank-42642

2021b. "The African Development Bank Extends a Grant of $2 Million to Strengthen Cybersecurity and Boost Financial Inclusion in Africa." https://www.afdb.org/en/news-and-events/press-releases/african-development-bank-extends-grant-2-million-strengthen-cybersecur ity-and-boost-financial-inclusion-africa-42526

AfDB, ADB, EBRD, and IDB. 2018. *The Future of Work: Regional Perspectives.* Washington, DC.

AfDB, OECD, and UNDP. 2017. *African Economic Outlook 2017.* www .africa.undp.org/content/rba/en/home/library/reports/african-eco nomic-outlook-2017.html

Affectiva. 2016. "Emotion AI Leader Affectiva Announces $14 Million in Growth Capital." https://www.affectiva.com/news-item/emotion-ai-leader-affectiva-announces-14-million-in-growth-capital/

AFP. 2013. "Cameroon Former Health Minister Gets 20 Years for Graft." *FoxNews.com.* www.foxnews.com/world/cameroon-former-health-minister-gets-20-years-for-graft

Africa Business. 2018. "Improving Conditions for Investing in the Information Technology Sector in Egypt." http://africabusiness.com/2018/09/19/egypt-it-sector/

Africa CDC. 2021a. "African Union and Africa CDC Launches Partnerships for African Vaccine Manufacturing (PAVM), Framework to Achieve It and Signs 2 MoUs." *African Union and Africa CDC.* https://africacdc.org/news-item/african-union-and-africa-cdc-launches-partnerships-for-african-vaccine-manufacturing-pavm-framework-to-achieve-it-and-signs-2-mous/

2021b. "Our Vision." *African Union and Africa CDC.* https://africacdc.org/about-us/vision/

Africa News. 2017. "Africa Gradually Embracing Tech to Promote Good Governance." *Africa News.* https://www.africanews.com/2017/10/25/africa-gradually-embracing-tech-to-promote-good-governance-hi-tech//

African Development Bank. 2013. *Health in Africa over the Next 50 Years.* Abidjan: African Development Bank.

African News Agency. 2020. "Focus on Good Practice: The Digital Transformation Center of Tunisia." https://www.africanewsagency.fr/focus-sur-une-good-practice-le-centre-de-transformation-digitale-de-tunisie/?lang=en

African Union and Africa CDC. 2021, March 26. "Africa's Telecom and Technology Industry Leads the Charge against COVID-19 by Backing AU Covid-Tech & Vaccine Passport System." https://africacdc.org/news-item/africas-telecom-and-technology-industry-leads-the-charge-against-covid-19-by-backing-au-covid-tech-vaccine-passport-system/

Afshar, Vala. 2017. "Cisco: Enterprises Are Leading the Internet of Things Innovation." *Huffington Post.* www.huffingtonpost.com/entry/cisco-enterprises-are-leading-the-internet-of-things_us_59a41fcee4b0a62d0987b0c6

Agarwal, Dimple, Josh Bersin, Gaurav Lahiri, Jeff Schwartz, and Erica Volini. 2018. "AI, Robotics, and Automation: Putting Humans in the Loop." *Deloitte 2018 Global Human Capital Trends.* www2.deloitte.com/insights/us/en/focus/human-capital-trends/2018/ai-robotics-intelligent-machines.html

Agence Française de Développement. 2019. "By 2050, More than Half of Africa's Population Will Be under 25 Years Old." *République Française.* https://www.afd.fr/en/actualites/2050-more-half-africas-population-will-be-under-25-years-old

Aglionby, John. 2018. "Africa's Banks Lag behind on Innovation in Financial Services." *Financial Times.* https://www.ft.com/content/68788cbc-221f-11e8-9a70-08f715791301

Agostinelli, Simone, Andrea Marrella, and Massimo Mecella. 2020. "Towards Intelligent Robotic Process Automation for BPMers." https://www.researchgate.net/publication/338401505_Towards_Intelligent_Robotic_Process_Automation_for_BPMers

Agyenim-Boateng, Yaw, Richard Benson-Armer, and Bill Russo. 2015. "Winning in Africa's Consumer Market." *McKinsey & Company*. https://www.mckinsey.com/industries/consumer-packaged-goods/our-insights/winning-in-africas-consumer-market

Akileswaran, Kartik, and Georgina Hutchinson. 2019. "Adapting to the 4IR: Africa's Development in the Age of Automation." *Tony Blair Institute for Global Change*. https://institute.global/advisory/adapting-4ir-africas-development-age-automation

Akinwande, Victor. 2018. "Artificial Intelligence in Healthcare: Where Does Africa Lie?" *Techpoint Africa*. https://techpoint.africa/2018/03/26/artificial-intelligence-healthcare-africa/

Akuta, Eric, Isaac Ong'oa, and Chanika Jones. 2011. "Combating Cyber Crime in Sub-Saharan Africa: A Discourse on Law, Policy, and Practice." *Journal of Peace, Gender, and Development Studies* 1(4): 129–137.

Alaa El-Din, Mohamed. 2021. "Egypt Builds Strong AI Industry to Serve Development Goals: Official." https://dailynewsegypt.com/2021/05/31/egypt-builds-strong-ai-industry-to-serve-development-goals-official/

Alesina, Alberto, and Roberto Perotti. 1996. "Income Distribution, Political Instability, and Investment." *European Economic Review* 40(6): 1203–1228.

Alfa Shaban, Abdur Rahman. 2020. "Ex-DRC Health Minister Jailed for Stealing Ebola Funds." *Africanews*. www.africanews.com/2020/03/24/ex-drc-health-minister-jailed-for-stealing-ebola-funds/

Allen, Tim, and Susette Heald. 2004. "HIV/AIDS Policy in Africa: What Has Worked in Uganda and What Has Failed in Botswana?" *Journal of International Development* 16(8): 1141–1154.

Alley, Tahrir. 2017. "Egypt's Start-Up 'Revolution' Is Set to Boost Africa's Tech Landscape." *Quartz Africa*. https://qz.com/africa/1146981/egypts-tahrir-alley-boosts-start-ups-despite-political-instability-and-violence

Alo, Babajide. n.d. "Nanotechnology in a Developing Country – Applications and Challenges." *World Health Organization*. https://www.who.int/ifcs/documents/forums/forum6/ppt_nano_alo.pdf

Alur, Rajeev. 2015. *Principles of Cyber-Physical Systems*. Cambridge, MA: MIT Press. https://mitpress.mit.edu/books/principles-cyber-physical-systems

Amref Health Africa. 2021 February 9. "Using the Leap mHealth platform Remotely to Train Community Health Volunteers about COVID-19."

https://newsroom.amref.org/innovative-health-services-solutions/2021/
02/using-the-leap-mhealth-platform-remotely-to-train-community-
health-volunteers-about-covid-19/

Andrew, James P., Emily Stover DeRocco, and Andrew Taylor. 2009. *The
Innovation Imperative in Manufacturing: How the United States Can
Restore Its Edge.* Boston: Boston Consulting Group. www.themanufactur
inginstitute.org/~/media/6731673D21A64259B081AC8E083AE091.ashx

Andrianaivo, Mihasonirina, and Kangni Kpodar. 2011. "ICT, Financial
Inclusion, and Growth: Evidence from African Countries." IMF Working
Paper 11/73.

Andriole, J. Stephen. 2019. "Artificial Intelligence, Machine Learning, and
Augmented Analytics [Life in C-Suite]." *IT Professional* 21(6): 56–59.
doi: 10.1109/MITP.2019.2941668

Ane, Tanjea, and Suraiya Yasmin. 2019. "Agriculture in the Fourth Industrial
Revolution." *Annals of Bangladesh Agriculture* 23. doi: 10.3329/aba.
v23i2.50060

Anyango, Anita. 2018. "Construction Industry Goes Robotic." *Construction
Review Online.* https://constructionreviewonline.com/2018/09/construc
tion-industry-goes-robotic/

Arezki, Rabah, Ferid Belhaj, and Parmesh Shah. 2019. *Promoting a New
Economy for the Middle East and North Africa.* Washington, DC:
World Bank Group. http://documents1.worldbank.org/curated/en/
781781561575850158/pdf/Promoting-a-New-Economy-for-the-Middle-
East-and-North-Africa.pdf

Arnold, Craig. 2019. "How to Turn Africa's Manufacturing Sector into a High-
Tech Powerhouse." *World Economic Forum.* https://www.weforum.org/
agenda/2019/08/how-to-turn-africas-manufacturing-sector-into-a-high-
tech-powerhouse/

Asongu, Simplice. 2014. "Software Piracy, Inequality and the Poor: Evidence
from Africa." *Journal of Economic Studies* 41(4): 526–553. doi: 10.1108/
JES-10-2012-0141

Asongu, Simplice, and Jacinta C. Nwachukwu. 2016. "The Role of Governance in
Mobile Phones for Inclusive Human Development in Sub-Saharan Africa."
Working Papers of the African Governance and Development Institute 16/
007. African Governance and Development Institute.

Assegaf, Zaenab, Denys Cherepakha, Aleck Matambo, and Jan Weydringer.
2017. "Africa: Mapping New Opportunities for Sourcing." *McKinsey
& Company.* https://www.mckinsey.com/featured-insights/middle-east-
and-africa/africa-mapping-new-opportunities-for-sourcing

Atieno, Milicent. 2017. "How Technology Can Improve Healthcare in Sub-
Saharan Africa." *Innov8tiv.* https://innov8tiv.com/technology-can-
improve-healthcare-sub-saharan-africa/

Atiku, Sulaiman, and Frank Boateng. 2020. *Rethinking Education System for the Fourth Industrial Revolution*. doi: 10.4018/978-1-5225-9810-7.ch001

Atzori, Luigi, Antonio Iera, and Giacomo Morabito. 2010. "The Internet of Things: A Survey." *Computer Networks* 54(15): 2787–2805.

AUC/OECD. 2021. *Africa's Development Dynamics 2021: Digital Transformation for Quality Jobs*. AUC, Addis Ababa/OECD Publishing, Paris. https://doi.org/10.1787/0a5c9314-en

Aufait Team. 2020. "Digital Competitiveness: Mauritius Loses Ground on African Counterparts." https://aufait.media/2020/09/11/digital-competitiveness-mauritius-loses-ground-on-african-counterparts/

Auty, Richard. 1993. *Sustaining Development in the Mineral Economies: The Resource Curse Thesis*. London: Routledge.

Axxsys. 2018. *The Fourth Industrial Revolution: Impact on Financial Services*. http://axxsysconsulting.com/wp-content/uploads/2018/03/FinTech-White-paper.pdf

Aykut, Dilek, and Monika Blaszkiewicz-Schwartzman. 2018. *Shaping the Future of Africa*. International Finance Corporation. www.ifc.org/wps/wcm/connect/5c9e9f2f-779a-4ab7-beb6-e3aa65b00a85/Africa+CEO+Forum+Report_FIN3_Web-lores.pdf?MOD=AJPERES

Banda, Honoré. 2015. "ICT: Outsourcing in Mauritius Faces New Challenges." *The Africa Report*. www.theafricareport.com/Southern-Africa/outsourcing-in-mauritius-faces-new-challenges.html

Banga, Karishma, and Dirk Willem te Velde. 2018. "Digitalisation and the Future of Manufacturing in Africa." *Supporting Economic Transformation*. https://set.odi.org/wp-content/uploads/2018/03/SET_Digitalisation-and-future-of-African-manufacturing_Final.pdf

Barrow, Keith. 2018. "Construction 4.0: Delivering an Infrastructure Revolution." *International Railway Journal*. www.railjournal.com/in_depth/construction-40-delivering-an-infrastructure-revolution

Barteit, Sandra, Albrecht Jahn, Sekelani Banda, et al. 2019. "E-Learning for Medical Education in Sub-Saharan Africa and Low-Resource Settings: Viewpoint." *Journal of Medical Internet Research* 21(1): e12449.

Bastos de Morais, Jean Claude. 2017. "Digital Technologies Can Deliver Better Healthcare to Sub-Saharan Africa. Here's How." *World Economic Forum*. https://www.weforum.org/agenda/2017/10/digital-paths-for-better-health care-in-sub-saharan-africa/

Batzilis, Dimitrios, Taryn Dinkelman, Emily Oster, Rebecca Thornton, and Deric Zanera. 2010. "New Cellular Networks in Malawi: Correlates of Service Rollout and Network Performance." National Bureau of Economic Research Working Paper No. 16616.

Baumann, Bauke, and Anja Hoffmann. 2020. "Digitalization and the Coronavirus in Morocco: From Care to Control?" https://eu.boell.org/en/2020/04/09/digitalisation-and-coronavirus-morocco-care-control

Bayen, Maxime. 2018a. "1000 Tech Hubs Are Powering Ecosystems in Asia Pacific and Africa." *GSMA*. www.gsma.com/mobilefordevelopment/programme/ecosystem-accelerator/1000-tech-hubs-are-powering-ecosystems-in-asia-pacific-and-africa/

2018b. "A Look at Morocco's Tech Ecosystem and Learnings from the Future. E.S. in Africa Conference." *GSMA*. www.gsma.com/mobilefordevelopment/programme/ecosystem-accelerator/look-moroccos-tech-ecosystem-learnings-futur-e-s-africa-conference/

Brown, Will. 2020. "Rwanda Deploys Robots to Fight COVID-19." *Telegraph*. https://www.telegraph.co.uk/global-health/science-and-disease/rwanda-deploys-robots-fight-covid-19/

BCEAO. 2015. "Instruction N° 009-06-2015 Relative aux dispositifs de Sécurité des systèmes d'information des Bureaux d'Information sur le credit."

Ben-Hassine, Wafa. 2019. "New Technologies for a New Tunisia." *Atlantic Council*. www.atlanticcouncil.org/blogs/menasource/new-technologies-for-a-new-tunisia

Besaw, Clayton, and John Filitz. 2019. "AI & Global Governance: AI in Africa Is a Double-Edged Sword." *Centre for Policy Research at United Nations University*. cpr.unu.edu/ai-in-africa-is-a-double-edged-sword.html

Bhalla, Nita. 2021. "Africa's Farmers Click with Digital Tools to Boost Crops." *Reuters*. https://www.reuters.com/article/africa-tech-farming/feature-africas-farmers-click-with-digital-tools-to-boost-crops-idUSL4N2QU29J

Bhargava, Alok, Dean Jamison, Lawrence Lau, and Christopher Murray. 2001. "Modeling the Effects of Health on Economic Growth." *Journal of Health Economics* 20(3): 423–440.

Bholanauth, Jason. 2021. "What Lies Ahead in Mauritius' Digital Landscape?" https://inboundmauritius.com/blog/what-lies-ahead-in-mauritius-digital-landscape/

Bhorat, Haroon, Ravi Kanbur, Christopher Rooney, and François Steenkamp. 2017. "Sub-Saharan Africa's Manufacturing Sector: Building Complexity." African Development Bank Group Working Paper No. 256.

Bissel, Kelly, Ryan M. Lassale, and Paolo Dal Cin. 2019. "Ninth Annual Cost of Cybercrime Study." *Accenture*. https://www.accenture.com/us-en/insights/security/cost-cybercrime-study

Bitok, Kipchirchir. 2016. "Biotechnology Hubs and Future Incubators in Africa." *Prescouter.* https://www.prescouter.com/2016/08/biotechnol ogy-hubs-future-incubators-africa/

Bloom, David E., and David Canning. 2008. "Population Health and Economic Growth." Commission on Growth and Development Working Paper No. 24.

Bloom, David E., David Canning, Rainer Kotschy, Klaus Prettner, and Johannes Schünemann. 2019. "Health and Economic Growth: Reconciling the Micro and Macro Evidence." National Bureau of Economic Research Working Paper No. 26003.

Bloom, David E., David Canning, and Jaypee Sevilla. 2001. "The Effect of Health on Economic Growth: Theory and Evidence." National Bureau of Economic Research Working Paper No. 8587.

2004. "The Effect of Health on Economic Growth: A Production Function Approach." *World Development* 32(1): 1–13.

Bond, Michael, Heba Maram, Asmaa Soliman, and Riham Khattab. 2012. "Science and Innovation in Egypt." *Royal Society.* https://royalsociety .org/~/media/policy/projects/atlas-islamic-world/atlas-egypt-report.pdf

Borgen Project. 2020. "Maternal Mortality in Sub-Saharan Africa." https:// borgenproject.org/maternal-mortality-in-sub-saharan-africa/

Bornet, Pascal, Ian Barkin, and Jochen Wirtz. 2021. *Intelligent Automation: Welcome to the World of Hyperautomation: Learn How to Harness Artificial Intelligence to Boost Business & Make Our World More Human.* Singapore: World Scientific Publishing. https://EconPapers.repec .org/RePEc:wsi:wsbook:12239

Botes, Anton, Hannah Marais, and Andrew Lane. 2019. "Winning in the African Oil and Gas Industry." *Deloitte.* https://www2.deloitte.com/us/ en/insights/industry/oil-and-gas/africa-oil-gas-industry-energy-reserves .html

Boudway, Ira. 2021. "Medical Drone Startup to Begin Covid Vaccine Delivery in April." *Bloomberg.* www.bloomberg.com/news/articles/2021-02-04/ medical-drone-startup-to-begin-covid-vaccine-delivery-in-april

Boum, Yap, and Yvonne Mburu. 2020. "Burden of Disease in Francophone Africa 1990–2017: The Triple Penalty?" *The Lancet Global Health* 8 (3): E306–E307.

Boumedjout, Hichem. 2010. "Tunisia Launches First Nanotech Project." *SciDevNet.* https://www.scidev.net/global/pollution/news/tunisia-launches-first-nanotech-project.html

Breckenridge, Keith. 2005. "The Biometric State: The Promise and Peril of Digital Government in the New South Africa." *Journal of Southern African Studies* 31(2): 267–282.

Breedon, Robert, and Jonathan Brufal. 2016. "Comment: Investing in Africa's Healthcare Sector." *African Business Magazine*. http:// africanbusinessmagazine.com/sectors/finance/comment-investing-afri cas-healthcare-sector

Breedon, Robert, and Tom Gray. 2016. "Maximizing the Return on Healthcare Investment in Africa." *Lexology*. www.lexology.com/ library/detail.aspx?g=6727424b-f66c-46aa-aa6a-a2b31993c52e

Bremmer, Ian. 2017. "The Wave to Come." *Time*. http://time.com/4775441/ the-wave-to-come

Briggs, Ray, Ed Dobner, Jennifer Dul, Joe Mariani, and Pankaj Kishnani. 2018. "Digital Reality in Government." *Deloitte Insights*. www.deloitte .com/insights/us/en/industry/public-sector/augmented-virtual-reality-government-services.html

Bright, Jake. 2018. With a $10 Million Round, Nigeria's Paga Plans Global Expansion. TechCrunch. https://techcrunch.com/2018/09/06/paga/

Brodsky, Paul. 2021. International Bandwidth Soars to New Heights. TeleGrography. https://blog.telegeography.com/2021-international-bandwidth-trends-demand-global-networks

Broadband Commission Working Group on Broadband for All: A "Digital Infrastructure Mo-onshot" for Africa. 2019. *Connecting Africa through Broadband: A Strategy for Doubling Connectivity by 2021 and Reaching Universal Access by 2030*. www.worldbank.org/en/news/press-release/ 2019/10/17/achieving-broadband-access-for-all-in-africa-comes-with-a-100-billion-price-tag

BroadReach Consulting. 2019. "4IR Technology Holds Key to Better Healthcare in Africa." *BroadReach*. www.broadreachcorporation.com/ 4ir-technology-holds-key-to-better-healthcare-in-africa/

Bryan, Lowell, Michael Conway, Tineke Keesmaat, Sorcha McKenna, and Ben Richardson. 2010. "Strengthening Sub-Saharan Africa's Health Systems: A Practical Approach." *McKinsey & Company*. www .mckinsey.com/industries/healthcare-systems-and-services/our-insights/ strengthening-sub-saharan-africas-health-systems-a-practical-approach

Burpee, Julia. 2015. "Canadian Team Uses 3D Printer to Make Artificial Legs for Ugandans." *CBC News*. www.cbc.ca/news/technology/canadian-team-uses-3d-printer-to-make-artificial-legs-for-ugandans-1.2953620

Burt, Martin. 2016. "The Poverty Stoplight: A New Metric for Microfinance." Dissertation for Tulane University Law School.

Business Chief. 2019. "Digitally Disrupting the Oil and Gas Industry." *The Journal of Petroleum Technology*. https://jpt.spe.org/digitally-disrupt ing-oil-and-gas-industry

Business Software Alliance. 2016. "Seizing Opportunity through License Compliance." https://globalstudy.bsa.org/2016/downloads/studies/BSA_ GSS_US.pdf#page=5

Byanyima, Winnie, and Caroline Kende-Robb. 2021. "Five Ways Women Are Driving Africa's Transformation and Contributing to a Global Reset." *Brookings Institution*. https://www.brookings.edu/blog/africa-in-focus/2021/03/05/5-ways-women-are-driving-africas-transform ation-and-contributing-to-a-global-reset/

Caisse Centrale de Garantie. 2017. "Lancement des principals composantes du 'Fonds Innov Invest.'" www.ccg.ma/fr/espace-media/actualites/lance ment-des-principales-composantes-du-fonds-innov-invest

"Cameroon: According to the CEO of Antic, Cybercrime Has Caused Cameroonian Banks to Lose More Than 3 Billion CFA Francs in 2015." 2016. *Camernews*. http://www.camernews.com/62699-2/

Campbell, Keith. 2015. "South Africa Aiming to Become a Leader in Additive Manufacturing." *Engineering News*. https://www .engineeringnews.co.za/article/south-africa-aiming-to-become-a-leader-in-additive-manufacturing-2015-12-04

Candelon, François, Hind El Bedraoui, and Hamid Maher. 2021. "Developing an Artificial Intelligence for Africa Strategy." *OECD Development Matters*. https://oecd-development-matters.org/2021/02/09/developing-an-artificial-intelligence-for-africa-strategy/#more-14109

Casey, Eoin. 2015. "Morocco Leads the Way in Hi-Tech Financial Services." *European Bank for Reconstruction and Development (EBRD)*. www.ebrd .com/news/2015/morocco-leads-the-way-in-hitech-financial-services.html

Chakchouk, Moez. 2017. "Blockchain in Tunisia: From Experimentations to a Challenging Commercial Launch." ITU Workshop on Security Aspects of Blockchain.

Champlin, Cary, David Bell, and Celina Schocken. 2017. "AI Medicine Comes to Africa's Rural Clinics." *IEEE Spectrum*. https://spectrum .ieee.org/biomedical/devices/ai-medicine-comes-to-africas-rural-clinics

Chan, Rosanna. 2018. "Foresight Africa Viewpoint – Rethinking African Growth and Service Delivery: Technology as a Catalyst." *The Brookings Institution*. www.brookings.edu/blog/africa-in-focus/2018/01/12/foresight-africa-viewpoint-rethinking-african-growth-and-ser vice-delivery-technology-as-a-catalyst/

Chatora, Rufaro. 2003. "An Overview of the Traditional Medicine Situation in the African Region." *African Health Monitor* 4(1): 4–7.

Chen, Guangzhe, Michael Geiger, and Minghui Fu. 2015. *Manufacturing FDI in Sub-Saharan Africa: Trends, Determinants, and Impact*. Washington, DC: World Bank.

Chen, Lincoln, David Evans, Tim Evans, et al. 2006. *Working Together for Health: The World Health Report 2006*. Geneva: World Health Organization.

Chironga, Mutsa, Luis Cunha, Hilary de Grandis, and Mayowa Kuyoro. 2018. "African Retail Banking's Next Growth Frontier." *McKinsey &*

Company. https://www.mckinsey.com/industries/financial-services/our-insights/african-retail-bankings-next-growth-frontier

Chironga, Mutsa, Hilary de Grandis, and Yassir Zouaoui. 2017. "Mobile Financial Services in Africa: Winning the Battle for the Customer." *McKinsey & Company.* https://www.mckinsey.com/industries/finan cial-services/our-insights/mobile-financial-services-in-africa-winning-the-battle-for-the-customer

Chiweche, Manase Kudzai. 2019. "Fourth Industrial Revolution: What's in It for African Women?" South African Institute of International Affairs. https://www.africaportal.org/documents/19280/Chiweshe__Fourth_industrial_revolution.pdf

CIA. 2019. "The World Factbook: South Africa." https://www.cia.gov/library/publications/the-world-factbook/geos/sf.html

CIAT. 2017. "Using Big Data and Machine Learning to Power a Nutrition Early Warning System (NEWS) for Africa." http://blog .ciat.cgiar.org/good-news-for-the-fight-against-malnutrition/

Cilliers, Jakkie. 2018. "Made in Africa: Manufacturing and the Fourth Industrial Revolution." *Institute for Security Studies.* https://issafrica .org/research/africa-report/made-in-africa-manufacturing-and-the-fourth-industrial-revolution

Cirera, Xavier, Filipe Lage, and Leonard Sabetti. 2016. "ICT Use, Innovation, and Productivity: Evidence from Sub-Saharan Africa." World Bank Policy Research Working Paper No. 7868.

Clapper, James. 2016. "Statement for the Record: Worldwide Threat Assessment of the US Intelligence Community." https://arstechnica .com/wp-content/uploads/2016/02/clappertestimony.pdf

Clausen, Lily B. 2015. "Taking on the Challenges of Health Care in Africa." *Stanford Graduate School of Business.* www.gsb.stanford .edu/insights/taking-challenges-health-care-africa

Clemens, Michael A., and Gunilla Pettersson. 2008. "New Data on African Health Professionals Abroad." *Human Resources for Health* 6(1).

Cohen, Boyd. 2014. "The Smartest Cities in the World 2015: Methodology." *Fast Company.* https://www.fastcompany.com/3038818/the-smartest-cities-in-the-world-2015-methodology

Collier, P., and A. Hoeffler. 1998. "On the Economic Causes of Civil War." *Oxford Economic Papers* 50: 563–573.

Collon, Cyril. 2018. "In Another Record-Breaking Year, African Tech Start-Ups Raised US$560 Million in VC Funding in 2017, a 53% YoY Growth." *Partech Africa.* https://cdn-website.partechpartners .com/media/documents/2018.02.19_-_Africa_Tech_Startups_raises_560M_in_2017_FINAL.pdf

Colombo, Armando W., Stamatis Karnouskos, Okyay Kaynak, Yang Shi, and Shen Yin. 2017. "Industrial Cyberphysical Systems: A Backbone of the Fourth Industrial Revolution." *IEEE Industrial Electronics Magazine* 11 (1): 6–16.

Conway, Michael, Tania Holt, Adam Sabow, and Irene Yuan Sun. 2019. "Should Sub-Saharan Africa Make Its Own Drugs?" *McKinsey & Company.* https://www.mckinsey.com/industries/public-sector/our-insights/should-sub-saharan-africa-make-its-own-drugs

Cornell University, INSEAD, and WIPO. 2018. *The Global Innovation Index 2018: Energizing the World with Innovation.* Ithaca, Fontainebleau, and Geneva.

Coulibaly, Brahima. 2017. Africa's Race against the Machines. Project Syndicate. https://www.project-syndicate.org/commentary/automation-africa-industrialization-by-brahima-coulibaly-2017-06

    2018. "Africa's Alternative Path to Development." *The Brookings Institution.* www.brookings.edu/opinions/africas-alternative-path-to-development/

Crandall, Robert W., William Lehr, and Robert Litan. 2007. "The Effects of Broadband Deployment on Output and Employment: A Cross-Sectional Analysis of US Data." *Issues in Economic Policy* 6: 1–34.

Crocker, Chester A. 2019. "African Governance: Challenges and Their Implications." *Hoover Institution.* www.hoover.org/research/african-governance-challenges-and-their-implications

Dadios, Elmer P., Alvin B. Culaba, Jose Ramon G. Albert, et al. 2018. "Preparing the Philippines for the Fourth Industrial Revolution: A Scoping Study." Philippine Institute for Development Studies Discussion Paper No. 2018-11.

Dahshan, Mohamed. 2020. "Fragile States and the Fourth Industrial Revolution." *African Business.* https://african.business/2020/02/economy/fragile-states-and-the-fourth-industrial-revolution/

Dannouni, Amane, Hamid Maher, Jan Gildemeister, et al. 2020. "The Race for Digital Advantage in Africa." BCG. https://www.bcg.com/publications/2020/race-digital-advantage-in-africa

Daramola, Justine Olawande. 2019. "African Countries Should Reconsider How They Use e-Government Platforms." *The Conversation.* https://theconversation.com/african-countries-should-rethink-how-they-use-e-government-platforms-108689

David-West, Olayinka, and Nkemdilim Iheanachor. 2016. "Constraints of the Nigerian Mobile Money Ecosystem." https://www.lbs.edu.ng/lbsinsight/constraints-of-the-nigerian-mobile-money-ecosystem-a-study/

David-West, Olayinka, Nkemdilim Iheanachor, and Ikechukwu Kelikume. 2018. "A Resource-Based View of Digital Financial

Services (DFS): An Exploratory Study of Nigerian Providers." *Journal of Business Research* 88. doi: 10.1016/j.jbusres.2018.01.034

Davis, Nicholas, and Klaus Schwab. 2018. *Shaping the Future of the Fourth Industrial Revolution*. Geneva: World Economic Forum.

de Beer, D., W. du Preez, H. Greyling, et al. 2016. "A South African Additive Manufacturing Strategy." Council for Scientific and Industrial Research, commissioned by South Africa Department of Science and Technology. https://site.rapdasa.org/wp-content/uploads/2017/02/South-African-Additive-Manufacturing-Strategy.pdf

de León, Riley. 2020. "Zipline Begins Drone Delivery of Covid-19 Test Samples in Ghana." *CNBC*. www.cnbc.com/2020/04/20/zipline-begins-drone-delivery-of-covid-19-test-samples-in-ghana.html

Deaton, Angus S., and Robert Tortora. 2015. "People in Sub-Saharan Africa Rate Their Health and Health Care among the Lowest in the World." *Health Affairs* 34(3): 519–527.

Deen-Swarray, M. 2016. "Toward Digital Inclusion: Understanding the Literacy Effect on Adoption and Use of Mobile Phones and the Internet in Africa." *Information Technologies & International Development* 12(2): 29–45.

Dele-Olowu, Shola, Temidayo Ogunrinu, Destiny Chukwu, Akachi Mbogu, Abubakar Mohammed, and Owes Wiwa. 2020. "Leveraging e-Learning to Train Health Workers during the COVID-19 Pandemic in Nigeria." *Clinton Health Access Initiative*. https://www.clintonhealthaccess.org/leveraging-e-learning-to-train-health-workers-during-the-covid-19-pandemic-in-nigeria/

Deloitte. 2014. "Africa Is Ready to Leapfrog the Competition." www2.deloitte.com/za/en/pages/public-sector/articles/smart-cities.html

    2015. "A 360° View: Africa Construction Trend Report." https://www2.deloitte.com/content/dam/Deloitte/fpc/Documents/secteurs/immobilier/deloitte_etude-africa-construction-trends_edition-2016.pdf

    2016. "Africa's Changing Infrastructure Landscape: Africa Construction Trends Report." https://www2.deloitte.com/content/dam/Deloitte/fpc/Documents/secteurs/immobilier/DeloitteAfrica_Construction_Trends_2017_Nov2016.pdf

    2018a. "Global Human Capital Trends 2018." www2.deloitte.com/insights/us/en/focus/human-capital-trends/2018/ai-robotics-intelligent-machines.html

    2018b. "Preparing Tomorrow's Workforce for the Fourth Industrial Revolution." https://www2.deloitte.com/content/dam/Deloitte/global/Documents/About-Deloitte/gx-preparing-tomorrow-workforce-for-4IR.pdf

2020. "Africa Construction Trend Report 2020." https://www2.deloitte
.com/za/en/pages/energy-and-resources/articles/africa-construction-
trends-2020.html

2021. "Morocco, from Resilience to Emergence?" https://www2.deloitte
.com/content/dam/Deloitte/fpc/Documents/nous-connaitre/policy-
paper-deloitte-maroc-juillet-2021-an.pdf

Deloitte Insights. 2020a. "The Fourth Industrial Revolution at the
Intersection of Readiness and Responsibility." https://www2.deloitte
.com/content/dam/Deloitte/de/Documents/human-capital/Deloitte_
Review_26_Fourth_Industrial_Revolution.pdf

2020b. "Tech Trends 2020." https://www2.deloitte.com/content/dam/
Deloitte/cz/Documents/technology/DI_TechTrends2020.pdf

Diabaté, Abdoulaye. 2021. "Results from Months of Monitoring Following
the First Release of Non Gene Drive Genetically Modified Mosquitoes
in Africa." *Target Malaria*. https://targetmalaria.org/results-from-
months-of-monitoring-following-the-first-release-of-non-gene-drive-gen
etically-modified-mosquitoes-in-africa/

Dialani, Priya. 2018. "Augmented Analytics is the Tomorrow of Business
Intelligence." Analytics Insight. https://www.analyticsinsight.net/aug
mented-analytics-is-the-tomorrow-of-business-intelligence/

"Digital Mauritius 2030 Strategy: Maurice avance vers l'ère 4.0 grâce au
TIC." 2018. *Call Center Ile Maurice*. www.callcenterilemaurice.com/
digital-mauritius-2030-strategy

Digitalist. 2019. "The Digital Paradox of Change in the Oil and Gas
Industry." *The Journal of Petroleum Technology*. https://jpt.spe.org/
digital-paradox-change-oil-and-gas-industry

Disrupt Africa. 2020. *African Tech Startups: Funding Report 2020*. https://
disruptafrica.gumroad.com/l/njrzl

Doroba, Hendrina, Tochukwu Mbanugo, and Uyoyo Edosio. 2020. "The
Relevance of Digital Skills in the COVID-19 Era." *African Development
Bank*. https://www.afdb.org/fr/news-and-events/relevance-digital-skills-
covid-19-era-36244

Drath, Rainier, and Alexander Horch. 2014. "Industries 4.0 – Hit or Hype?"
IEEE Industrial Electronics Magazine 8(2): 56–58.

Drummond, P., V. Thakoor, and S. Yu. 2014. "Africa Rising: Harnessing
the Demographic Dividend." IMF Working Paper No. 14143.

DTI (Department of Trade and Industry of the Republic of South Africa).
2018. "The Digital Industrial Revolution." http://www.dti.gov.za/indus
trial_development/fipt.jsp

Duara, P. 2018. *Nationalism and Development in Asia*. Helsinki: UNU-
WIDER. www.wider.unu.edu/publication/nationalism-and-development-
asia

Duffy, Ryan. 2021. "'Imagine How You Would Use Teleportation': Drone Delivery Unicorn Zipline's CEO on Plans for $250 Million Funding." *Morning Brew.* https://www.morningbrew.com/emerging-tech/stories/2021/06/30/imagine-use-teleportation-drone-delivery-unicorn-ziplines-ceo-plans-250-million-funding

Duricic, A. 2018. Care AI: A Solution for African Health Care? Masters of Media. https://mastersofmedia.hum.uva.nl/blog/2018/09/23/careai-a-solution-for-african-healthcare/

Duvivier, Robbert J., Vanessa C. Burch, and John R. Boulet. 2017. "A Comparison of Physician Emigration from Africa to the United States of America between 2005 and 2015." *Human Resources Health* 15(41).

Ecofin Agency. 2018. "Tunisia: 5G Licenses Will Probably Be Available in 2021, According to the Minister of Digital Economy." www.ecofinagency.com/telecom/2112-39465-tunisia-5g-licenses-will-probably-be-available-in-2021-according-to-the-minister-of-digital-economy

Economic Development Board of Mauritius. 2021. "Showcasing the Shining Resilience of the ICT/BPO Industry." https://www.linkedin.com/pulse/showcasing-shining-resilience-ictbpo-industry-edb-mauritius

EDCI (European Digital City Index). 2016. "Methodology." https://media.nesta.org.uk/documents/2016_EDCi_Construction_Methodology_FINAL.pdf

"Egypt Riding the Gas Wave to Self Sufficiency." 2018. *Africa Oil Week.* https://www.africa-oilweek.com/Articles/7-worldwide-oil-gas-projects-to-watch-in-2018

Ehui, S. 2018. "Why Technology Will Disrupt – and Transform – Africa's Agriculture Sector in a Good Way." In *Foresight Africa: Top Priorities for the Continent in 2018*: 96. www.brookings.edu/wp-content/uploads/2018/01/foresight-2018_full_web_final2.pdf

Ekekwe, Ndubuisi. 2018. "How New Technologies Could Transform Africa's Health Care System." *Harvard Business Review.* https://hbr.org/2018/08/how-new-technologies-could-transform-africas-health-care-system

El-Behary, Hend. 2016. "Egypt Missing Targets on Research and Development: UNESCO." *Egypt Independent.* https://www.egyptindependent.com/egypt-missing-targets-research-and-development-unesco/

El-Darwiche, B., E. Friedrich, A. Koster, and M. Singh. 2013. "Digitization for Economic Growth and Job Creation: Regional and Industry Perspectives." *PwC Strategy&.* www.strategyand.pwc.com/media/file/Strategyand_Digitization-for-Economic-Growth-and-Job-Creation.pdf

El Elj, Moez. 2012. "Innovation in Tunisia: Empirical Analysis for Industrial Sector." *Journal of Innovation Economics and Management* 1(9): 183–197.

El Masaiti, Amira. 2017. "Morocco Leads in Science, Technology and Innovation in Africa: Report." *Morocco World News.* www .moroccoworldnews.com/2017/03/212434/morocco-leads-in-science-technology-and-innovation-in-africa-report/

Engelke, Peter. 2018. "Three Ways the Fourth Industrial Revolution Is Shaping Geopolitics." *World Economic Forum.* www.weforum.org/agenda/2018/08/three-ways-the-fourth-industrial-revolution-is-shaping-geopolitics/

Euphemia, Nwokorie, Juliet Odii, and Donatus Njoku. 2019. "Cyberspace Activities Awareness and Security Strategies in Tertiary Institutions in Nigeria." *IRE Journals* 3(2). https://www.researchgate.net/publication/338225751_Cyberspace_Activities_Awareness_and_Security_Strategies_in_Tertiary_Institutions_in_Nigeria

European Commission. 2015. *Supply and Demand Side Innovation Policies.* https://op.europa.eu/en/publication-detail/-/publication/ef276884-0dce-11e6-ba9a-01aa75ed71a1

Eusébio, Celeste, Leonor Teixeira, and Maria João Carneiro (Eds.). 2021. *ICT Tools and Applications for Accessible Tourism.* IGI Global. http://doi:10.4018/978-1-7998-6428-8

Evans, Dave. 2011. "The Internet of Things: How the Next Evolution of the Internet is Changing Everything." *Cisco Internet Business Solutions Group.* www.cisco.com/c/dam/en_us/about/ac79/docs/innov/IoT_IBSG_0411FINAL.pdf

Exportiamo. 2018. "Tunisia Digital 2020 Strategy: Why Invest in Tunisia." https://www.exportiamo.it/aree-tematiche/13719/%E2%80%9Ctunisia-digital-2020%E2%80%9D-why-invest-in-tunisia/#:~:text=%E2%80%9CTunisia%20Digital%202020%E2%80%9D%20is%20a,lever%20for%20socio%2Deconomic%20development

EY Global. 2021. "Will Digital Help Us Do Less or Become More?" https://www.ey.com/en_gl/oil-gas/how-digitalization-can-streamline-oil-and-gas-operations

"Facts about Health in the African Region of WHO." 2018. *All Countries.* https://allcountries.org/health/facts_about_health_in_the_african_region_of_who.htm

FAO. 2016. *The State of Food and Agriculture: Climate Change, Agriculture, and Food Security.* www.fao.org/3/a-i6030e.pdf

2017. *The State of Food and Agriculture: Leveraging Food Items for Inclusive Rural Transformation.* https://www.fao.org/family-farming/detail/en/c/1043688/

Faria, Julia. 2021. "Registered Mobile Money Accounts in Kenya 2019–2021." *Statista.* https://www.statista.com/statistics/1188510/registered-mobile-money-accounts-in-kenya/

Farmcrowdy. 2022. farmcrowdy.com

FDI Intelligence. 2016. *The Africa Investment Report 2016: Foreign Investment Broadens Its Base.* https://www.camara.es/sites/default/files/publicaciones/the-africa-investment-report-2016.pdf

Feldman, Amy. 2020. "Inside a Silicon Valley Unicorn's Urgent Dash to 3D-Print Face Shields and Test Swabs to Battle COVID-19." *Forbes.* www.forbes.com/sites/amyfeldman/2020/03/25/inside-a-silicon-valley-unicorns-urgent-dash-to-3d-print-face-shields-and-test-swabs-to-battle-covid-19/#1e9ecacc4370

Fengler, Wolfgang. 2013. "Big Data and Development: 'The Second Half of the Chess Board.'" *World Bank.* https://blogs.worldbank.org/category/tags/kenya-ict

Financial Services Commission of Mauritius. 2018. *Regulatory Framework for the Custodian Services (Digital Asset) License.* https://www.fscmauritius.org/media/70752/communiqu%C3%A9-regulatory-framework-for-the-custodian-services-digital-asset-licence.pdf

Fleming, Sean. 2018. "In Rwanda, High-Speed Drones Are Delivering Blood to Remote Communities." *World Economic Forum.* https://www.weforum.org/agenda/2018/12/in-rwanda-drones-are-delivering-blood-to-remote-communities/

Flood, Z. 2018. "Zimbabwe and Kenya Lead the Way in Africa's Dash from Cash." *The Guardian.* https://www.theguardian.com/world/2018/feb/22/kenya-leads-way-mobile-money-africa-shifts-towards-cash-free-living

Fox, L., and L. Signé. 2021. "The Fourth Industrial Revolution (4IR) and the Future of Work: Could This Bring Good Jobs to Africa?" *Include Platform.* https://includeplatform.net/publications/the-fourth-industrial-revolution-4ir-and-the-future-of-work-could-this-bring-good-jobs-to-africa/

Fraser, M., T. Anastaselos, and G. V. V. Ravikumar. 2018. "The Disruption in Oil and Gas Upstream Business by Industry 4.0." Infosys White Papers. www.infosys.com/engineering-services/white-papers/Documents/disruption-oil-gas-upstream.pdf

Freedom House. 2017. "Nigeria Country Profile." *Freedom House: Freedom on the Net.* https://freedomhouse.org/report/freedom-net/2017/nigeria
  2018. *Freedom on the Net 2018: The Rise of Digital Authoritarianism.* https://freedomhouse.org/sites/default/files/FOTN_2018_Final%20Booklet_11_1_2018.pdf

Frehywot, Seble, Chulwoo Park, and Alexandra Infanzon. 2019. "Medical Diaspora: An Underused Entity in Low- and Middle-Income Countries' Health System Development." *Human Resources for Health* 17(Article number: 56).

Frey, Carl, Michael Osborne, and Craig Holmes. 2016. *Technology at Work v2.0: The Future Is Not What It Used to Be.* Citi GPS: Global Perspectives and Solutions. University of Oxford. www.oxfordmartin .ox.ac.uk/downloads/reports/Citi_GPS_Technology_Work_2.pdf

Frost and Sullivan. 2016. *African Pharmaceuticals Market Forecast 2020: Assessing Market Potential with a Focus on Kenya and Nigeria.* https:// store.frost.com/african-pharmaceuticals-market-forecast-to-2020.html

Frost & Sullivan and Principal. 2018. *5G: The Foundation for a Hyper-Connected World.* https://www.principalglobal.com/knowledge/ insights/5g-foundation-a-hyper-connected-world

Fu, X. 2020. *Innovation under the Radar: The Nature and Sources of Innovation in Africa.* Cambridge: Cambridge University Press. https:// doi.org/10.1017/9781316869482

"Gabon: La BGFI-Bank secouée par une fraude massive aux cartes Visa prépayées." 2017. *Jeune Afrique.* https://www.jeuneafrique.com/ 404469/economie/gabon-bgfi-bank-secouee-fraude-massive-aux-cartes-visa-prepayees/

"Gabon-Côte d'Ivoire: Quand un conseiller d'Alassane Ouattara aide Jean Ping à l'insu de son patron…" 2016. *Jeune Afrique.* https://www .jeuneafrique.com/353085/politique/gabon-cote-divoire-conseiller-dalas sane-ouattara-aide-jean-ping-a-linsu-de-patron/

Gadzala, Aleksandra. 2018. "3D Printing: Shaping Africa's Future." *The Atlantic Council.* https://www.atlanticcouncil.org/images/publications/ 3D_Printing_Africa_WEB.pdf

Galasso, V. N., G. N. Feroci, K. Pfeifer, and M. Walsh. 2017. "The Rise of Populism and Its Implications for Development NGOs." Oxfam Research Backgrounder series. www.oxfamamerica.org/riseofpopulism

Gandhi, Prashant, Somesh Khanna, and Sree Ramaswamy. 2016. "Which Industries Are the Most Digital (And Why)?" *Harvard Business Review.* https://hbr.org/2016/04/a-chart-that-shows-which-industries-are-the-most-digital-and-why

Ganguly, S., H. Harreis, B. Margolis, and K. Rowshankish. 2017. "Digital Risk: Transforming Risk Management for the 2020s." *McKinsey & Company.* https://www.mckinsey.com/business-functions/risk/our-insights/digital-risk-transforming-risk-management-for-the-2020s

Gebre, S. 2018. "Blockchain Opens Up Kenya's $20 Billion Informal Economy." *Bloomberg.* www.bloomberg.com/news/articles/2018-06-14/blockchain-is-opening-up-kenya-s-20-billion-informal-economy

Gentner, S. 2016. "Industry 4.0: Reality, Future or Just Science Fiction? How to Convince Today's Management to Invest in Tomorrow's Future! Successful Strategies for Industry 4.0 and Manufacturing IT." *Chimia* 70(9): 628–633.

Gerbert, P., S. Catagnino, C. Rothballer, A. Renz, and F. Rainer. 2016. *Digital in Engineering and Construction*. The Boston Consulting Group. http://futureofconstruction.org/content/uploads/2016/09/BCG-Digital-in-Engineering-and-Construction-Mar-2016.pdf

Ghafar, Adel Abdel. 2016. "Educated but Unemployed: The Challenge Facing Egypt's Youth." *Brookings Institution*. https://www.brookings.edu/wp-content/uploads/2016/07/en_youth_in_egypt-1.pdf

Gilga, S., G. Hrkac, C. Donnelly, et al. 2017. "Emergent Dynamic Chirality in a Thermally Driven Artificial Spin Ratchet." *Nature Materials* 16(11): 1106.

Giuliani, Dario, and Sam Ajadi. 2019. "618 Active Tech Hubs: The Backbone of Africa's Tech Ecosystem." GSMA Mobile for Development. https://www.gsma.com/mobilefordevelopment/blog/618-active-tech-hubs-the-backbone-of-africas-tech-ecosystem/

Goad, Kimberly. 2021. "How Drones Are Being Used to Deliver Lifesaving HIV Drugs to Remote Areas of the World." Johnson & Johnson. https://www.jnj.com/innovation/medical-drones-deliver-hiv-medicine

Goldstein Research. 2016. *African Pharmaceutical Market – Industry Analysis & Forecast 2017–2030*. New York: Goldstein Research. www.goldsteinresearch.com/report/africa-pharmaceutical-industry-market-size-forecast

2019. *Africa Healthcare Market Outlook: Opportunity and Demand Analysis, Market Forecast, 2016–2024*. New York: Goldstein Research. https://www.goldsteinresearch.com/report/africa-healthcare-market-outlook-opportunity-and-demand-analysis-market-forecast-2016-2024

Government of Canada. 2020. "Secteur des Technologies de l'Information et de la Communication (TIC) en Tunisie." https://www.tradecommissioner.gc.ca/tunisia-tunisie/market-reports-etudes-de-marches/0002801.aspx?lang=eng

Government of Kenya. 2008. "Kenya Vision 2030." http://vision2030.go.ke/enablers-and-macros

Government of the Republic of Mauritius. 2018. "Digitalisation Will Usher Mauritius into Industrial Age 4.0, Says Minister." *Innoviva Inc.* www.publicnow.com/view/01E4E12E54C9D4338982E132A445D77CB7E36CED?2018-06-07-13:00:14 01:00-xxx2916

Great Lakes St. Lawrence Governors and Premiers Africa Trade Office. 2017. Sub-*Saharan Africa: Healthcare Market Opportunities*. https://ihif.org/wp-content/uploads/2017/03/Southern-Africa-Healthcare-Brief-for-GSGP-Companies-2017.pdf

Gretzel, U., L. Zhong, and C. Koo. 2016. "Application of Smart Tourism to Cities." *International Journal of Tourism Cities* 2(2).

Grigorov, Vladimir. 2009. "Healthcare in Africa." *Cardiovascular Journal of Africa* 20(5): 275–277.

Gruber, H., and P. Koutroumpis. 2011. "Mobile Telecommunications and the Impact on Economic Development." Wiley-Blackwell 52nd Panel Meeting of Economic Policy: 1–41.

GSMA. 2017. "Egypt." *GSMA Mobile Connectivity Index*. https://www.mobileconnectivityindex.com/#year=2017&zoneIsocode=EGY

2018a. "Access to Mobile Services and Proof-of-Identity: Global Policy Trends, Dependencies and Risks." https://www.gsma.com/mobilefordevelopment/wp-content/uploads/2018/02/Access-to-Mobile-Services-and-Proof-of-Identity.pdf

2018b. *The Mobile Economy: Sub-Saharan Africa 2018*. https://www.gsma.com/r/mobileeconomy/sub-saharan-africa/

2020. *The State of Mobile Internet Connectivity 2020*. https://www.gsma.com/r/wp-content/uploads/2020/09/GSMA-State-of-Mobile-Internet-Connectivity-Report-2020.pdf

2021a. *State of the Industry Report on Mobile Money*. https://www.gsma.com/mobilefordevelopment/wp-content/uploads/2021/03/GSMA_State-of-the-Industry-Report-on-Mobile-Money-2021_Full-report.pdf

2021b. *The Mobile Economy Sub-Saharan Africa 2021*. https://www.gsma.com/mobileeconomy/sub-saharan-africa/

Guttentag, D. 2010. "Virtual Reality: Applications and Implications for Tourism." *Tourism Management* 31(5): 637–651.

Gwagwa, A., E. Kraemer-Mbula, N. Rizk, I. Rutenberg, and J. Beer. 2020. "Artificial Intelligence (AI) Deployments in Africa: Benefits, Challenges and Policy Dimensions." *The African Journal of Information and Communication*. http://dx.doi.org/10.23962/10539/30361

Hafkin, Nancy. 2009. "E-Government in Africa: An Overview of Progress Made and Challenges Ahead." Prepared for the UNDESA/UNPAN workshop on electronic/mobile government in Africa: Building Capacity in Knowledge Management through Partnership, held at the United Nations Economic Commission for Africa. wisa.org/wp-content/uploads?unpan034002.pdf

Hallward-Driemeier, Mary, and Gaurav Nayyar. 2017. *Trouble in the Making? The Future of Manufacturing-Led Development*. Washington, DC: World Bank.

Hamann, Jasper. 2021. "Study: Morocco Ranks Second in Africa on Digital Transformation." *Morocco World News*. https://www.moroccoworldnews.com/2021/04/338879/study-morocco-ranks-second-in-africa-on-digital-transformation

Hamuth, Shaffick. 2017. "The Digital Economy: Opportunities Abound, Initiatives Lacking." *Le Defi Media Group*. defimedia.info/digital-economy-opportunities-abound-initiatives-lacking

Happi, Christian. 2020. "Nigerian Scientists Have Identified Seven Lineages of SARS-CoV-2." *Quartz Africa*. https://qz.com/africa/1900397/nigerian-scientists-identified-seven-lineages-of-sars-cov-2-covid/

Harvey, Ross. 2017. "The 'Fourth Industrial Revolution': Potential and Risks for Africa." *The Conversation*. https://theconversation.com/the-fourth-industrial-revolution-potential-and-risks-for-africa-75313

Hatch, Grant, Pieter Becker, and Michelle van Zyl. 2011. "The Dynamic African Consumer Market: Exploring Growth Opportunities in Sub-Saharan Africa." *Accenture*. https://studylib.net/doc/8721889/the-dynamic-african-consumer-market–exploring

Hatim, Yahia. 2020. "Is Digitization the Future for Morocco's Business Sector?" https://www.moroccoworldnews.com/2020/01/292042/digitization-future-morocco-business-sector

Hayden, E. C. 2014. "Technology: The $1,000 Genome." *Nature* 507 (7492): 294–295.

Heberger, Matthew. 2013. "Five Facts about Health in Africa." *The Dokotoro Project*. http://dokotoro.org/five-facts

Heilbron, Miguel. 2013. "Ten Innovative African Healthcare Startups." *VC4A*. https://vc4a.com/blog/2013/01/24/10-innovative-african-healthcare-startups

Heldreth, Courtney, Fernanda Viégas, Titi Akinsanmi, and Diana Akrong. 2019. "AI in Nigeria." Google Whitepaper, Policy Perspectives + People Insights. https://research.google/pubs/pub48985/

Heney, Paul. 2020. "Global R&D Investments Unabated in Spending Growth." *R&D World*. https://www.rdworldonline.com/global-rd-investments-unabated-in-spending-growth/

Henn, Brynne. 2021. "Augmented Analytics Use Cases and Examples." *Sisu*. https://sisudata.com/blog/augmented-analytics-use-cases-and-examples

Heuler, Hilary. 2014. "With a Piracy Rate of 80 Percent, Can the Tech World Convince Africa to Buy Legitimate Software?" *ZDNet*. https://www.zdnet.com/article/with-a-piracy-rate-of-80-percent-can-the-tech-world-convince-africa-to-buy-legitimate-software/

Höller, J., V. Tsiatsis, C. Mulligan, S. Karnouskos, S. Avesand, and D. Boyle. 2014. *From Machine-to-Machine to the Internet of Things*. https://www.sciencedirect.com/book/9780124076846/from-machine-to-machine-to-the-internet-of-things

Hollingworth, S. 2019. *Coffee, Cocoa, and the Cutting Edge*. Project Syndicate. https://www.project-syndicate.org/commentary/technology-data-finance-sustainable-farming-by-steve-hollingworth-2019-03

Holmås, H., O. Sjåtil, S. Santamarta, S. Lindseth, and P. Romanin. 2019. "Creating Value with Digital Twins in Oil and Gas." *BCG*. https://www.bcg.com/publications/2019/creating-value-digital-twins-oil-gas

Holt, Tania, Mehdi Lahrichi, Jean Mina, and Jorge Santos da Silva. 2015. *Insights into Pharmaceuticals and Medical Products: Africa, a Continent of Opportunity for Pharma and Patients.* Johannesburg: McKinsey & Company.

Howard, Philip N. 2015. *Pax Technica.* New Haven and London: Yale University Press.

Howell, Jenalea. 2017. "Number of Connected IoT Devices Will Surge to 125 Billion by 2030, IHS Markit says." *IHS*. https://technology.ihs.com/596542/number-of-connected-iot-devices-will-surge-to-125-billion-by-2030-ihs-markit-says

Huet, Jean-Michel. 2016. "Smart Cities: The Key to Africa's Third Revolution." *Bearing Point Institute.* www.bearingpoint.com/en-us/our-success/thought-leadership/smart-cities-the-key-to-africas-third-revolution/

IBL Group. 2020. Diya Nababsing-Jetshan: "Digital Transformation Can Be a Powerful Driver for Business Outcomes." https://www.iblgroup.com/diya-nababsing-jetshan-digital-transformation-can-be-powerful-driver-business-outcomes

IBM. 2017. *IBM's African Scientists Look to Tackle the Continent's Pressing Healthcare Challenges with AI.* https://www.ibm.com/blogs/research/2017/11/ibms-african-scientists-look-tackle-continents-pressing-health care-challenges-ai/

Ichikowitz, Ivor. 2017. "Africa Is Stoking the Fire of the Fourth Industrial Revolution." *Paramount Group Perspective: African Business.* www.paramountgroup.com/media/1502/africa-is-stoking-the-fire-of-the-fourth-industrial-revolution.pdf

IDG. 2013. *Africa 2013: Cyber-Crime, Hacking and Malware.* https://www.idgconnect.com/idgconnect/analysis-review/1009430/africa-2013-cyber-crime-hacking-malware

IDRC. 2022. "Bajenu Gox: A Community Approach to Maternal and Child Health in Senegal (IMCHA)." www.idrc.ca/en/project/bajenu-gox-com munity-approach-maternal-and-child-health-senegal-imcha

IFC. 2018. *Digital Access: The Future of Financial Inclusion in Africa. Interpol to Launch Crime Control Platform in Nigeria in Partnership with VoguePay.* Finextra. https://www.finextra.com/pressarticle/72585/interpol-to-launch-crime-control-platform-in-nigeria-in-partnership-with-voguepay

2020. "e-Conomy Africa – Africa's $180 Billion Internet Economy Future." https://www.ifc.org/wps/wcm/connect/publications_ext_content/ifc_exter nal_publication_site/publications_listing_page/google-e-conomy

IFR. 2020. "IFR Presents World Robotics Report 2020." https://ifr.org/ifr-press-releases/news/record-2.7-million-robots-work-in-factories-around-the-globe

Ikegbune, Cassandra. 2021. "ACEGID-Africa Pathogen Genomics Initiative Trains African Scientists in Next Generation Sequencing." *ACEGID Redeemer's University*. https://acegid.org/2021/06/21/acegid-africa-pathogen-genomics-initiative-trains-african-scientists-in-ngs/

IMF. 2018. *Financial Access Survey*. http://data.imf.org/?sk=E5DCAB7E-A5CA-4892-A6EA-598B5463A34C&sId=1460040555909

IndyGeneUS AI. 2021. "IndyGeneUS AI Secures Pathogen Sequencing Capability to Support COVID-19 Genomic Surveillance Initiatives." *PRNewswire*. https://www.prnewswire.com/news-releases/indygeneus-ai-secures-pathogen-sequencing-capability-to-support-covid-19-genomic-surveillance-initiatives-301294883.html

International Federation of Robotics. 2020. "IFR Presents World Robotics Report." https://ifr.org/ifr-press-releases/news/record-2.7-million-robots-work-in-factories-around-the-globe

2021. *IFR Presents World Robotics Report*. https://ifr.org/ifr-press-releases/news/robot-sales-rise-again

International Finance Corporation. 2008. *The Business of Health in Africa: Partnering with the Private Sector to Improve People's Lives*. Washington, DC: World Bank.

International Trade Administration. 2019a. "Kenya – Medical Equipment." *Export.gov*. www.export.gov/article?id=Kenya-medical-equipment

2019b. "South Africa – Medical Devices." *Export.gov*. www.export.gov/article?id=South-Africa-medical-devices

2019c. "Botswana – Medical Equipment and Pharmaceuticals." *Export.gov*. www.export.gov/article?id=Botswana-Medical-Equipment-and-Pharmaceuticals

2022. "Tunisia – Commercial Country Guide." https://www.trade.gov/country-commercial-guides/tunisia-telecommunications-equipment-services

Ismaili, Fayçal. 2018. "Développement Technologique: Le Maroc leader en Afrique." LE 360. fr.le360.ma/economie/developpement-technologique-le-maroc-leader-en-afrique-165423

ISO. 2017. "ISO Survey of Certifications to Management System Standards." https://isotc.iso.org/livelink/livelink?func=ll&objId=18808772&objAction=browse

2020. "ISO Survey of Certifications to Management System Standards." https://isotc.iso.org/livelink/livelink?func=ll&objId=18808772&objAction=browse

Israel Ministry of Foreign Affairs. 2019. "Israel and Cameroon Inaugurate State of the Art 3D Printing Facility in Yaoundé." https://mfa.gov.il/

MFA/AboutTheMinistry/Events/Pages/Israel-and-Cameroon-inaugur
ate-3D-facility-in-Yaounde-16-April-2019.aspx

Issahaku, A., and A. Kimbu. 2020. "Strategies Africa's Tourism Requires to Manage Blow from Coronavirus." *The Conversation.* https://theconversation.com/strategies-africas-tourism-requires-to-manage-blow-from-coronavirus-135858

ITA. 2020. "Information and Communications Technology; and Digital Economy." https://www.trade.gov/country-commercial-guides/egypt-infor mation-and-communications-technology-and-digital-economy

Itcovitz, Hannah. 2020. "Advancing Africa's Capabilities." *Include Platform.* https://includeplatform.net/wp-content/uploads/2020/01/Advancing-Africas-Capabilities.pdf

ITU. 2017. "Africa Global Cybersecurity Index." https://www.itu.int/en/ITU-D/Cybersecurity/Documents/Africa_GCIv2_report.pdf

2018. "Global Cybersecurity Index 2018." https://www.itu.int/dms_pub/itu-d/opb/str/D-STR-GCI.01-2018-PDF-E.pdf

2021. "Digital Trends in Africa 2021." https://www.itu.int/dms_pub/itu-d/opb/ind/D-IND-DIG_TRENDS_AFR.01-2021-PDF-E.pdf

ITU News. 2019. "The Digital Transformation of Mauritius: Q+A with Minister Sawmynaden." https://www.itu.int/en/myitu/News/2020/03/23/15/33/The-digital-transformation-of-Mauritius-QplusA-with-Minister-Sawmynaden

Jackson, Tom. 2015. "Kenya's Weza Tele Acquired by AFB for $1.7m." *Disrupt Africa.* http://disrupt-africa.com/2015/05/kenyas-weza-tele-acquired-by-afb-for-1-7m/

2020a. "Kenya's Ilara Health Raises $3.75m Series A Funding Round." *Disrupt Africa.* https://disrupt-africa.com/2020/12/16/kenyas-ilara-health-raises-3-75m-series-a-funding-round/

2020b. "Nigerian Startup 54gene Partners US Firm Illumina to Launch Lagos Genomics Facility." *Disrupt Africa.* https://disrupt-africa.com/2020/09/07/nigerian-startup-54gene-partners-us-firm-illumina-to-launch-lagos-genomics-facility/

2021. "Ghanaian e-Health Startup mPharma Makes Ethiopia Its 6th Market in Africa." *Disrupt Africa.* https://disrupt-africa.com/2021/03/15/ghan aian-e-health-startup-mpharma-makes-ethiopia-its-6th-market-in-africa/

Jamii Afriica. 2017. "About Us." www.jamiiafrica.com

Jamrisko, Michelle, and Lu Wei. 2017. "These Are the World's Most Innovative Economies." *Bloomberg.* www.bloomberg.com/news/art icles/2017-01-17/sweden-gains-south-korea-reigns-as-world-s-most-innovative-economies

Jamwal, Ankit. 2016. "The Fourth Industrial Revolution: Challenges for Enterprises and Their Stakeholders." *Information Services Group.*

https://www.isg-one.com/industries/manufacturing/articles/the-fourth-industrial-revolution-challenges-for-enterprises-and-their-stakeholders

Jansen van Vuuren, J. C., and Louise Leenen. 2019. "Framework for the Development and Implementation of a Cybercrime Strategy in Africa." *Conference: International Conference on Cyber Warfare and Security.* https://www.researchgate.net/publication/336605756_Framework_for_the_Development_and_Implementation_of_a_Cybercrime_Strategy_in_Africa

Jasanoff, Sheila. 2015. "Future Imperfect: Science, Technology, and the Imaginations of Modernity." In Sheila Jasanoff and Sang-Hyun Kim (Eds.), *Dreamscapes of Modernity: Sociotechnical Imaginaries and the Fabrication of Power.* Chicago: University of Chicago Press, pp. 1–33. https://doi.org/10.7208/chicago/9780226276663.003.0001

Jensen, R. 2007. "The Digital Provides: Information (Technology), Market Performance and Welfare in the South Indian Fisheries Sector." *The Quarterly Journal of Economics* 122(3): 879–924.

Jezard, Adam. 2018. "Morocco Is Building a Giant Thermosolar Farm in the Sahara Desert." *World Economic Forum.* https://www.weforum.org/agenda/2018/05/morocco-is-building-a-solar-farm-as-big-as-paris-in-the-sahara-desert/

JICA. 2019. "The Youth behind Rwanda's ICT Sector." https://www.jica.go.jp/english/publications/j-world/c8h0vm0000f4ng2q-att/1907_03.pdf

Jimenez, Joseph. 2015. "Three Ways to Improve Healthcare in Africa." *World Economic Forum.* www.weforum.org/agenda/2015/01/3-ways-to-improve-healthcare-in-africa

Kallel, Anis. 2018. "The Next Wave of Innovation Will Come from Tunisia – Here Is Why." *Medium.* https://medium.com/@akallel/the-next-wave-of-innovation-will-come-from-tunisia-here-is-why-c6892addd564

Kamel, S. H., & N. Rizk. 2019. "The Role of Innovative and Digital Technologies in Transforming Egypt into a Knowledge-Based Economy." In M. Habib (Ed.), *Handbook of Research on the Evolution of IT and the Rise of E-Society.* IGI Global, pp. 386–400. http://doi:10.4018/978-1-5225-7214-5.ch017

Kamineni, Shobana. 2019 July 15. "Five Ways to Bridge the Global Health Worker Shortage." *World Economic Forum.* https://www.weforum.org/agenda/2019/07/5-ways-to-bridge-the-global-health-worker-shortage/

Kande, M., and M. Sonmez. 2020. "Don't Fear AI. It Will Lead to Long-Term Job Growth." *World Economic Forum.* https://www.weforum.org/agenda/2020/10/dont-fear-ai-it-will-lead-to-long-term-job-growth/

Kariuki, H. 2018. "Innovation Is Key to Curbing Post-Harvest Losses in Africa." *Medium*. https://medium.com/@harriet436/innovation-is-key-to-curbing-post-harvest-losses-in-africa-755f2cde0b2f

Kaseje, Dan. 2006. "Health Care in Africa: Challenges, Opportunities and an Emerging Model for Improvement." *The Woodrow Wilson International Center for Scholars*. https://www.wilsoncenter.org/publi cation/health-care-africa-challenges-opportunities-and-emerging-model-for-improvement

Kasilo, Ossy M. J. 2003. "Enhancing Traditional Medicine Research and Development in the African Region." *African Health Monitor* 4(1): 15–18.

Katz, R. L., S. Vaterlaus, P. Zenhaüsern, and S. Suter. 2010. "The Impact of Broadband on Jobs and the German Economy." *Intereconomics* 45(1): 26–34.

Kazimierczuk, Agnieszka. 2020. "Will the Future of Work Create Two Speeds in Africa?" *Include Platform*. https://includeplatform.net/wp-content/uploads/2020/02/Will-the-future-of-work-create-two-speeds-in-Africa-022020.pdf

Kaushal, Mohit, and Sheel Tyle. 2015. "The Blockchain: What It Is and Why It Matters." *Brookings TechTank* blog. www.brookings.edu/blog/tech tank/2015/01/13/the-blockchain-what-it-is-and-why-it-matters/

Kemp, Simon. 2020. "Digital 2020: Mauritius." *Kepios*. https://datareport .com/reports/digital-2020-mauritius

2021a. "Digital 2021: Egypt." *Kepios*. https://datareportal.com/reports/ digital-2021-egypt

2021b. "Digital 2021: Kenya." *Kepios*. https://datareportal.com/reports/ digital-2021-kenya

2021c. "Digital 2021: Nigeria." *Kepios*. https://datareportal.com/reports/ digital-2021-nigeria

2021d. "Digital 2021: Rwanda." *Kepios*. https://datareportal.com/reports/ digital-2021-rwanda

Kene-Okafor, Tage. 2021. "How African Startups Raised Investments in 2020." *TechCrunch*. https://techcrunch.com/2021/02/11/how-african-startups-raised-investments-in-2020/

2021. "RxAll Grabs $3.15M to Scale Its Drug and Counterfeiting Tech across Africa." *TechCrunch*. https://techcrunch.com/2021/07/20/rxall-grabs-3-15m-to-scale-its-drug-checking-and-counterfeiting-tech-across-africa/

Khan, Themrise. 2020. "Young, Female and African: Barriers, Interventions and Opportunities for Female Youth Employment in Africa." *Include Platform*. https://includeplatform.net/wp-content/uploads/2020/04/Khan-

2020-Young-female-and-African-barriers-interventions-and-opportun
ities-for-female-youth-employment-in-Africa-INCLUDE.pdf

Khurana, A., and M. Shaban. 2018. *The Future of Manufacturing –
Morocco.* PwC Global Manufacturing and Industrialization Summit.
http://gmisummit.com/wp-content/uploads/2018/07/20180214_
GMIC_GMIS-Morocco_v4.0.pdf

Kigen, Paula Musuva, Carol Muchai, Kevin Kimani, et al. 2015. "Kenya
Cyber Security Report 2015." *Serianu.* https://www.serianu.com/down
loads/KenyaCyberSecurityReport2015.pdf

Kihara, Patrick, and Juliet Njeri. 2016. "Africa Cracks Down on Social
Media." *BBC.* https://www.bbc.com/news/world-africa-37300272

Kinai, A. 2018. "IBM and Twiga Foods Introduce Blockchain-Based
MicroFinancing for Food Kiosk Owners in Kenya." *IBM.* https://www
.ibm.com/blogs/research/2018/04/ibm-twiga-foods/

Kirigia, Joses Muthuri, and Saidou Pathe Barry. 2008. "Health Challenges in
Africa and the Way Forward." *International Archives of Medicine* 1:
27.

Kizza, Joseph M. 2016. "Can Implementing Smart City Technologies Save
the African Cities? – Part 2." *International Journal of Computing and
ICT Research (IJCIR)* 10(2): 6–9. http://www.ijcir.org/volume10-
issue2/article1.pdf

Klonner, S., and P. Nolen. 2010. "Cell Phones and Rural Labor Markets:
Evidence from South Africa." Proceedings of the German Development
Economics Conference, Verein fuer Socialpolitik, Research Committee
Development Economics.

Knapp, Tim, Ben Richardson, and Shrey Viranna. 2010. "Three Practical
Steps to Better Health. In Africa." *McKinsey & Company.* www
.mckinsey.com/industries/healthcare-systems-and-services/our-insights/
three-practical-steps-to-better-health-for-africans#

Kodjani, David. 2021. "The Cost of Cybercrime in Africa." *AfroAware.*
https://afroaware.com/cybercrime-cost-africa

Koigi, Bob. 2021. "Egypt Government Partners with Siemens to Establish First
Industry 4.0 Innovation Center." https://africabusinesscommunities.com/
tech/tech-news/egypt-government-partners-with-siemens-to-establish-
first-industry-4.0-innovation-center/

Kolodziejczyk, Bart. 2018. "Why Do We Fail to Measure the Most
Innovative Countries?" *Brookings TechTank.* www.brookings.edu/
blog/techtank/2018/01/22/why-do-we-fail-to-measure-the-most-innova
tive-countries/

Kontzer, Tony. 2018. "Nigerian Startup Aims to Save Lives by Analyzing
Infant Cries with AI." *NVIDIA* blog. https://blogs.nvidia.com/blog/
2018/10/05/ubenwa-startup-deep-learning-infant-cries/

Kortuem, Gerd, Fahim Kawsar, Vasughi Sundramoorthy, and Daniel Fitton. 2010. "Smart Objects as Building Blocks for the Internet of Things." *IEEE Internet Computing* 14(1): 44–51.

Koundouno, Tamba François. 2018. "Morocco among the Most Innovative Countries of the MENA Region." *Morocco World News*. www .moroccoworldnews.com/2018/07/250516/morocco-innovative-mena-region/

Koutroumpis, P. 2009. "The Economic Impact of Broadband on Growth: A Simultaneous Approach." *Telecommunications Policy* 33(9): 471–485.

KPMG. 2017. *The Changing Landscape of Disruptive Technologies*. https:// assets.kpmg/content/dam/kpmg/tw/pdf/2017/04/changing-landscape-disruptive-tech-2017.pdf

Kramer, F. D., S. H. Starr, and L. K. Wentz. 2009. "Cyber Power and National Security." *Center for Technology and National Security Policy and National Defense University*.

Kritzinger, E., and S. H. von Solms. 2011. "A New Role for Information Service Providers as Part of Critical Information Infrastructure Protection in Africa." *Center for Infrastructure Protection and Homeland Security at George Mason University* 9(12).

2012. "A Framework for Cybersecurity in Africa." *Journal of Information Assurance & Cybersecurity* 2012: 1–10.

Kshetri, Nir. 2019. "Cybercrime and Cybersecurity in Africa." *Journal of Global Information Technology Management* 22(2): 77–81. doi: 10.1080/1097198X.2019.1603527

Kubayi-Ngubane, M. T. 2018. "Draft White Paper on Science, Technology and Innovation." *Department of Science and Technology of the Republic of South Africa*. https://www.csir.co.za/sites/default/files/DST %20Draft%20White%20Paper%20on%20STI_Web%20version_ FINAL_12092018.pdf

Kumar, N. 2010. "Africa Could Become the Cybercrime Capital of the World." https://www.psfk.com/2010/04/africa-could-become-the-cyber crime-capital-of-the-world.html

Kumar, N., K. Mohan, and R. Holowczak. 2008. "Locking the Door but Leaving the Computer Vulnerable: Factors Inhibiting Home Users' Adoption of Software Firewalls." *Decision Support System* 46: 254–264.

Ladimeji, Dapo. 2020. "4IR and Nigeria. Pan – African." Volume 83. https://www.researchgate.net/publication/340266793_4IR_and_ Nigeria

Laitinen, Anni, Annarinna Koivu, Pirkko Nykanen, and Honest Kimaro. 2019. "Healthcare Workers' eHealth Competences in Private Health

Centres in Urban Tanzania." *Journal of Health Informatics in Developing Countries* 14(1).

Lakmeeharan, K., Q. Manji, R. Nyario, and H. Poeltner. 2020. "Solving Africa's Infrastructure Paradox." *McKinsey & Company*. https://www.mckinsey.com/business-functions/operations/our-insights/solving-africas-infrastructure-paradox

Lancaster, Henry. 2017. "Fixed and Mobile Broadband in Africa: An Executive Summary." *Africology: The Journal of Pan African Studies* 10(10). http://www.jpanafrican.org/docs/vol10no10/10.10-15-Lancaster.pdf

Latif Dahir, Abdi. 2017. "Kenya's Newest Tech Hubs Are Sprouting outside Its 'Silicon Savannah' in Nairobi." *Quartz Africa*. https://qz.com/africa/1059305/kenyas-newest-tech-hubs-are-sprouting-outside-its-silicon-savannah-in-nairobi/

Latif Dahir, Abdi, and Yomi Kazeem. 2018. "Tunisia's 'Startup Act' Could Show Other African Governments How to Support Tech Ecosystems." *Quartz Africa*. https://qz.com/africa/1252113/tunisia-startup-act-to-boost-african-tech-ecosystem-and-innovation/

Lee, M., J. J. Yun, A. Pyka, et al. 2018. "How to Respond to the Fourth Industrial Revolution, or the Second Information Technology Revolution? Dynamic New Combinations between Technology, Market, and Society through Open Innovation." *Journal of Open Innovation: Technology, Market, and Complexity* 4(3): 21.

Lewin, D. M., B. Williamson, and M. E. Cave. 2009. *Regulating Next-Generation Fixed Access to Telecommunications Services*. SSRN.

Lewis, Nell. 2019. "Drones, Apps and Smart Lockers: The Technology Transforming Healthcare in Africa." *CNN Business*. www.cnn.com/2019/10/15/tech/tech-africahealthcare/index.html

Li, G., Y. Hou, and A. Wu. 2017. "Fourth Industrial Revolution: Technological Drivers, Impacts and Coping Methods." *Chinese Geographical Science* 27(4): 626–637.

Liao, Yongxin, Fernando Deschamps, Eduardo de Freitas Rocha Loures, and Luiz Felipe Pierin Ramos. 2017. "Past, Present and Future of Industry 4.0 – A Systematic Literature Review and Research Agenda Proposal." *International Journal of Production Research* 55(12): 3609–3629.

Lightfoot, G., and T. Wisniewski. 2014. "Information Asymmetry and Power in a Surveillance Society." MPRA Paper No. 58726. https://mpra.ub.uni-muenchen.de/58726/8/MPRA_paper_58726.pdf

Linsky, Marty, and Ghaleb Darabya. 2019. "Leadership in the Fourth Industrial Revolution." *Dubai Policy Review*. http://dx.doi.org/10.46993/DPR/EN002

Liu, Peter, and Timothy Reuter. 2021. "Five Lessons from Africa on How Drones Could Transform Medical Supply Chains." *World Economic*

Forum. https://www.weforum.org/agenda/2021/04/5-lessons-from-africa-on-how-drones-could-transform-medical-supply-chains/

Lotz, Brendyn. 2015. "African Countries Top List for Mobile Malware Attacks." *Hypertext*. https://www.htxt.co.za/2015/12/22/mobile-is-the-weak-link-in-business-network-security/

Lou, Karine Kouassi, Francie Sadeski, and Matthieu Lacave. 2019. "Study on Unlocking the Potential of the Fourth Industrial Revolution in Africa. Morocco Country Case Study." *Technopolis & Research ICT Africa & Tambourine Innovation Ventures, African Development Bank*. https://4irpotential.africa/

Ly, Racine. 2021. "Machine Learning Challenges and Opportunities in the African Agricultural Sector – A General Perspective." arXiv preprint arXiv:2107.05101. https://arxiv.org/abs/2107.05101

Lye, David. 2017. "The Fourth Industrial Revolution and Challenges for Government." *Brink*. www.brinknews.com/the-fourth-industrial-revolution-and-challenges-for-government

Maaref, Slaheddine. 2012. "Cloud Computing in Africa: Situation and Perspectives." *ITU*. https://www.itu.int/ITU-D/treg/publications/Cloud_Computing_Afrique-e.pdf

Maclean, Ruth, and Simon Marks. 2020 April 18. "10 African Countries Have No Ventilators. That's Only Part of the Problem." *The New York Times*. https://www.nytimes.com/2020/04/18/world/africa/africa-coronavirus-ventilators.html?smid=url-share

Madden, Payce. 2020. "Africa's Preparedness for the Fourth Industrial Revolution." *Brookings*. https://www.brookings.edu/blog/africa-in-focus/2020/03/11/figures-of-the-week-africas-preparedness-for-the-fourth-industrial-revolution/

Mahajan, Vijay. 2009. *Africa Rising: How 900 Million African Consumers Offer More Than You Think*. Upper Saddle River, NJ: Pearson.

2011 [2009]. *Africa Rising: How 900 Million African Consumers Offer More Than You Think*. FT Press (initially published in 2008).

Maisha Meds. 2020. *2019 Annual Report*. https://maishameds.org/wpcontent/uploads/2020/07/Maisha-Meds-2019-Annual-Report.pdf

Makaka, Andrew, Sarah Breen, and Agnes Binagwaho. 2012. "Universal Health Coverage in Rwanda: A Report of Innovations to Increase Enrolment in Community-Based Health Insurance." *The Lancet* 380(7).

Makuvaza, Leonard, Chernay Johnson, and Herman Smit. 2018. "The Rise of African Digital Platforms." *Insight2Impact*. http://i2ifacility.org/insights/blog/the-rise-of-african-digital-platforms?entity=blog

Manson, Katrina. 2015. "GE and Philips Scan Africa Medical Market." *Financial Times.* www.ft.com/content/6cf30f9e-c26c-11e4-ad89-00144feab7de

Manyika, J., M. Chui, J. Bughin, R. Dobbs, P. Bisson, and A. Marrs. 2013. "Disruptive Technologies: Advances That Will Transform Life, Business, and the Global Economy." *McKinsey Global Institute.* www.mckinsey.com/~/media/McKinsey/Business%20Functions/McKinsey%20Digital

Manyika, J., M. Chui, J. Bughin, R. Dobbs, P. Bisson, J. Woetzel, and D. Aharon. 2015. "Unlocking the Potential of the Internet of Things." *McKinsey Global Institute.* www.mckinsey.com/business-functions/mckinsey-digital/our-insights/the-internet-of-things-the-value-of-digitizing-the-physical-world

Manyika, J., M. Chui, M. Miremadi, J. Bughin, K. George, P. Willmott, and M. Dewhurst. 2017. "A Future That Works: Automation, Employment, and Productivity." *McKinsey Global Institute.* www.mckinsey.com/featured-insights/digital-disruption/harnessing-automation-for-a-future-that-works

Marinchenko, T. E. 2021. "Digital Transformations in Agriculture." In A. V. Bogoviz (Eds.), *Complex Systems: Innovation and Sustainability in the Digital Age.* Studies in Systems, Decision and Control, vol. 283. Cham: Springer. https://doi.org/10.1007/978-3-030-58823-6_45

Maritz, Jaco. 2013. "Private Sector Eyeing Opportunities in Africa's Healthcare Industry." *How We Made It in Africa.* www.howwemadeitinafrica.com/private-sector-eyeing-opportunities-in-africas-healthcare-sector

Marr, Bernard. 2018. "Nine Powerful Real-World Applications of Augmented Reality (AR) Today." *Forbes.* www.forbes.com/sites/bernardmarr/2018/07/30/9-powerful-real-world-applications-of-augmented-reality-ar-today/#29e6f23c2fe9

Mashrou3i. 2020. "About Mashrou3i." https://mashrou3i.net/en/what-is-mashrou3i/

Mastercard Foundation. 2021a. "Mastercard Foundation to Deploy $1.3 Billion in Partnership with Africa CDC to Save Lives and Livelihoods." https://mastercardfdn.org/mastercard-foundation-to-deploy-1-3-billion-in-partnership-with-africa-cdc-to-save-lives-and-livelihoods/

2021b. "New Platform Curates African Perspectives on the COVID-19 Pandemic." https://mastercardfdn.org/new-platform-curates-african-perspectives-on-the-covid-19-pandemic/

Matchaba, Patrice. 2018. "How New Tech Can Propel Africa to the Forefront of Healthcare." *World Economic Forum.* www.weforum.org/agenda/2018/01/africa-lead-healthcare-fourth-industrial-revolution/

Mathe, Amanda. 2019. "The Misunderstood World of Cybersecurity in Africa. Policy Center." https://www.policycenter.ma/opinion/misunder stood-world-cybersecurity-africa#.YRVTYI5Kg2w

"Mauritius' Financial Sector to Launch Digital-Asset Licensing Program." 2019. *Africa Times.* africatimes.com/2019/02/20/mauritius-financial-sector-to-launch-digital-asset-licensing-program/

"Mauritius Is Willing to Adapt Distributed Ledger Technology and Acknowledge the Cryptocurrency as Digital Asset." 2018. *Offshore License.* offshorelicense.com/blog/detail/mauritius-willing-adapt-distributed-ledger-technology-and-acknowledge-cryptocurrency-digital-asset

Mauritius Ministry of Technology, Communication, and Innovation. 2018. "Digital Mauritius 2030 Strategic Plan." mtci.govmu.org/English/Documents/2018/Launching Digital Transformation Strategy 191218/DM 2030 17 December 2018 at 12.30hrs.pdf

Mayo Clinic. 2019. "MRI." www.mayoclinic.org/tests-procedures/mri/about/pac-20384768

Mazambani, L., T. Rushwaya, and E. Mutambara. 2018. "Financial Inclusion: Disrupted Liquidity and Redundancy of Mobile Money Agents in Zimbabwe." *Investment Management and Financial Innovations* 15(3): 131–142.

McHugh, Lauren. 2017. "How Global Pharma Players Can Gain Traction in Africa." *Wharton School of the University of Pennsylvania.* https://knowledge.wharton.upenn.edu/article/global-pharma-players-can-gain-traction-africa

McKinsey Global Institute. 2020. "Risk, Resilience, and Rebalancing in Global Value Chains." https://www.mckinsey.com/business-functions/operations/our-insights/risk-resilience-and-rebalancing-in-global-value-chains

Meads, David. 2017. "Here's How Africa Can Take Advantage of the Fourth Industrial Revolution." *World Economic Forum.* www.weforum.org/agenda/2017/05/heres-how-africa-can-take-advantage-of-the-fourth-industrial-revolution/

Meijia, P., and V. Castel. 2012. *Could Oil Shine like Diamonds? How Botswana Avoided the Resource Curse and Its Implications for a New Libya.* AfDB Chief Economist Complex.

Mellah, Mohamed. 2018. "Transformation digitale: Le Maroc à la recherche de son second souffle." *Al HuffPost Maghreb.* www.huffpostmaghreb.com/mohamed-mellah/transformation-digitale-le-maroc-a-la-recherche-de-son-second-souffle_b_19085134.html

Mercy Corps. 2019. "Towards a Digital Workforce: Understanding the Building Blocks of the Kenya Gig Economy." https://www.mercycorps

.org/sites/default/files/2020-01/Youth_Impact_Labs_Kenya_Gig_
Economy_Report_2019_1.pdf

MINDEX. 2018. "GMEX Leads Consortium to Launch a Mauritius Based
International Commodities and Derivatives Exchange (MINDEX)
Ecosystem." www.mindex.mu/gmex-leads-consortium-to-launch-a-
mauritius-based-international-commodities-and-derivatives-exchange-
mindex-ecosystem/

Minishi-Majanja, Mabel, and Ezra Ondari-Okemwa. 2009. "Enhancing
Government Basic Service Delivery and Performance Effectiveness in
Sub-Saharan Africa through e-Governance." *Mousaion* 27(2): 17–35.

Ministry of Communications and Information Technology. 2020. "Egypt
Telecom Sector Grows by 15.2% Despite COVID-19: Cabinet Report.
Ahram Online. https://mcit.gov.eg/Upcont/MediaCenter/EN_Egypt_
Telecom_Sector_Grows_by_15.2_Despite_COVID_19_Cabinet_
Report%20.pdf

2021. "Digital Egypt." https://mcit.gov.eg/en/Digital_Egypt

Minu, M. S., and Zoya Ahmed. 2020. "Augmented Analytics: The Future of
Business Intelligence." *Recent Trends in Computer Science and
Software Technology* 5: 7–13. doi: 10.5281/zenodo.3757837

MISC. 2018. *MISC Industrial Automation Systems.* https://www.miscegypt
.com/

Mistra, M. 2019. *Epidemics and the Health of African Nations.* African
Books Collective. https://www.africanbookscollective.com/books/epi
demics-and-the-health-of-african-nations

Mlambo, Perseus. 2019. *Africa's Digital Generation Gap.* Project Syndicate.
https://www.project-syndicate.org/commentary/africa-overregulation-
digital-economy-by-perseus-mlambo-2019-02

Mogo, Ebele. 2021. "The AfCFTA Agreement Should Be Radical in
Prioritizing Africa's Health." *Quartz Africa.* https://qz.com/africa/
1977159/?utm_term=mucp

Monks, Kieron. 2017. "M-Pesa: Kenya's Mobile Money Success Story Turns
10." *CNN.* https://edition.cnn.com/2017/02/21/africa/mpesa-10th-anni
versary/index.html

Monostori, László. 2014. "Cyber-Physical Production Systems: Roots,
Expectations and R&D Challenges." *Procedia CIRP* 17: 9-13. http://
www.sciencedirect.com/science/article/pii/S2212827114003497

Moore, Jan, Vinay Chandran, and Jörg Schubert. 2018. "Are Middle East
Workers Ready for the Impact of Automation?" *McKinsey and
Company.* https://www.mckinsey.com/featured-insights/middle-east-
and-africa/are-middle-east-workers-ready-for-the-impact-of-
automation

Mordor Intelligence. 2021. *Africa Automative Market – Growth, Trends, COVID-19 Impact, and Forecasts (2021–2026)*. https://www .mordorintelligence.com/industry-reports/africa-automotive-industry-outlook

Morel, Benoit. 2016. "The Challenge of Building Cyber Security Capability in Africa." *Africa Policy Review*. http://africapolicyreview.com/the-chal lenge-of-building-cyber-security-capability-in-africa/

"Morocco Has Second Highest Potential for Automation in Africa – McKinsey Says." 2017. *The North Africa Post*. http://northafricapost .com/17406-morocco-second-highest-potential-automation-africa-mckinsey-says.html

"Morocco Seeks Digital Transformation for Economic, Social Development." 2019. *Morocco World News*. www.moroccoworldnews.com/2019/01/ 263828/morocco-digital-economic-social-development/

Mothobi, Onkokame, and Lukasz Grzybowski. 2017. "Infrastructure Deficiencies and Adoption of Mobile Money in Sub-Saharan Africa." *Information Economics and Policy* 40: 71–79.

Mourdoukoutas, Eleni. 2017. "Africa's Digital Rise Hooked on Innovation." *UN Africa Renewal*. https://www.un.org/africarenewal/ magazine/may-july-2017/africa%E2%80%99s-digital-rise-hooked-innovation

Mpala, Daniel. 2018. "Five SA Biotech Companies to Watch in 2018." *Ventureburn*. http://ventureburn.com/2018/05/x-south-african-biotech-companies-watch-2018-digital-stars/

Mphidi, Hamilton. 2008. "Digital Divide and e-Governance in South Africa." *Research, Innovation and Partnerships, Tshwane University of Technology*.

Muggah, Robert, and Katie Hill. 2018. "African Cities Will Double in Population by 2050. Here Are 4 Ways to Make Sure They Thrive." *World Economic Forum*. https://www.weforum.org/agenda/2018/06/ Africa-urbanization-cities-double-population-2050-4%20ways-thrive/

Mureithi, Carlos. 2021a. "The Covid-19 Pandemic Has Created Africa's Next Big Investment Opportunity." *Quartz Africa*. https://qz.com/ africa/1986528/the-covid-19-pandemic-has-boosted-african-health-tech-startups/

  2021b. "African Telemedicine Startups Need Regulation to Reach More Patients." *Quartz Africa*. https://qz.com/africa/2010661/africas-grow ing-telemedicine-space-has-a-regulation-problem/

Muto. 2008. "The Impact of Mobile Phone Coverage Expansion on Market Participation: Panel Data Evidence from Uganda." *World Development* 37(12): 1887–1896.

Mwanza, Kevin, and Henry Wilkings. 2018. "African Startups Bet on Blockchain to Tackle Land Fraud." *Reuters*. www.reuters.com/article/us-africa-landrights-blockchain/african-startups-bet-on-blockchain-to-tackle-land-fraud-idUSKCN1G00YK

Myovella, Godwin, Mehmet Karacuka, and Justus Haucap. 2020. "Digitalization and Economic Growth: A Comparative Analysis of Sub-Saharan Africa and OECD Economies." *Telecommunications Policy* 44(2): S0308596119302290.

Narayanan, Anjana. 2020. "How Data Analytics Skills Can Open New Opportunities for Oil and Gas Professionals." *The Journal of Petroleum Technology*. https://jpt.spe.org/how-data-analytics-skills-can-open-new-opportunities-for-oil-and-gas-professionals

Nasman, Nina, Dan Dowling, Benjamin Combes, and Celine Herweijer. 2017. *Fourth Industrial Revolution for the Earth: Harnessing the 4th Industrial Revolution for Sustainable Emerging Cities*. PricewaterhouseCoopers. https://www.pwc.com/gx/en/sustainability/assets/4ir-for-the-earth.pdf

Nathaniel, Allen. 2021. "Africa's Evolving Cyber Threats. Spotlight, Africa Center for Strategic Studies." https://africacenter.org/spotlight/africa-evolving-cyber-threats/

Nathaniel, Allen, and Noëlle van der Waag-Cowling. 2021. "How African States Can Tackle State-Backed Cyber Threats." *Brookings*. https://www.brookings.edu/techstream/how-african-states-can-tackle-state-backed-cyberthreats/#:~:text=African%20states%20can%20benefit%20from,threat%20of%20state%2Dsponsored%20cyberattacks.&text=African%20actors%20are%20increasingly%20prioritizing%20cybersecurity%20at%20a%20continental%20and%20regional%20level

National Computer Board. 2020. "National Computer Board." *1 World Connected*. https://1worldconnected.org/project/africa_digitalskills_nationalcomputerboardmauritius

National Nanotechnology Initiative. 2021. "NNI Budget." *United States of America*. https://www.nano.gov/about-nni/what/funding

Nature Index. 2018. "Egypt." https://www.natureindex.com/country-out puts/egypt

Naudé, Wim. 2017. "Entrepreneurship, Education and the Fourth Industrial Revolution in Africa." *Institute of Labor Economics*. www.iza.org/publications/dp/10855/entrepreneurship-education-and-the-fourth-industrial-revolution-in-africa

2018. "Brilliant Technologies and Brave Entrepreneurs: A New Narrative for African Manufacturing." *Journal of International Affairs* 72(1): 143–158.

Navas-Sabater, Juan. 2015. "World Bank Regional Broadband Programs and Proposed Central Asian Regional Fiber Optic Network (CARFON)." UN SPECA Project Working Group on Knowledge-based Development, Dushanbe, Tajikistan. https://www.unescap.org/sites/default/d8files/knowledge-products/World%20Bank%20Regional%20Broadband%20Programs%20and%20CARFON%20-%20Dushanbe%20workshop%20June%202015.pdf

Necdem, Assongmo. 2015. "Cameroun: 22,2 milliards FCfa de pertes en 2015 sur les appels frauduleux par Simbox." *Investir au Cameroun.* https://www.investiraucameroun.com/telecom/0910-6775-cameroun-22-2-milliards-fcfa-de-pertes-en-2015-sur-les-appels-frauduleux-par-simbox

Ncube, Mtuli. 2015. "Inclusive Growth in Africa." In Celestin Monga and Justin Yifu Len (Eds.), *The Oxford Handbook of Africa and Economics*, vol. 1. Oxford: Oxford University Press.

Ndemo, Bitange. 2015. "Effective Innovation Policies for Development: The Case of Kenya." *Global Innovation Index 2015: Effective Innovation Policies for Development.* https://www.globalinnovationindex.org/user files/file/reportpdf/GII-2015-v5.pdf

2016. "The Paradigm Shift: Disruption, Creativity, and Innovation in Kenya." In Bitange Ndemo and Tim Weiss (Eds.), *Digital Kenya: An Entrepreneurial Revolution in the Making.* London: Palgrave Macmillan, pp. 1–23.

Ndung'u, Njuguna. 2018. "Next Steps for the Digital Revolution in Africa." The Brookings Institution Working Paper 20. www.brookings.edu/wp-content/uploads/2018/10/Digital-Revolution-in-Africa_Brookings_AGI_20181022.pdf

2019. "Could Taxation of Mobile Banking in Africa Stall Financial Inclusion?" In *Foresight Africa.* Washington, DC: The Brookings Institution.

Ndung'u, Njuguna, and Landry Signé. 2020. "The Fourth Industrial Revolution and Digitization Will Transform Africa into a Global Powerhouse." www.brookings.edu/wp-content/uploads/2020/01/ForesightAfrica2020_Chapter5_20200110.pdf

NEPAD. 2012. *Africa Information and Communications Technology Sector Outlook 2030.* https://www.nepad.org/publication/africa-ict-sector-out look-2030-0

NEPAD, AU, and AfDB. 2011. *Study on Program for Infrastructure Development in Africa: Study Synthesis.* http://www.au-pida.org/down load/study-on-pida-phase-iii-reports/

Neudert, Lisa-Maria. 2018. "Future Elections May Be Swayed by Intelligent, Weaponized Chatbots." *MIT Technology Review.* www

.technologyreview.com/s/611832/future-elections-may-be-swayed-by-intelligent-weaponized-chatbots/

Newfarmer, Richard, John Page, and Finn Tarp. 2018. *Industries without Smokestacks: Industrialization in Africa Reconsidered.* Oxford: Oxford University Press.

Newman, Carol, John Page, and Finn Tarp. 2017. "Made in Africa – The Future of Production on the Continent." *World Economic Forum.* www .weforum.org/agenda/2017/01/made-in-africa-the-future-of-production-on-the-continent/

Nigeria Communications Commission. 2021. "ICT Development: Nigeria Seeks Increased Regional Collaboration among West African States." https://www.ncc.gov.ng/media-centre/news-headlines/965-ict-develop ment-nigeria-seeks-increased-regional-collaboration-among-west-african-states

Nijhuis, Sebastiaan, and Iris Herrmann. 2019. *The Fourth Industrial Revolution in Agriculture.* Strategy+Business. https://www.strategy-business.com/article/The-fourth-industrial-revolution-in-agriculture

Norbrook, Nicholas, Marième Soumaré, Quentin Velluet, and Mathier Galtier. 2020. "Tech Hubs across Africa to Incubate the Next Generation." *The Africa Report.* https://www.theafricareport.com/23434/tech-hubs-across-africa-to-incubate-the-next-generation/

Nsehe, Mfonobong. 2014. "Seven Innovative Products from Africa You Should Know." *Forbes.* www.forbes.com/sites/mfonobongnsehe/2014/02/13/seven-innovative-products-from-africa-you-should-know/#1da38a5f7f1c

2018. "Meet Piggybank.ng, the Nigerian FinTech Startup That Just Raised $1.1 million." *Forbes.* https://www.forbes.com/sites/mfono bongnsehe/2018/05/31/meet-piggybank-ng-the-nigerian-fintech-startup-that-just-raised-1-1million/#bb8db1310ca2

Nsengimana, Jean Phibert. 2018. "How Africa Wins The 4th Industrial Revolution." *Forbes.* https://www.forbes.com/sites/startupnationcen tral/2018/10/10/how-africa-wins-the-4th-industrial-revolution/ #66f14c7c2f37

Nyakanini Grace, Sayinzoga Maurice, Gates Nicholas, Almqvist Erik, and Erkan Kutay. 2020. "Unlocking the Digital Economy in Africa: Benchmarking the Digital Transformation Journey." *Dial-Smart Africa.* https://digitalimpactalliance.org/wp-content/uploads/2020/10/ SmartAfrica-DIAL_DigitalEconomyInAfrica2020-v7_ENG.pdf

OC&C. 2018. "Tech Entrepreneurship Ecosystem in Nigeria." https://www .occstrategy.com/media/1307/tech-eship-in-nigeria.pdf

OECD. 2018. *Digital Government Review of Morocco: Laying the Foundations for the Digital Transformation of the Public Sector in Morocco.* Paris: OECD Digital Government Studies, OECD Publishing.

Ogaugwu, Christian, Stanley Agbo, and Moninat Adekoya. 2019. "CRISPR in Sub-Saharan Africa: Applications and Education." *Trends in BioTechnology* 7: 3. https://doi.org/10.1016/j.tibtech.2018.07.012

Ogbole, Godwin I., Adekunle O. Adeyomoye, Augustina Badu-Peprah, Yaw Mensah, and Donald Amasike Nzeh. 2018. "Survey of Magnetic Resonance Imaging Availability in West Africa." *Pan African Medical Journal* 30(1): 240.

Ogbuoji, Osondu, Ipchita Bharali, Natalie Emergy, and Kaci Kennedy McDade. 2019. "Closing Africa's Health Financing Gap." *Brookings.* www.brookings.edu/blog/future-development/2019/03/01/closing-afri cas-health-financing-gap/

Okonkwo, Judith. 2018. "Africa's Largest Augmented and Virtual Reality Event Supported by VR First." *Medium.* https://medium.com/vr-first/vr-first-supports-africas-largest-augmented-and-virtual-reality-event-f33397799677

Olyaei, Sam. 2017. "Gartner Says Middle East and North Africa Information Security Spending Will Grow 11 Percent to Reach $1.8 Billion in 2017." *Gartner.* https://www.gartner.com/en/newsroom/press-releases/2017-10-16-gartner-says-middle-east-and-north-africa-information-security-spend ing-will-grow-11-percent-to-reach-1-billion-in-2017

Ong, S. K., and Andrew Y. C. Nee. 2013. *Virtual and Augmented Reality Applications in Manufacturing.* Springer Science & Business Media. Singapore: National University of Singapore.

Onwughalu, Vincent, and Victor Ojakorotu. 2020. "The 4th Industrial Revolution: an Opportunity for Africa's 'Decolonization' and Development or Recolonization?" *African Renaissance; London. United Kingdom* 17(1): 75–93. https://journals.co.za/doi/10.31920/2516-5305/ 2020/17n1a4

Oolun, Krishna, Suraj Ramgolam, and Vasenden Dorasami. 2012. "The Making of a Digital Nation: Toward i-Mauritius." *The Global Information Technology Report* 161–168.

Orange. 2017. *Orange Middle East and Africa: Partner for Digital Transformation.* www.orange.com/en/content/download/38172/ 1160229/version/6/file/MEA_Plaquette_2017_EN_PDF_Web_Page.pdf

Osuagwu, Prine. 2021. "Why ICT Will Remain Nigeria's Top GDP Earner." *Vanguard.* https://www.vanguardngr.com/2021/09/why-ict-will-remain-nigerias-top-gdp-earner/

Oughton, Edward J., Niccolo Comini, Vivien Foster, and Jim W. Hall. 2021. "Policy Choices Can Help Keep 4G and 5G Universal Broadband Affordable." Policy Research Working Paper No. 9563. Washington, DC: World Bank. https://openknowledge.worldbank.org/handle/10986/ 35212

Owoyemi, Ayomide, Andy Boyd, Adeneken Osiyemi, and Joshua Owoyemi.
    2020. *Artificial Intelligence for Healthcare in Africa*. Frontiers in Digital
    Health. https://doi.org/10.3389/fdgth.2020.00006
Oxford Business Group. 2017a. "Nigeria Makes Significant Progress
    towards Universal Health Care Coverage." *The Report: Nigeria 2017*.
    https://oxfordbusinessgroup.com/overview/prioritising-care-new-
    developments-health-care-signify-progress-towards-universal-cover
    age-political
    2017b. "Tunisia's Education Sector to Be Overhauled." https://
    oxfordbusinessgroup.com/overview/track-series-reforms-are-set-over
    haul-sector
    2018a. "Skilled Workforce, Low Costs and State Support Offer an
    Attractive Environment for Technological Investment in Egypt." *The
    Report: Egypt 2018*. https://oxfordbusinessgroup.com/overview/top-
    ranks-highly-skilled-workforce-low-costs-and-government-support-
    offer-attractive-environment
    2018b. "Young Egyptians Gain ICT Capabilities and Entrepreneurial
    Skills with New Programs." *The Report: Egypt 2018*. https://
    oxfordbusinessgroup.com/analysis/brain-gain-multiple-initiatives-
    launched-develop-ict-capabilities-and-entrepreneurial-skills-young
    2020. "Tunisia's Government Works to Develop the Start-Up Ecosystem
    Using New Policies and Incentives." https://new.oxfordbusinessgroup
    .com/article/tunisias-government-works-to-develop-the-start-up-ecosys
    tem-using-new-policies-and-incentives/
    2021a. "E-Commerce in Sub-Saharan Africa: Can Covid-19 Growth Be
    Sustained?" https://oxfordbusinessgroup.com/news/e-commerce-sub-
    saharan-africa-can-covid-19-growth-be-sustained
    2021b. "The Fourth Industrial Revolution in Sub-Saharan Africa: Key to
    the Coronavirus Recovery?" https://oxfordbusinessgroup.com/news/
    fourth-industrial-revolution-sub-saharan-africa-key-coronavirus-
    recovery
    2021c. "What Infrastructure Will Aid in Egypt's Digital Transformation?"
    https://oxfordbusinessgroup.com/overview/mobile-connection-new-
    legislation-and-continuing-investment-communications-infrastructure-
    set
Oyelola, Folake Olagunju. 2016. "Cybersecurity and the Fight against
    Cybercrimes in West Africa: Current Status, Challenges and the
    Future." *Global Forum on Cyber Expertise*. https://www.thegfce.com/
    news/news/2016/12/07/cybersecurity-and-fight-against-cybercrimes
Panayotou, Todor. 1993. "Empirical Tests and Policy Analysis of
    Environmental Degradation at Different Stages of Economic

Development." ILO Working Papers 992927783402676. International Labour Organization.

Panayotou, Todor. 2003. *Economic Growth and the Environment.* United Nations Economic Commission for Europe Spring Seminar.

Pandey, Piyush, Deborah Golden, Sean Peasley, and Mahesh Kelkar. 2019. "Making Smart Cities Cybersecure: Ways to Address Distinct Risks in an Increasingly Connected Urban Future." *Deloitte.* https:// www2.deloitte.com/insights/us/en/focus/smart-city/making-smart-cities-cyber-secure.html

Pape. 2019. "Transformation Digitale. Inwi dote le Maroc de la plus grande infrastructure datacenter." *Micromagma Magazine.* www .micromagma.ma/actualites/maroc/item/8774-transformation-digi tale-inwi-dote-le-maroc-de-la-plus-grande-infrastructure-datacenter

Paracha, Zubair Naeem. 2018. "A Guide to Egypt's Tech Startup Ecosystem." *Menabytes.* https://www.menabytes.com/egypt-tech-startup-ecosystem-guide/

Pensulo, Charles. 2021. "Could 3D Printed Schools Be 'Transformative' for Education in Africa?" *World Economic Forum.* https://www .weforum.org/agenda/2021/07/could-3d-printed-schools-be-trans formative-for-education-in-africa/

Pepper, Robert, John Garrity, and Connie LaSalle. 2016. "Cross-Border Data Flows, Digital Innovation, and Economic Growth." *Global Information Technology Report.* https://reports.weforum.org/ global-information-technology-report-2016/1-2-cross-border-data-flows-digital-innovation-and-economic-growth/

Peters, Michael A. 2017. "Technological Unemployment: Educating for the Fourth Industrial Revolution." *Journal of Self-Governance and Management Economics* 5(1): 25–33.

Pharatlhatlhe, Kesaobaka, and Bruce Byiers. 2019. "Youth Unemployment and the Role of Regional Organisations: The Case of the Southern African Development Community (SADC)." https:// ecdpm.org/publications/youth-unemployment-and-the-role-of-regional-organisations/

PND. 2016. "Gates Foundation to Invest $5 Billion in Africa over Five Years." *PND by Candid.* https://philanthropynewsdigest.org/news/ gates-foundation-to-invest-5-billion-in-africa-over-five-years

Ponelis, Shana R., and Marlene A. Holmner. 2015. "ICT in Africa: Building a Better Life for All." *Information Technology for Development* 21(2): 163–177.

Poverty Spotlight. 2021. "The Impact." https://www.povertystoplight .org/en/impact/

Power Africa. 2020. "Cybersecurity for Transmission and Distribution in Africa." *Power Africa.* https://powerafrica.medium.com/cybersecurity-for-transmission-and-distribution-in-africa-475676074534

Prakash, Chander, Sunpreet Singh, Bs Pabla, and Grzegorz Krolczyk. 2020. *Advances in Materials Science and Engineering.* Singapore: Springer. http://dx.doi.org/10.1007/978-981-15-4059-2

Prisecaru, Petre. 2016. "Challenges of the Fourth Industrial Revolution." *Knowledge Horizons – Economics* 8(1)" 57–62. https://EconPapers.repec .org/RePEc:khe:journl:v:8:y:2016:i:1:p:57-62

Puchooa, Daneshwar. 2004. "Biotechnology in Mauritius: Current Status and Constraints." *Electronic Journal of Biotechnology* 7(2).

PwC. 2015. *Global State of Information Security Survey 2015.*

   2016. *The Choice to Change: Africa Oil and Gas Review.* https://dpe.pwc .com/content/dam/pwc/za/en/assets/pdf/africa-oil-and-gas-review-2016 .pdf

   2017. "Fighting Counterfeit Pharmaceuticals: New Defenses for an Underestimated – and Growing – Menace." *Strategy&.* www .strategyand.pwc.com/gx/en/insights/2017/fighting-counterfeit-pharma ceuticals/fighting-counterfeit-pharmaceuticals.pdf

Qiang, C. Z., and C. M. Rossotto. 2009. "Economic Impacts of Broadband." In *Information and Communications for Development 2009: Extending Reach and Increasing Impact.* Washington, DC: World Bank, pp. 35–50.

Quarshie, Henry Osborn, and Alexander Martin-Odoom. 2012. *Ethical Dilemma in a Computerized Society: Computer Ethics and Society.* Mauritius: Lambert Academic Publishing.

Quartz Staff. 2019. "Quartz Africa Innovators 2019: Leading the Change for Africa's Future." *Quartz.* https://qz.com/africa/1700312/quartz-africa-innovators-2019

Qui, Winston. 2020. "A study on Submarine Cables Crossing Egypt and Their Costs." *Submarine Networks.* https://www.submarinenetworks .com/en/services/research/submarine-cables-crossing-egypt-and-cost

Radwan, Ismail, and Giulia Pellegrini. 2010. *Knowledge, Productivity, and Innovation in Nigeria: Creating a New Economy.* Washington, DC: The World Bank Group. https://openknowledge.worldbank.org/handle/ 10986/2424

Rao, Pavithra. 2020 June 25. "Nigerian Digital Healthcare Startup Helps Triage COVID-19 Cases." *Africa Renewal.* https://www.un.org/africar enewal/magazine/june-2020/coronavirus/nigerian-digital-healthcare-startup-helps-triage-covid-19-cases

Ratcheva, Vesselina Stefanova, and Till Leopold. 2018. "Five Things to Know about the Future of Jobs." *World Economic Forum.* https://www.weforum .org/agenda/2018/09/future-of-jobs-2018-things-to-know/

Razavi, Lauren. 2018. "How Rwanda's Capital Became an African Tech Leader." *Medium.* https://medium.com/s/story/how-rwandas-capital-became-an-african-tech-leader-66e00edc74d

Rehr, David K., and Dorin Munteanu. 2021. "The Promise of Robotic Process Automation for the Public Sector." Center for Business Civic Engagement George Mason University. https://cbce.gmu.edu/wp-content/uploads/2021/06/The-Promise-of-RPA-For-The-Public-Sector.pdf

Republic of Rwanda Ministry of Finance and Economic Planning. 2000. *Rwanda Vision 2020.* Kigali, Rwanda: Republic of Rwanda. https://www.sida.se/globalassets/global/countries-and-regions/africa/rwanda/d402331a.pdf

Retief, Chanel. 2021. "The Cost of CO2VID." *Forbes Africa.* https://www.forbesafrica.com/focus/2021/08/04/the-cost-of-co$_2$vid/

Richard, Stéphane. 2019. "Three Reasons Why Most Africans Aren't on the Internet – And How to Connect Them." *World Economic Forum.* https://www.weforum.org/agenda/2019/08/3-reasons-why-most-africans-arent-on-the-internet-and-how-to-connect-them/

Richards, Kevin. 2017. "2017 Cost of Cyber Crime Study." *Accenture Security.* https://www.accenture.com/us-en/insight-cost-of-cybercrime-2017

Riley, Thyra, and Anoma Kulathunga, 2017. *Bringing E-money to the Poor: Successes and Failures.* Washington, DC: World Bank.

Roman, Rodrigo, Pablo Najera, and Javier Lopez. 2011. "Securing the Internet of Things." *IEEE Computer* 44: 51–58.

Root, Tik. 2016. "Start-Ups for the State." *Foreign Policy.* https://foreignpolicy.com/2016/06/26/start-ups-for-the-state-rwanda-entrepreneurship/

Ross, Michael. 1999. "The Political Economy of the Resource Curse." *World Politics* 51: 297–322.

Rouse, M. Stella, and Grietjie Verhoef. 2016. "Mobile Banking in Africa: The Current State of Play." In B. Batiz-Lazo and L. Efthymiou (Eds.), *The Book of Payments: Historical and Contemporary Views of the Cashless Economy.* London: Palgrave Macmillan, pp. 233–257. https://doi.org/10.1057/978-1-137-60231-2_21

Rowe, Brent, Doug Reeves, Dallas Wood, and Fern Braun, 2010. "Estimating the Market for Internet Service Provider-Based Cybersecurity Solutions." *Institute for Home Security Solutions.*

Russo, Amanda, and Harrison Wolf. 2019. "What the World Can Learn from Rwanda's Approach to Drones." *World Economic Forum.* https://www.weforum.org/agenda/2019/01/what-the-world-can-learn-from-rwandas-approach-to-drones/.

Russo, Giuliano, Gerald Bloom, and David McCoy. 2017. "Universal Health Coverage, Economic Slowdown and System Resilience: Africa's Policy Dilemma." *BMJ Global Health* 2(3).

Rwanda Energy Group. 2021. "Electricity Access." https://www.reg.rw/
what-we-do/access/

Sahadut, Muhammad Ridwan, Mohammad Hashim Bundhoo, and Pierre
Clarel Catherine. 2015. "The Establishment of Smart Cities in
Mauritius: Requirements, Challenges and Opportunities." *The Second
International Conference on Data Mining, Internet Computing, and Big
Data (Big Data 2015)*.

Salient. 2021. *Innovations in Health Product Distribution in Sub-Saharan
Africa: Market Intelligence Report*. https://healthtech.salientadvisory
.com/reports/african-health-product-distribution-2021/

Sawahel, Wagdy. 2021. "Africa Launches Powerful Supercomputer."
University World News. https://www.universityworldnews.com/post
.php?story=20210228193908881

SAS. 2019. "Big Data: What It Is and Why It Matters." https://www.sas
.com/en_us/insights/big-data/what-is-big-data.html

Schaffer, Mark, Andre Steenkamp, Wayde Flowerday, and John Gabriel
Goddard. 2018. *Innovation Activity in South Africa: Measuring the
Returns to R&D*. Washington, DC: International Bank for
Reconstruction and Development / The World Bank. https://elibrary
.worldbank.org/doi/pdf/10.1596/30265

Schmidt, Oliver. 2018. "Digitalization, Servitization and 'Leapfrogging' –
The Case of Mobile Financial Services in East Africa." In *Die informa-
tisierte Service-Ökonomie*. Fachmedien Wiesbaden GmbH: Springer.

Schneier. 2007. "Home Users: A Public Health Problem?" *Schneier on
Security*. http://www.schneier.com/blog/archives/2007/09/

Schultz, Ivy. 2018. "International Entrepreneurship: Exposure to Micro-
Markets in Tunisia." *Forbes*. https://www.forbes.com/sites/columbiabu
sinessschool/2018/12/03/international-entrepreneurship-exposure-to-
micro-markets-in-tunisia

Schwab, Klaus. 2016a. *The Fourth Industrial Revolution*. New York:
Crown Publishing Group.

   2016b. "The Fourth Industrial Revolution: What It Means, How to
   Respond." *World Economic Forum*. www.weforum.org/agenda/2016/
   01/the-fourth-industrial-revolution-what-it-means-and-how-to-
   respond/

   2018. *The Global Competitiveness Report 2018*. Cologny/Geneva: World
   Economic Forum. www3.weforum.org/docs/GCR2018/05FullReport/
   TheGlobalCompetitivenessReport2018.pdf

Schwab, Klaus, and Nicholas Davis. 2018. *Shaping the Fourth Industrial
Revolution*. Cologny/Geneva: World Economic Forum.

Scott, Kate. 2018. "Drones Driven by AI Will Track Illegal Fishing in African Waters." *CNN*. https://www.cnn.com/2018/08/15/africa/atlan-space-ai-drone-morocco/index.html

Seo, Michael. 2019. "Can a Mobile Health Payment Platform Reshape Kenya's Health Care System?" *Global Innovations in Health Care*. https://international.kaiserpermanente.org/wp-content/uploads/2019/08/Carepay-MTiba_final_080519.pdf

Serianu. 2016. *Africa Cyber Security Report 2016: Achieving Cyber Security Resilience*. https://www.serianu.com/downloads/AfricaCyberSecurity Report2016.pdf

2017. *Africa Cyber Security Report 2017: Demystifying Africa's Cyber Security Poverty Line*. https://www.serianu.com/downloads/ AfricaCyberSecurityReport2017.pdf

"Seven Worldwide Oil and Gas Projects to Watch in 2018." 2017. *Africa Oil Week*. https://www.africa-oilweek.com/Articles/7-worldwide-oil-gas-projects-to-watch-in-2018

Shahan, Zachary. 2021. "Morocco Aims for 50% Renewable Energy by 2030." *Clean Technica*. https://cleantechnica.com/2021/01/22/morocco-aims-for-50-renewable-energy-by-2030/

Shapshak, Toby. 2019. "Africa Now Has 643 Tech Hubs Which Play 'Pivotal' Role for Business." *Forbes*. https://www.forbes.com/sites/toby shapshak/2019/10/30/africa-now-has-643-tech-hubs-which-play-piv otal-role-for-business/?sh=168446184e15

Sharma, Abhinav, Arpit Jain, Prateek Gupta, and Vinay Chowdary. 2020. "Machine Learning Applications for Precision Agriculture: A Comprehensive Review." *IEEE Access* 9: 4843–4873. doi: 10.1109/ACCESS.2020.3048415

Shekar, Meera, and Kate Otto. 2014. *ICT for Health in Africa*. Washington, DC: World Bank. https://openknowledge.worldbank.org/handle/10986/19020

Sher, Davide. 2014. "3D Printing Takes Hold in Egypt." *3D Printing Industry*. https://3dprintingindustry.com/news/osama-kamals-open-source-project-just-beginning-new-movement-eygpt-32952

Siba, Eyerusalem, and Mariama Sow. 2017. "Smart City Initiatives in Africa." *The Brookings Institution*. www.brookings.edu/blog/africa-in-focus/2017/11/01/smart-city-initiatives-in-africa/

Sibanda, Tawanda. 2019. "Digital Reinvention Can Spur South Africa's Economy." *McKinsey*. https://www.mckinsey.com/featured-insights/middle-east-and-africa/digital-reinvention-can-spur-south-africas-economy

Sicari, S., A. Rizzardi, L. A. Grieco, and A. Coen-Porisini. 2015. "Security, Privacy and Trust in Internet of Things: The Toad Ahead." *Computer Networks* 76: 146–164.

Siderska, Julia. 2021. "The Adoption of Robotic Process Automation Technology to Ensure Business Processes during the COVID-19 Pandemic." *Sustainability* 13(14): 8020. doi: 10.3390/su13148020

Siemens. 2017. *Africa Digitalization Maturity Report 2017*. www.siemens .co.za/pool/about_us/Digitalization_Maturity_Report_2017.pdf

Signé, Landry. 2018a. "Capturing Africa's High Returns." *The Brookings Institution*. www.brookings.edu/opinions/capturing-africas-high-returns/

2018b. "Africa's Consumer Market Potential: Trends, Drivers, Opportunities, and Strategies." *The Brookings Institution*. https://www .brookings.edu/wp-content/uploads/2018/12/Africas-consumer-market-potential.pdf

2018c. "Africa's Tourism Potential: Trends, Drivers, Opportunities, and Strategies." *The Brookings Institution*. https://www.brookings. edu/wp-content/uploads/2018/12/Africas-tourism-potential_Landry Signe1.pdf

2020a. "The Potential of Manufacturing and Industrialization in Africa." *The Brookings Institution*. https://www.brookings.edu/wp-content/ uploads/2018/09/Manufacturing-and-Industrialization-in-Africa-Signe-20180921.pdf

2020b. *Unlocking Africa's Business Potential: Trends, Opportunities, Risks and Strategies*. Washington, DC: The Brookings Institution Press.

2021a. "Capturing Africa's Insurance Potential for Shared Prosperity." *Brookings*. https://www.brookings.edu/blog/africa-in-focus/2021/07/02/ capturing-africas-insurance-potential-for-shared-prosperity/

2021b. "Strategies for Effective Health Care for Africa in the Fourth Industrial Revolution: Bridging the Gap between the Promise and Delivery." *Africa Growth Initiative at Brookings*. https://www.brookings .edu/wp-content/uploads/2021/10/Strategies-for-effective-health-care-deliv ery-in-Africa_FINAL.pdf

Signé, Landry, and Louise Fox. 2021. "The Fourth Industrial Revolution (4IR) and the Future of Work: Could This Bring Good Jobs to Africa?" *INCLUDE Knowledge Platform*. https://includeplatform.net/wp-con tent/uploads/2021/06/Book-ESP-Fox-FINAL.pdf

Signé, Landry, and Chelsea Johnson. 2018. *Africa's Tourism Potential: Trends, Drivers, Opportunities, and Strategies*. Africa Growth Initiative at Brookings. https://www.brookings.edu/wp-content/uploads/2018/12/ Africas-tourism-potential_LandrySigne1.pdf

Signé, Landry, and Kevin Signé. 2018. "Cybersecurity in Africa: Securing Businesses with a Local Approach with Global Standards." *The Brookings Institution*. www.brookings.edu/blog/africa-in-focus/2018/06/04/cybersecurity-in-africa-securing-businesses-with-a-local-approach-with-global-standards/

2021. "African States Can Improve Their Cybersecurity." *The Brookings Institution*. https://www.brookings.edu/techstream/how-african-states-can-improve-their-cybersecurity/.

Signé, Landry, and Colette van der Ven. 2019. *Keys to Success for the AfCFTA Negotiations*. Washington: Brookings Africa Growth Initiative.

Singh, Rishi. 2018. "Mauritius Must Look to the Example of Singapore to Build Its Own Global Digital Revolution." *Maunews Online*. maunewsonline.uitvconnect.com/mauritius-must-look-to-the-example-of-singapore-to-build-its-own-globaldigital-revolution/

Sirkin, Hal, Michael Zinser, and Justin Rose. 2015. "The Robotics Revolution: The Next Great Leap in Manufacturing." *Boston Consulting Group*. https://www.bcg.com/publications/2015/lean-manufacturing-innovation-robotics-revolution-next-great-leap-manufacturing.aspx

Slav, Irina. 2019. "Oil Rises Amid Nigerian Oil Terminal Shutdown." *Oilprice.com*. https://oilprice.com/Energy/Crude-Oil/Oil-Rises-Amid-Nigeria-Oil-Terminal-Shutdown.html

Slavova, Mira, and Ekene Okwechime. 2016. "African Smart Cities Strategies for Agenda 2063." *Africa Journal of Management* 2(2): 210–229.

Smit, Janine. 2013. "Africa's First Virtual Reality Mine Design Center." *University of Pretoria – Innovate*. https://www.up.ac.za/media/shared/Legacy/sitefiles/file/44/1026/2163/8121/innovate8/2829africas_first_virtual_reality_mine_design_centrebyjaninesmit.pdf

Smith, Stephen. 2019. *The Scramble for Europe: Young Africa on Its Way to the Old Continent*, 1st ed. London: Polity.

"Software Piracy in Africa Double Global Rate." 2011. *Daily Nation*. https://www.nation.co.ke/business/Tech/Software-piracy-in-Africa-double-global-rate/1017288-1161742-sn0mknz/index.html

Solomon, Edna, and Aaron van Klyton. 2020. "The Impact of Digital Technology Usage on Economic Growth in Africa." *Utilities Policy* 67. doi: 10.1016/j.jup.2020.101104

"Sound Energy Are Plotting a Path to Develop Their Assets in Western Morocco." 2019. *Africa Oil Week*. https://www.africa-oilweek.com/Articles/httpsafrica-oilweekcomarticlessound-energy

Spivey, Lori, Patrick Dupoux, Stefano Niavas, Tenbite Ermia, and Stéphane Heuze. 2013. "Ten Things to Know about African Consumers:

Capturing the Emerging Consumer Class." *Bcg.perspectives*. www
.bcgperspectives.com/content/articles/globalization_consumer_insight_
ten_things_to_know_about_african_consumers/

Stankovic, Mirjana, Ravi Gupta, Francie Sadeski, and Matthieu Lacave.
2019. "Study on Unlocking the Potential of the Fourth Industrial
Revolution in Africa. Final Report – Country Case: Uganda." *African
Development Bank.*

Statista. 2021. "Number of Public and Private Tertiary Education
Institutions in Tunisia from 2013/2014 to 2018/2019." https://www
.statista.com/statistics/1241507/number-of-public-and-private-tertiary-
education-institutions-in-tunisia/

Statistics South Africa. 2018. *Quarterly Labor Force Survey: Quarter 2:
2018*. Pretoria, South Africa: Statistics South Africa. http://www
.statssa.gov.za/publications/P0211/P02112ndQuarter2018.pdf

Steyn, Gabriella. 2018. "Aerobotics Uses Artificial Intelligence to Make
Farming Easier." *Business Report*. https://www.iol.co.za/business-
report/technology/watch-aerobotics-uses-artificial-intelligence-to-make-
farming-easier-17505625

Stork, Cristoph, Enrico Calandro, and Alison Gillwald. 2013. "Internet
Going Mobile: Internet Access and Use in 11 African Countries." *info*
15(5): 34–51.

Stroetmann, Karl. 2018. "Digital Health Ecosystem for African Countries:
A Guide for Public and Private Actors for Establishing Holistic Digital
Health Ecosystems in Africa." *Federal Ministry for Economic
Cooperation and Development (BMZ).*

Suberg, William. 2018. "Egypt's Central Bank Conducting 'Feasibility
Studies' Around Digital Currency Issuance." *Cointelegraph*. https://
cointelegraph.com/news/egypts-central-bank-conducting-feasibility-
studies-around-digital-currency-issuance

Sun, Irene Y., Kartik Jarayam, and Omid Kassiri. 2017. "Dance of the Lions
and Dragons: How Are Africa and China Engaging, and How Will the
Partnership Evolve?" *McKinsey & Company*. https://www.mckinsey
.com/~/media/McKinsey/Featured%20Insights/Middle%20East%
20and%20Africa/The%20closest%20look%20yet%20at%20Chinese
%20economic%20engagement%20in%20Africa/Dance-of-the-lions-
and-dragons.ashx

Sustainable Energy for All. 2021. "Power Africa, SEforALL to Accelerate
Health Facility Electrification in Sub-Saharan Africa." https://www
.seforall.org/news/health-facility-electrification-in-sub-saharan-africa.

Sutherland, Ewan. 2017. "Governance of Cybersecurity: The Case of South
Africa." *African Journal of Information and Communication* 20:
83–112.

Swan, Melanie. 2015. *Blockchain: Blueprint for a New Economy.* Sebastopol, CA: O'Reilly Media.

Symantec. 2017. *Internet Security Threat Report.* https://www.symantec.com/content/dam/symantec/docs/reports/gistr22-government-report.pdf

Tan, Joy. 2018. "Cloud Computing Is Crucial to the Future of Our Societies – Here's Why." *Forbes.* https://www.forbes.com/sites/joytan/2018/02/25/cloud-computing-is-the-foundation-of-tomorrows-intelligent-world/#22abc1564073

Tanner, Maureen. 2009. "Communication and Culture in Global Software Development: The Case of Mauritius and South Africa." *Journal of Information, Information Technology, and Organizations* 4: 57–86.

Taylor, Ian. 2014. *Africa Rising? BRICS – Diversifying Dependency.* Rochester, NY: Boydell & Brewer.

Te Velde, Dirk. 2016. *Why African Manufacturing Is Doing Better than You Think.* Overseas Development Institute. https://www.odi.org/comment/10382-why-african-manufacturing-doing-better-you-think

Terebey, Skye. 2016. "African Union Cybersecurity Profile: Seeking a Common Continental Policy." *University of Washington Henry M. Jackson School of International Studies.* https://jsis.washington.edu/news/african-union-cybersecurity-profile-seeking-common-continental-policy

"The Battle against Ransomware." 2017. *African Business Magazine.* https://africanbusinessmagazine.com/sectors/technology/the-battle-against-ransomware/

The Conversation. 2021. "African Countries Must Muscle up Their Support and Fill Massive R&D Gap." https://theconversation.com/african-countries-must-muscle-up-their-support-and-fill-massive-randd-gap-161024

The Economist. 2017. "What Technology Can Do for Africa." https://www.economist.com/special-report/2017/11/10/what-technology-can-do-for-africa

The Medical Futurist. 2020. *Ten Ways Technology Is Changing Healthcare.* https://medicalfuturist.com/ten-ways-technology-changing-healthcare/

Theunissen, Ian. 2015. "E-agriculture: How ICT Is Taking Farming into the Future." *IT News Africa.* https://www.itnewsafrica.com/2015/11/e-agriculture-how-ict-is-taking-farming-into-the-future/

Thompson, Herbert, and Christopher Garbacz. 2008. "Broadband Impacts on State GDP: Direct and Indirect Impacts." Paper presented at the International Telecommunications Society 17th Biennial Conference, Montreal, Canada.

Times Higher Education. 2021. "Best Universities in Africa 2022." https://www.timeshighereducation.com/student/best-universities/best-universities-africa

Trade Commissioner. 2021. "Cybersecurity Market in Morocco." Government of Canada. https://www.tradecommissioner.gc.ca/morocco-maroc/market-reports-etudes-de-marches/0005881.aspx?lang=eng

Tsagkalidis, Christos, Luigi Matrone, Zineb El Ouazzani, et al. 2018. "Trade 2030 and the Fourth Industrial Revolution (4IR): Bringing the Vision and Thoughts of Youth to the World." *Global Shapers Community and WTO.* https://www.wto.org/english/forums_e/public_forum18_e/fly_64.pdf

Tshabalala, Sim. 2017. "South Africa in the Fourth Industrial Revolution: A New Opportunity to Create More Jobs and a Better Society." *Standard Bank.* https://standardbank.com/CIB/About-us/Insights-Hub/South-Africa-in-the-fourth-industrial-revolution:–A-new-opportunity-to-create-more-jobs-and-a-better-society

Tshiani, Valerie, and Maureen Tanner. 2018. "South Africa's Quest for Smart Cities: Privacy Concerns of Digital Natives of Cape Town, South Africa." *Interdisciplinary Journal of e-Skills and Lifelong Learning* 14: 55–76.

Tsuyoshi, Kano, and Kentaro Toyama. 2020. "Bottlenecks of ICT Innovation in Rwanda." In *Proceedings of the 2020 International Conference on Information and Communication Technologies and Development (ICTD2020).* Association for Computing Machinery, New York, Article 16, 1–11. DOI: https://doi.org/10.1145/3392561.3394644.

Tugizimana Fidele, Jasper Engel, Reza Salek, Ian Dubery, Lizelle Piater, and Karl Burgess. 2020. "The Disruptive 4IR in the Life Sciences: Metabolomics." In Wesley Doorsamy, Babu Paul, and Tshilidzi Marwala (Eds.), *The Disruptive Fourth Industrial Revolution.* Lecture Notes in Electrical Engineering, vol. 674. Cham: Springer. https://doi.org/10.1007/978-3-030-48230-5_10

Turianskyi, Yarik, and Steven Gruzd. 2016. "Can Technological Advances Improve Governance in Africa?" *The Mail & Guardian.* mg.co.za/article/2016-04-27-can-technological-advances-improve-governance-in-africa

Uche Ordu, Aloysius. 2020. "The Coming of Age of the African Centers for Disease Control." *Brookings Africa in Focus* blog. www.brookings.edu/blog/africa-in-focus/2020/04/15/the-coming-of-age-of-the-africa-centers-for-disease-control/

Uchechukwu, Nnamani, and Makwe Stella. 2019. "Impact of Electronic Banking on Customer Satisfaction." *IDOSR Journal of Science and Technology* 4(1): 23–35. https://www.idosr.org/wpcontent/uploads/2019/04/IDOSRJST-41-23-35-2019.-OL.pdf

UNCTAD. 2017. "Robots, Industrialization, and Inclusive Growth." In *Trade and Development Report 2017*. Beyond Austerity: Towards a Global New Deal.

    2019. *Foreign Direct Investment to Africa Defies Global Slump, Rises 11%*. https://unctad.org/en/pages/newsdetails.aspx?OriginalVersionID=2109

    2020a. Discussion on "Harnessing Rapid Technological Change for Inclusive and Sustainable Development." *Kenya's Position Paper*. https://unctad.org/system/files/non-official-document/ecn162020_s06_rapidtech_space_Kenya_en.pdf

    2020b. *World Investment Report 2020*. https://unctad.org/system/files/official-document/wir2020_en.pdf

UNCTAD and UNIDO. 2011. *Economic Development in Africa Report 2011*. https://unctad.org/en/Docs/aldcafrica2011_en.pdf

UNDP. 2018. "Rwanda: Human Development Indicators." http://hdr.undp.org/en/countries/profiles/RWA

    2020. "Human Development Report 2020." http://hdr.undp.org/en/countries/profiles/EGY

"Une directive de BAM sur la fiabilité et la sécurité systèmes d'information des banques." 2016. *La Tribune*. https://lnt.ma/une-directive-de-bam-sur-la-fiabilite-et-la-securite-systemes-dinformation-des-banques/

UNECA. 2014. "Tackling the Challenges of Cybersecurity in Africa." *UNECA Policy Brief* NTIS/002/2014.

    2017. *Towards Improved Access to Broadband in Africa*. https://www.uneca.org/sites/default/files/PublicationFiles/towards_improved_access_to_broadband_inafrica.pdf

    2020a. *Economic Report on Africa 2020: Innovative Finance for Private Sector Development in Africa*. https://uneca.org/sites/default/files/fullpublicationfiles/ERA_2020_mobile_20201213.pdf

    2020b. "Questions and Answers." www.uneca.org/publications/african-continental-free-trade-area-questions-answers

UNECA, GBCHealth, and Aliko Dangote Foundation. 2019. *Healthcare and Economic Growth in Africa*. Addis Ababa: United Nationals Economic Commission for Africa.

UNESCO. 2016. "Green Technologies a Focus of Innovation in Morocco." www.unesco.org/new/en/member-states/single-view/news/green_technologies_a_focus_of_innovation_in_morocco/

    2017a. "Stratégie Maroc Digital 2020." https://en.unesco.org/creativity/periodic-reports/measures/strategie-maroc-digital-2020

    2017b. *Country Profile – Rwanda*. http://www.unesco.org/new/fileadmin/MULTIMEDIA/HQ/SC/pdf/FEI_Country_profile_Rwanda.pdf

UNFPA, World Health Organization, UNICEF, World Bank Group, the United Nations Population Division. 2019. *Trends in Maternal Mortality 2000 to 2017.* https://www.unfpa.org/featured-publica tion/trends-maternal-mortality-2000-2017

UNICEF. 2016. "mTrac: Using Innovations to Improve Healthcare." www.unicef.org/uganda/what-we-do/mtrac

2017. *Education Budget Brief: Investing in Child Education in Rwanda.* https://www.unicef.org/rwanda/RWA_resources_budgetbriefseducation. pdf

2019. "Children in Africa: Key Statistics on Child Survival and Population." https://data.unicef.org/resources/children-in-africa-child-sur vival-brochure/

2020. "E-Learning Tools Help to Ensure Continuity of Services in Somalia during the COVID-19 Pandemic." https://www.unicef.org/ esa/documents/e-learning-tools-help-ensure-continuity-services-soma lia-during-covid-19-pandemic

United Nations. 2019. "World Population Prospects." https://population.un .org/wpp

2020. "E-Government Survey 2020: Digital Government in the Decade of Action for Sustainable Development – With Addendum on COVID-19 Response." *United Nations.* https://publicadministration .un.org/egovkb/Portals/egovkb/Documents/un/2020-Survey/2020% 20UN%20E-Government%20Survey%20(Full%20Report).pdf

UNWTO. 2019. *Tourism Highlights 2017 Edition.* https://www.e-unwto.org/ doi/pdf/10.18111/9789284421152

USAID. 2016. "Data-driven Strategy to Improve Health Outcomes in Sub-Saharan Africa." *BroadReach/Regional Action through Data* Fact Sheet. www.usaid.gov/sites/default/files/documents/1864/Fact_Sheet_RAD_ IGAD_WAHO_508.pdf

Vahabi, Mehrdad. 2017. *A Critical Survey of the Resource Curse Literature through the Appropriability Lens.* Document de travail du CEPN N°2017-14. https://hal.archives-ouvertes.fr/hal-01583559/document

van der Stelt, Merel, Arico C. Verhulst, Jonathan H. Vas Nunes, et al. 2020. "Improving Lives in Three Dimensions: The Feasibility of 3D Printing for Creating Personalized Medical Aids in a Rural Area of Sierra Leone." *American Journal of Tropical Medicine and Hygiene* 102: 4. doi: 10.4269/ajtmh.19-0359.

van der Waag-Cowling, Noëlle. 2020. "Living below the Cyber Poverty Line: Strategic Challenges for Africa." *International Committee of the Red Cross.* https://blogs.icrc.org/law-and-policy/2020/06/11/cyber-poverty-line-africa/

Vasconcellos, G. Alexandre , Bruna de Paula Fonseca e Fonseca, and Carlos M. Morel. 2018. "Revisiting the Concept of Innovative Developing Countries (IDCs) for Its Relevance to Health Innovation and Neglected Tropical Diseases and for the Prevention and Control of Epidemics." *PLoS Neglected Tropical Diseases* 12(7).

V.e.n.t.u.r.e.s Onsite & Construct East Africa. 2015. *The Emerging East Africa Construction Market 2015: Focus on Uganda, Ethiopia, Tanzania, Mozambique and Kenya.* www.enterprisegreece.gov.gr/files/TRADE/ THE_BIG_5_CONSTRUCT_EAST_AFRICA/The%20Emerging% 20East%20Africa%20Construction%20Market%202015.pdf

Veselinovic, Milena. 2018. "Alain Nteff, Savior of Cameroon's Mothers and Babies." *CNN.* www.cnn.com/2015/02/17/africa/gifted-mom-camer oon-alain-nteff/index.html

Vidal, Maria. 2017. "Mapping Africa's Latest Innovations in Digital Finance." *CGAP.* https://www.cgap.org/blog/mapping-africas-latest- innovations-digital-finance

Vithani, Priya. 2017. "Government and Private Sector Team up to Support Startups in Egypt." *Wamda.* https://www.wamda.com/2017/06/govern ment-private-sector-team-support-startups-egypt

VOA. 2011. "Ethiopia Recruits Health 'Army' to Combat Child Mortality, Malnutrition." *VOA.* www.voanews.com/africa/ethiopia-recruits- health-army-combat-child-mortality-malnutrition

Wadekar, Neha. 2020 April 15. "Kenya's 3D Printing Community Is Making Covid-19 Equipment to Fill a Deficit as Caseloads Rise." *QuartzAfrica.* https://qz.com/africa/1838608/?utm_term=mucp

Wamboye, Evelyn, Abel Adekola, and Bruno Sergi. 2016. "ICTs and Labor Productivity Growth in Sub-Saharan Africa." *International Labor Review* 155(2): 231–252.

Waluyo, B. Agustinus, and Ling Tan (Eds.). 2022. *Mobile Computing and Technology Applications in Tourism and Hospitality.* IGI Global. http:// doi:10.4018/978-1-7998-6904-7

We Robotics. 2020. "How Delivery Drones Are Being Used to Tackle COVID-19." https://blog.werobotics.org/2020/04/25/cargo-drones- covid-19/

Wegner, Phillip. 2021. "Global IoT Spending to Grow 24% in 2021, Led by Investments in IoT Software and IoT Security." *IoT Analytics.* https:// iot-analytics.com/2021-global-iot-spending-grow-24-percent/

Weil, David N. 2007. "Accounting for the Effect of Health on Economic Growth." *The Quarterly Journal of Economics* 122(3): 1265–1306.

2014. "Chapter 3 – Health and Economic Growth." *Handbook of Economic Growth* 2: 623–682.

Westby, Jody R. 2015. "Governance of Cybersecurity: 2015 Report." *Georgia Tech Information Security Center.*

WHO Regional Office for Africa. 2018. *Atlas of African Health Statistics 2018: Universal Health Coverage and the Sustainable Development Goals in the WHO African Region.* Brazzaville.

2019. *Preventing and Responding to HIV Drug-Resistance in the African Region: Regional Action Plan 2019–2023.* https://www.afro.who.int/publications/preventing-and-responding-hiv-drug-resistance-african-region-regional-action-plan-2019

Wijkman, Anders, and Mona Afifi. 2002. "Technology Leapfrogging and the Digital Divide." *Ainability* A. https://people.eecs.berkeley.edu/~jfc/mattkam/tased/wijkman2002.pdf

Wille, John. 2017. "Home-Grown Technology Firms Help Drive eGovernment Expansion in East Africa." *World Bank.* http://blogs.worldbank.org/psd/home-grown-technology-firms-help-drive-egovernment-expansion-east-africa

Wood, Johnny. 2018. "Morocco Will Soon Unveil Africa's First High-Speed Rail Link." *World Economic Forum.* www.weforum.org/agenda/2018/08/morocco-high-speed-rail-link/

World Bank. 2010. *Kenya Economic Update.* Washington, DC: The World Bank Group Poverty Reduction and Economic Management Unit Africa Region. http://siteresources.worldbank.org/KENYAEXTN/Resources/KEU-Dec_2010_with_cover_e-version.pdf

2015a. "Medium and High-Tech Exports (% Manufactured Exports)." https://data.worldbank.org/indicator/TX.MNF.TECH.ZS.UN?locations=ZA

2015b. "Physicians (per 1,000 People) – Sub-Saharan Africa." https://data.worldbank.org/indicator/SH.MED.PHYS.ZS?locations=ZG

2016a. *Financial Services in Côte d'Ivoire: Banks Set Aside in Favor of Mobile Money.* https://www.worldbank.org/en/country/cotedivoire/publication/financial-services-in-cote-divoire-banks-set-aside-in-favor-of-mobile-money

2016b. "Access to Electricity (% of Population)." https://data.worldbank.org/indicator/EG.ELC.ACCS.ZS

2016c. "Mobile Cellular Subscriptions (per 100 People)." https://data.worldbank.org/indicator/IT.CEL.SETS.P2

2017a. "People Using Safely Managed Drinking Water Services, Urban (% of Urban Population) – Sub-Saharan Africa." https://data.worldbank.org/indicator/SH.H2O.SMDW.UR.ZS?locations=ZG

2017b. "People Using Safely Managed Sanitation Services, Urban (% of Urban Population) – Sub-Saharan Africa." https://data.worldbank.org/indicator/SH.STA.SMSS.UR.ZS?locations=ZG

2017c. "People Using at Least Basic Sanitation Services (% of Population) – Sub-Saharan Africa." https://data.worldbank.org/indicator/SH.STA.BASS .ZS?locations=ZG

2017d. "People Using at Least Basic Drinking Water Services (% of Population) – Sub-Saharan Africa." https://data.worldbank.org/indica tor/SH.H2O.BASW.ZS?locations=ZG

2017e. *South Africa Economic Update: Innovation for Productivity and Inclusiveness*. Washington, DC: International Bank for Reconstruction and Development / The World Bank. (https://elibrary.worldbank.org/doi/ pdf/10.1596/28439)

2017–2018. "Individuals Using the Internet (% of population)." https://data .worldbank.org/indicator/it.net.user.zs

2018a. *Mauritius: Addressing Inequality through More Equitable Labor Markets*. https://www.worldbank.org/en/country/mauritius/publication/ mauritius-addressing-inequality-through-more-equitable-labor-markets

2018b. "Kenya." https://data.worldbank.org/country/kenya

2018c. "Rwanda." https://data.worldbank.org/country/rwanda

2018d. *Doing Business 2019: Economy Profile: Rwanda*. Washington, DC: The World Bank Group. http://www.doingbusiness.org/content/ dam/doingBusiness/country/r/rwanda/RWA.pdf

2018e. "Nigeria." https://data.worldbank.org/country/nigeria

2018f. "South Africa." https://data.worldbank.org/indicator/SE.TER .ENRR?locations=ZA

2019a. "Mortality rate, under-5 (per 1,000 live births) – Sub-Saharan Africa." https://data.worldbank.org/indicator/SH.DYN.MORT?loca tions=ZG

2019b. "Mortality Rate, Infant (per 1,000 Live Births) – Sub-Saharan Africa." https://data.worldbank.org/indicator/SP.DYN.IMRT.IN?loca tions=ZG

2019c. "Prevalence of HIV, Total (% of Population Ages 15–49) – Botswana." https://data.worldbank.org/indicator/SH.DYN.AIDS.ZS

2019d. "Access to Electricity, Rural (% of Rural Population) – Sub-Saharan Africa." https://data.worldbank.org/indicator/EG.ELC.ACCS .RU.ZS?locations=ZG

2019e. "Mortality Rate, Adult, Female (per 1,000 Female Adults – Sub-Saharan Africa, World)." https://data.worldbank.org/indicator/SP .DYN.AMRT.FE?locations=ZG-1W&most_recent_value_desc=false

2019f. "Life Expectancy at Birth, Total (Years) – Sub-Saharan Africa." https://data.worldbank.org/indicator/SP.DYN.LE00.IN?locations=ZG

2019g. "Immunization, Measles (% of Children Ages 12–23 Months) – Sub-Saharan Africa." https://data.worldbank.org/indicator/SH.IMM .MEAS?locations=ZG

2019h. "Antiretroviral Therapy Coverage (% of People Living with HIV) – Sub-Saharan Africa." https://data.worldbank.org/indicator/SH.HIV .ARTC.ZS?locations=ZG&most_recent_value_desc=false

2019i. "Prevalence of HIV, Total (% of Population Ages 15–49) – Sub-Saharan Africa." https://data.worldbank.org/indicator/SH.DYN.AIDS .ZS?locations=ZG

2019j. "Access to Electricity (% of population) – Kenya." https://data .worldbank.org/indicator/EG.ELC.ACCS.ZS?locations=KE

2019k. "Digital Development Partnership: Annual Review 2019 – Making Sure That No One Is Left Behind in the Digital Age." https:// documents1.worldbank.org/curated/en/848061587152231518/pdf/ Digital-Development-Partnership-Annual-Review-2019-Making-Sure-That-No-One-Is-Left-Behind-in-the-Digital-Age.pdf

2020a. "The African Continental Free Trade Area." https://www .worldbank.org/en/topic/trade/publication/the-african-continental-free-trade-area

2020b. "Individuals Using the Internet (% of Population) – Morocco." https://data.worldbank.org/indicator/IT.NET.USER.ZS?locations=MA

2020c. "Mobile Cellular Subscriptions (per 200 People) – Nigeria." https://data.worldbank.org/indicator/IT.CEL.SETS.P2?locations=NG

2020d. "Urban Development." https://www.worldbank.org/en/topic/ urbandevelopment/overview#1

2021a. "Africa's Scientific Solutions and Innovation in the Fight against COVID-19." https://www.worldbank.org/en/results/2021/07/14/africa-s-scientific-solutions-and-innovation-in-the-fight-against-covid-19

2021b. "Research and Development Expenditure (% of GDP) – Egypt, Arab Rep." https://data.worldbank.org/indicator/GB.XPD.RSDV.GD .ZS?locations=EG

2021c. "Unemployment, Youth Total (% of Total Labor Force Ages 15–24) (Modeled ILO Estimate) – Egypt, Arab Rep." https://data .worldbank.org/indicator/SL.UEM.1524.ZS?locations=EG

2021. "Widespread Informality Likely to Slow Recovery from COVID-19 in Developing Economies." https://www.worldbank.org/en/news/press-release/2021/05/11/widespread-informality-likely-to-slow-recovery-from-covid-19-in-developing-economies.

2021d. "World Bank's Response to COVID-19 (Coronavirus) in Africa." https://www.worldbank.org/en/news/factsheet/2020/06/02/world-banks-response-to-covid-19-coronavirus-in-africa

World Bank and ITU. 2020. *Digital Trends in Africa 2021.* https://www.itu.int/ dms_pub/itu-d/opb/ind/D-IND-DIG_TRENDS_AFR.01-2021-PDF-E.pdf

World Economic Forum. 2017a. "The Future of Jobs and Skills in Africa." http://www3.weforum.org/docs/WEF_Future_of_Jobs_2018.pdf

2017b. *The Global Human Capital Report 2017.* http://www3.weforum
.org/docs/WEF_Global_Human_Capital_Report_2017.pdf

2017c. "An Agenda for Leaders to Shape the Future of Education, Gender and Work." https://www.weforum.org/whitepapers/realizing-human-potential-in-the-fourth-industrial-revolution

2017d. "The Future of Jobs and Skills in the Middle East and North Africa: Preparing the Region for the Fourth Industrial Revolution." http://www3.weforum.org/docs/WEF_EGW_FOJ_MENA.pdf

2017e. "Meet the 100 Arab Start-Ups Shaping the Fourth Industrial Revolution." https://widgets.weforum.org/mena-startups-2017/

2018a. "The Future of Jobs Report 2018." www3.weforum.org/docs/ WEF_EGW_FOJ_Africa.pdf

2018b. *Insight Report. Advanced Drone Operations Toolkit: Accelerating the Drone Revolution.* http://www3.weforum.org/docs/WEF_Advanced_ Drone_Operations_Toolkit.pdf

2018c. *Shaping the Future of Construction: Future Scenarios and Implications for the Industry.* http://www3.weforum.org/docs/Future_ Scenarios_Implications_Industry_report_2018.pdf

2018d. *The Digital Arab World: Understanding and Embracing Regional Changes in the Fourth Industrial Revolution.* www3.weforum.org/docs/ WEF_Digital_Arab_World_White_Paper_2018.pdf

2018e. "Sub-Saharan Africa." *The Global Competitiveness Report.* http:// reports.weforum.org/global-competitiveness-report-2018/sub-saharan-africa/

2019a. *Insight Report. Health and Healthcare in the Fourth Industrial Revolution: Global Future Council on the Future of Health and Healthcare 2016–2018.* http://www3.weforum.org/docs/WEF_ Shaping_the_Future_of_Health_Council_Report.pdf

2019b. "Mapping Global Transformations: Fourth Industrial Revolution." https://toplink.weforum.org/knowledge/insight/a1Gb0000001RIhBEAW/ explore/summary

2019c. "Meet the 100 Start-Ups Shaping the Fourth Industrial Revolution." https://widgets.weforum.org/arabstartups/index.html

2020a. "The Future of Jobs Report 2020." http://www3.weforum.org/ docs/WEF_Future_of_Jobs_2020.pdf

2020b. "Global Competitiveness Report Special Edition 2020: How Countries Are Performing on the Road to Recovery. https://www .weforum.org/reports/the-global-competitiveness-report-2020.

2020c. "Global Technology Governance Report 2020." http://www3 .weforum.org/docs/WEF_Global_Technology_Governance_2020.pdf

2020d. "Recession and Automation Changes Our Future of Work, But There Are Jobs Coming, Report Says." https://www.weforum.org/press/

2020/10/recession-and-automation-changes-our-future-of-work-but-there-are-jobs-coming-report-says-52c5162fce/

World Economic Forum and Accenture. 2017. *Digital Transformation Initiative: Aviation, Travel, and Tourism Industry*. http://reports .weforum.org/digital-transformation/wp-content/blogs.dir/94/mp/files/ pages/files/wef-dti-aviation-travel-and-tourism-white-paper.pdf

World Economic Forum and A. T. Kearney. 2018. *Readiness for the Future of Production Report 2018*. http://www3.weforum.org/docs/FOP_ Readiness_Report_2018.pdf

World Health Organization. 2014. *The Health of the People: What Works. The African Regional Health Report 2014*. Geneva: World Health Organization.

   2016. *Atlas of African Health Statistics 2016: Health Situation Analysis of the African Region*. Geneva: World Health Organization.

   2017a. "What Needs to Be Done to Solve the Shortage of Health Workers in the African Region." www.afro.who.int/news/what-needs-be-done-solve-shortage-health-workers-african-region.

   2017b. *WHO Global Surveillance and Monitoring System for Substandard and Falsified Medical Products*. Geneva: World Health Organization.

   2019a. "Ten Threats to Global Health in 2019." https://www.who.int/ news-room/spotlight/ten-threats-to-global-health-in-2019

   2019b. *World Health Statistics 2019: Monitoring Health for the SDGs*. Geneva: World Health Organization.

   2020a. "COVID-19 Spurs Health Innovation in Africa." https://www.afro .who.int/news/covid-19-spurs-health-innovation-africa

   2020b. "Global Strategy on Human Resources for Health: Workforce 2030." https://www.who.int/publications/i/item/9789241511131

   2020c. "World Malaria Report 2020." https://www.who.int/publications/ i/item/9789240015791

   2021a. "Risk of Major Measles Outbreaks as Countries Delay Vaccination Drives." https://www.afro.who.int/news/risk-major-measles-outbreaks-countries-delay-vaccination-drives

   2021b. "The Global Health Observatory: Out-of-Pocket Expenditure as Percentage of Current Health Expenditure (CHE) (%)." https://www .who.int/data/gho/data/indicators/indicator-details/GHO/out-of-pocket-expenditure-as-percentage-of-current-health-expenditure-(che)-(-)

   2021c. *World Health Statistics 2021: Monitoring Health for the SDGs, Sustainable Development Goals*. https://apps.who.int/iris/bitstream/ handle/10665/342703/9789240027053-eng.pdf

   2021d. *Global Progress Report on HIV, Viral Hepatitis and Sexually Transmitted Infections, 2021. Accountability for the Global Health*

Sector Strategies 2016–2021: Actions for Impact. https://www.who.int/publications/i/item/9789240027077

2021e. "What Is Africa's Vaccine Production Capacity?" *WHO Africa.* https://www.afro.who.int/news/what-africas-vaccine-production-capacity

World Oil. 2018. *Exclusive Country-by-Country Data Point to Modest Growth outside U.S.* https://www.worldoil.com/forecast-data/2019-forecast-data/exclusive-country-by-country-data-point-to-modest-growth-outside-us

WTO. 2021. "Adapting to the Digital Trade Era: Challenges and Opportunities." https://www.wto.org/english/res_e/booksp_e/adtera_e.pdf

Wyche, Susan, and Jennifer Olson. 2018. "Kenyan Women's Rural Realities, Mobile Internet Access, and 'Africa Rising.'" *Information Technologies & International Development (Special Section)* 14: 33–47.

Xinhua. 2018. "Tunisia, China Sign Deal on Developing Digital Economy." *China Daily.* www.chinadaily.com.cn/a/201807/04/WS5b3c6a4fa3103349141e0a7f.html

Yarrow, Noah. 2017. "Education in Tunisia: Technology as a Tool to Support School Improvement." *The World Bank Blog.* blogs.worldbank.org/arabvoices/tunisia-technology-support-school-improvement

Yawson, Freda. 2021. "Challenges and Opportunities in the Innovation Ecosystem. Economic and Social Research Council, UK Ai, Growth Research Programme, ODI, ACET." https://acetforafrica.org/acet/wp-content/uploads/publications/2021/03/ACET-ODI-%E2%80%93-Challenges-and-Opportunities-in-the-Innovation-Ecosystem.pdf

Yazgan, Sekip, and Omer Yalcinkaya. 2018. "The Effects of Research and Development (R&D) Investments on Sustainable Economic Growth: Evidence from OECD Countries (1996–2015)." *Review of Economic Perspectives* 18(1): 3–23.

Yeboah, Stephen. 2018. "Fourth Industrial Revolution in Africa: It's the Energy." *BBN Times.* https://www.bbntimes.com/en/politics/society/fourth-industrial-revolution-in-africa-it-s-the-energy

Yeboah-Boateng, O. Ezer, Alexander Osei-Owusu, and Anders Henten. 2017. "ICT Developments in Africa – Infrastructures, Applications and Policies." *Telecommunications Policy* 41(7–8): 533–716.

Yli-Huumo, Jesse, Deokyoon Ko, Sujin Choi, Sooyong Park, and Kari Smolander. 2016. "Where Is Current Research on Blockchain Technology? A Systematic Review." *PLoS ONE* 11(10): e0163477. https://doi.org/10.1371/journal.pone.0163477

Yusuf, A. K. 2012. "An Appraisal of Research in Nigeria's University Sector." *JORIND* 10(2): 321–330.

Zaari Jabiri, Adil. 2017. "Technologie spatiale: Le Maroc désormais dans la cour des grands." *MAP Express.* www.mapexpress.ma/actualite/opin

ions-et-debats/technologie-spatiale-le-maroc-desormais-dans-la-cour-des-grands-2

Zawya. 2020. "Unemployment among Egypt's University Grads Exceeds 36% CAPMAS." https://www.zawya.com/mena/en/economy/story/Unemployment_among_Egypts_university_grads_exceeds_36_CAPMAS-SNG_181812803/

Zeufack, Albert G., Cesar Calderon, Gerard Kambou, et al. 2020. "An Analysis of Issues Shaping Africa's Economic Future." *Africa's Pulse*, No. 21, Spring 2020. World Bank. https://openknowledge.worldbank.org/handle/10986/33541

Zheng, Zibin, Shaoan Xie, Hong-Ning Dai, Xiangping Chen, and Huaimin Wang. 2018. "Blockchain Challenges and Opportunities: A Survey." *International Journal of Web and Grid Services* 14(4): 352–375.

Zhu, Yiqing, and Nan Li. 2021. "Virtual and Augmented Reality Technologies for Emergency Management in the Built Environments: A State-of-the-Art Review." *Journal of Safety Science and Resilience* 2 (1): 1–10. doi: 10.1016/j.jnlssr.2020.11.004

Zoltán, Kolozsváry. 2019. "The Relationship between Materials Science and the Fourth Industrial Revolution." *Acta Materialia Transylvanica* 2(1): 1–6. https://doi.org/10.33924/amt-2019-01-01

Index

Abuja Declaration, 156
ACEGID. *See* Africa Higher Education
  Center of Excellence for the
  Genomics of Infectious Diseases
additive manufacturing, 12. *See also* 3D
  printing
ADFI. *See* African Digital Financial
  Inclusion Facility
advanced materials science, 14
advanced robotics, 3
AfCFTA. *See* African Continental Free
  Trade Area
Africa. *See also* Fourth Industrial
  Revolution; Sub-Saharan Africa;
  specific countries; specific topics
  information and communication
    technology sector in, 24–25
  smart city technology in, research
    and initiatives on, 24
Africa Centers for Disease Control and
  Prevention (Africa CDC),
  146–147
Africa Higher Education Center of
  Excellence for the Genomics of
  Infectious Diseases (ACEGID),
  163–164
African Continental Free Trade Area
  (AfCFTA), 27, 176–177
  demand-side drivers and, 53–54
African Development Bank, 79
African Digital Financial Inclusion
  Facility (ADFI), 134
African Internet Group, 52
African Union Convention on the
  Confidence and Security in
  Cyberspace, 137
agile governance, in Rwanda, 164–166
agricultural sector
  agro-industries, 69–72
  agro-processing, 69–72

ICTs and, 70–71
climate change as influence on, 71–72
food insecurity and, 72
rural incomes, 72
strategic approaches to, 72
agro-industries, 69–72
agro-processing, 69–72
ICTs and, 70–71
AI. *See* artificial intelligence
Angola
  economic markets in, expansion of,
    30–31
  ransomware threats in, 133, 136
anti-money laundering operations, 78
artificial intelligence (AI), 5, 15
  big data in, 17
  in health care industry, 84–85,
    160–161
  in Mauritius, 101
  in Nigeria, 15
  oil and gas industry and, 65–66
  for security, 46
  in strategies to fight poverty, 36
  in tourism industry, 79–80
augmented reality. *See* virtual and
  augmented reality
automation technologies. *See also*
  robotics technologies
  in Egypt, 36–37
  in global manufacturing, 16
  in South Africa, 36
autonomous/near-autonomous
  vehicles, 3, 16–17

banking and financial services, 74–78
  access to, 74–76
  blockchain technology in, 75–78
  challenges for, 76–77
  constraints on, 76–77
    supply-side, 76–77

245

Ingram Content Group UK Ltd.
Milton Keynes UK
UKHW021414150623
423415UK00033B/654

9 781009 200011